D0917040

Social History in Perspective
General Editor: Jeremy Black

Social History in Perspective is a series of in-depth studies of the many topics in social, cultural and religious history for students. They also give the student clear surveys of the subject and present the most recent research in an accessible way.

PUBLISHED

John Belchem *Popular Radicalism in Nineteenth-Century Britain*
Sue Bruley *Women in Britain since 1900*
Simon Dentith *Society and Cultural Forms in Nineteenth-Century England*
Harry Goulbourne *Race Relations in Britain since 1945*
Tim Hitchcock *English Sexualities, 1700–1800*
Sybil M. Jack *Towns in Tudor and Stuart Britain*
Helen M. Jewell *Education in Early Modern England*
Alan Kidd *State, Society and the Poor in Nineteenth-Century England*
Hugh McLeod *Religion and Society in England, 1850–1914*
Donald M. MacRaild *Irish Migrants in Modern Britain, 1750–1922*
Christopher Marsh *Popular Religion in the Sixteenth Century*
Michael A. Mullett *Catholics in Britain and Ireland, 1558–1829*
Malcolm Smuts *Culture and Power in England, 1585–1685*
John Spurr *English Puritanism, 1603–1689*
W. B. Stephens *Education in Britain, 1750–1914*
Heather Swanson *Medieval British Towns*
David Taylor *Crime, Policing and Punishment in England, 1750–1914*
N. L. Tranter *British Populations in the Twentieth Century*
Ian D. Whyte *Scotland's Society and Economy in Transition, c.1500–c.1760*
Ian D. Whyte *Migration and Society in Britain, 1550–1830*

Please note that a sister series, *British History in Perspective,* is available which covers all the key topics in British political history.

Social History in Perspective
Series Standing Order
ISBN 0–333–71694–9 hardcover
ISBN 0–333–69336–1 paperback
(outside North America only)

You can receive future titles in this series as they are published by placing a standing order. Please contact your bookseller or, in the case of difficulty, write to us at the addresss below with your name and address, the title of the series and the ISBN quoted above.

Customer Services Department, Macmillan Distribution Ltd
Houndmills, Basingstoke, Hampshire RG21 6XS, England

By the same author

Climate Change and Human Society (1995)

Scotland before the Industrial Revolution: An Economic and Social History, c. 1050–c. 1750 (1995)

Scotland's Society and Economy in Transition, c. 1500–c. 1760 (1997)

Migration and Society in Britain 1550–1830

Ian D. Whyte

304.80941
W62 m

First published in Great Britain 2000 by
MACMILLAN PRESS LTD
Houndmills, Basingstoke, Hampshire RG21 6XS and London
Companies and representatives throughout the world

A catalogue record for this book is available from the British Library.

ISBN 0–333–71244–7 hardcover
ISBN 0–333–71245–5 paperback

First published in the United States of America by
ST. MARTIN'S PRESS, INC.,
Scholarly and Reference Division,
175 Fifth Avenue, New York, N. Y. 10010

ISBN 0–312–23175–X (cloth)

Library of Congress Cataloging-in-Publication Data
Whyte, Ian D., 1948–
Migration and Society in Britain: 1550–1830 / Ian D. Whyte.
p. cm. – (Social history in perspective)
Includes bibliographical references (p.) and index.
ISBN 0–312–23175–X (cloth)
1. Migration, Internal–Great Britain–History. 2. Great Britain–Emigration and immigration–History. 3. Great Britain–Social conditions. I. Title. II. Series.
HB2043.W49 2000
304,8'0941'0903–dc21

99–059336
CIP

© Ian D. Whyte 2000

All rights reserved. No reproduction, copy or transmission of this publication may be made without written permission.

No paragraph of this publication may be reproduced, copied or transmitted save with written permission or in accordance with the provisions of the Copyright, Designs and Patents Act 1988, or under the terms of any licence permitting limited copying issued by the Copyright Licensing Agency, 90 Tottenham Court Road, London W1P 0LP.

Any person who does any unauthorised act in relation to this publication may be liable to criminal prosecution and civil claims for damages.

The author has asserted his right to be identified as the author of this work in accordance with the Copyright Designs and Patents Act 1988.

This book is printed on paper suitable for recycling and made from fully managed and sustained forest resources.

10 9 8 7 6 5 4 3 2 1
09 08 07 06 05 04 03 02 01 00

Copy edited and typeset by Password, Norwich, UK.
Printed in Hong Kong

cak

For students, past and present, on Geography 337,
who have sat through so much of this.

University Libraries
Carnegie Mellon University
Pittsburgh, PA 15213-3890

CONTENTS

FIGURES

Tables

Introduction: The Significance of Migration in Early-Modern British Society

What is Migration?

In the past, as today, migration was an important demographic, social, economic and cultural process linking communities, regions and nations. In preindustrial Britain migration affected everyone, regardless of whether they were movers or stayers, for it determined the make up of every community by adding or subtracting people. It was an important element in social and economic change, but could sometimes have a conservative aspect, helping to maintain a traditional economy and a conservative society. Yet its significance is easily underestimated. Of the three basic demographic variables: fertility, mortality and migration, migration is the hardest to measure. Births and deaths are specific events, often well recorded. Migration, by contrast, is harder to define and frequently poorly documented. It is an imprecise variable which, in Early-Modern Britain, could include everything from a short-distance move within a small community to transatlantic emigration. The study of migration is interdisciplinary and, in an historical context, it has involved contributions from economic and social historians and historical geographers, as well as population specialists.

Migration has been defined as a residential change of a permanent or semi-permanent nature (Lee, 1969). However, this leaves ample scope for different interpretations. Some authors have restricted the term to changes of residence involving complete readjustment by the individual, with a change of job, friends and neighbours (Bogue, 1969).

Others have specified types of movement which do, or do not, constitute migration. Jones (1990), for example, excludes movements of temporary and seasonal labour, such as harvest workers. Within towns he also omits residential relocation. Nevertheless, the movement of seasonal workers has been considered a key element of migration in preindustrial societies by many historians (Devine, 1979; Johnson, 1967; Lucassen, 1987). Neither is the rationale for omitting intra-urban residential moves clear: many changes of residence within rural parishes operated over equally limited distances (Escott, 1988), while the impact of such movements on preindustrial urban communities may have been as significant as those in nineteenth-century towns (Boulton, 1987; Pooley, 1979). Not all people on the move, however, may be considered true migrants. Many historians omit vagrants, that is permanent migrants without a fixed residential base. Even more would exclude itinerant traders. Regular seasonal movements, such as those associated with transhumance, have generally been left out of historical studies of migration, as have moves which were short term, repetitive, cyclical and local in scale, such as journey to work, attendance at church or visiting local market centres. Such local movements around a fixed residential base have been termed circulation (Jones, 1990), locomotion (Clark and Souden, 1987) or, more generally, mobility (White and Woods, 1980) rather than migration. 'Mobility' is an ambiguous term though. It has been used by geographers and historians to refer to all population movements, of which migration is a subset, but it has also been used as synonymous with migration.

Migration has been classified in different ways, such as by the distances and time involved, the nature of people's origins and destinations, and the reasons for their movement. For Early-Modern times, it can be studied at geographical scales ranging from mobility within parishes, through regional, national and continental-scale migration (Lucassen, 1987) to transatlantic emigration. Migration studies can adopt a macro-scale approach, studying large numbers of movements in aggregate (Lucassen, 1987; Redford, 1926), or it can focus on the individual, based on detailed biographical material (Pooley and D. Cruz, 1995). Economic historians have often used macro-scale approaches, while social historians have been more concerned to evaluate community-based data. A distinction has often been drawn between internal migration, operating within a country, and international migration involving the crossing of state boundaries. The dividing line may be hard to draw in practice; does the migration of Scots to Ulster during the seventeenth century count as an internal or international flow? While there may be differences in the sources which capture migration within and between countries, such distinctions were probably less significant in the past than today as there was less government control on international population movements. Nor did crossing a national boundary necessarily turn migration into a different process. International movements, such as the emigration of indentured servants from Britain to America in the seventeenth and eighteenth centuries, may merely have been extensions of internal rural–urban migration (Souden, 1987; Wareing, 1981).

A differentiation of migration by the time period involved has included a division into seasonal movements, return migration and permanent moves. The movements involved in migration have usually been measured by straight-line distances between places of origin and destination. This is easy to measure, and over limited distances probably does not introduce significant distortions. Over longer distances, however, during a period when travel was slow and often difficult, it may not have been as good a reflection of reality, particularly where topographic barriers existed or where unrecorded intermediate stepwise movements may have occurred. Geographical distance may sometimes have been less significant than social or cultural differences between places. Classifying migration by environments of origin and destination is often based on distinctions such as movements within the countryside, rural to urban flows, and migration within the urban hierarchy. Attempts to classify migration by reasons for movement are limited by historical sources which rarely even hint at the motives involved. These can sometimes be inferred; a desire for upward social mobility is implicit in the taking up of an apprenticeship, for instance. However, many factors may have influenced the decision making which lay behind a migratory move, not all of them necessarily even conscious ones.

Migrants were not a random sample from the populations of their places of origin or destination (White and Woods, 1980). The dynamic element in the population of the source area might be over-represented in the stream of out-migrants, depriving communities of leadership and drive. Active, primary migrants were often the innovators, followed by more passive secondary ones. Primary migrants were often dominated by young adult males, secondary ones by their wives and children. In some cases, though, traditionalists moved in order to preserve their lifestyles, such as Irish harvest workers travelling to England and Scotland in the eighteenth century or Highlanders emigrating to North America. Migration was strongly related to age and life-cycle phase. It was most common among young, single adults searching for work. After marriage, especially once a family had been started, migration became less frequent.

The Impact of Migration

Only a handful of questions can be posed regarding migration; who moved, why, what were the patterns of origins, destinations and flows, and what were the effects on the societies migrants left and moved to? But these questions are fundamental for understanding preindustrial economies and societies. Migration was a dynamic force, not just responding to demographic, economic and social changes, but also influencing them. It changed the communities from which migrants were drawn, as well as those to which they moved. Because it was selective, migration could alter the age structures and sex ratios, and thus the fertility patterns of source areas and destinations. The migrants too were affected through changes in occupation, family status and cultural attitudes. The fact that a person had moved once may have predisposed them to move again. An influx of migrants to an area or town might have negative effects including competition for jobs, reductions in wage rates, an increased burden on poor rates, stress on housing, sanitation and water supply, social disturbance, crime and violence. But there were also positive features, such as increasing the demand for goods and services and the encouragement of industrial development by augmenting the labour force and introducing new skills. Although it was a transitory phenomenon, it could have profound, long-term effects on population structure and distribution through processes such as urban growth and rural depopulation. The problems of Ulster, still so prominent today, derive from the immigration of Scottish Protestant settlers in the seventeenth century (Percival-Maxwell, 1973). Migration to English towns, especially London, in the later sixteenth and seventeenth centuries was a major factor in checking national population growth, not merely because death rates were higher in the larger towns, but because the influx of female servants, particularly in the later seventeenth century, unbalanced sex ratios and lowered fertility rates in both the countryside and the towns (Wrigley, 1967). In Scotland emigration during the seventeenth century may have had a similar effect as a demographic safety valve (Smout, Devine and Landsman, 1991). Migration also had important social and cultural effects on patterns of language, religion and literacy.

The Ubiquity of Migration in Early-Modern England

Until the 1960s most historians believed that the population of Britain in preindustrial times was relatively immobile, with most people being born, living and dying in the same community. It was thought that a major change in levels of mobility occurred from the later eighteenth century with the onset of the industrialization. Early community studies, such as Hoskins (1957) on Wigston Magna in Leicestershire, gave little attention to migration. In the 1960s it became increasingly clear that migration had been much more frequent, the norm rather than the exception (Cornwall, 1967). The development of parish register demography with the first attempts at family reconstitution, studies of marriage registers and successive population listings all highlighted the high level of turnover that existed within rural communities (Constant, 1948; Laslett, 1977; Rich, 1950). Early research on sources such as apprenticeship records emphasized the importance of rural–urban migration, especially to London, in allowing the marked growth of towns that occurred in the sixteenth, seventeenth and eighteenth centuries (Buckatzsch, 1949–50; Wrigley, 1967). Within the last 30 years, research on migration in preindustrial Britain has pushed back into the fifteenth and even the fourteenth century, demonstrating that considerable mobility existed in English society even before the disruptions caused by the Black Death (Field, 1983; Poos, 1991).

Since then further research has reinforced this impression and extended our understanding of the nature and scale of migration in preindustrial Britain. High levels of mobility have been seen as causing Early-Modern English society to differ from the peasant societies of Continental Europe, contributing to English 'individualism' (Macfarlane, 1978). Many aspects of the mobility identified in England could also be seen in Wales. The considerable scale of Welsh immigration to England, following the Union of 1536, is now evident (Williams, 1987). For Scotland, emigration of Lowlanders to Ireland

and Europe in the seventeenth century, and of Highlanders to America in the eighteenth century, was already a familiar story. More recently it has been demonstrated that high levels of internal mobility also occurred in Lowland Scotland (Houston, 1985; Jones, 1986; Whyte, 1989). Irish emigration to Britain, once seen as resulting largely from the Great Famine of 1845–46, has been shown to have a history reaching back into the seventeenth century. There are still unanswered questions regarding the levels and nature of mobility within traditional Gaelic societies in Ireland and the Scottish Highlands.

Migration studies have benefited from the increasingly rigorous evaluation of sources, the development of more sophisticated techniques of analysis, and the formulation of new theoretical approaches, particularly by the Cambridge Group for the Study of Population and Social Structure (Wrigley and Schofield, 1989). Despite the detailed research which has been undertaken in recent years, many key themes in Early-Modern migration remain little studied. More work has been done on patterns of migration than on their effects on receiving and sending societies. Additionally, the counter-currents of migration – especially urban–rural movement – have been neglected. Migration has long been accepted as a key variable in the industrialized societies which developed in Britain, Europe and North America during the nineteenth century. It was also an important element in the transition to an industrialized society. Research is only now beginning to focus on the important transition phase of the later eighteenth and early nineteenth centuries (Pooley and Turnbull, 1998).

The relative importance of different types of migration varied between the sixteenth and the nineteenth centuries. Apprenticeship migration fell off in the seventeenth and eighteenth centuries as systems of apprenticeship declined, while the flow of indentured servants to the American colonies became correspondingly important. Long-distance subsistence migration, a characteristic feature of England in the late sixteenth and early seventeenth centuries, declined thereafter. The relatively undifferentiated pattern of longer-distance migration of the sixteenth and early seventeenth centuries gave way, in the later seventeenth and eighteenth centuries, to one increasingly characterized by specialized flows, a shift related to both economic and social changes. New forms of migration appeared: the seasonal movement of agricultural labour between regions, not significant in the seventeenth century, assumed great importance in the eighteenth with increasing regional agricultural specialization. For preindustrial

Britain, differences in the type and volume of migration, and the average distances covered, are gradually becoming clearer. No longer is the transition to an industrial society seen as involving a marked increase in the amount of mobility; the stress is on continuity as much as change.

1

Preindustrial Migration: Theories, Techniques and Sources

Theoretical Approaches

Much research on migration in preindustrial Britain has been empirical. There have been relatively few attempts to develop theoretical frameworks, although there has been considerable borrowing of ideas from research on migration in the nineteenth century and modern times. E. G. Ravenstein's 'laws' of migration (really hypotheses based on empirical data) have formed the basis for much work on migration in the nineteenth and twentieth centuries, and have also influenced research on migration in earlier periods. Ravenstein published his work, based on an analysis of birthplace data and current residence in the published British censuses of 1871 and 1881, in the 1870s and 1880s. This pioneering research in the development of theories in the social sciences based on historical data has tended to straitjacket much later work. It is important to appreciate that his ideas were developed in the context of a maturing industrial society and that, while they are often partially applicable to other periods, they have their limitations in explaining movement in preindustrial contexts. Ravenstein's laws may be summarized as follows (Grigg, 1977):

1. Most migrants move only short distances.

2. Migration proceeds step by step.
3. Migrants going long distances usually go to one of the great centres of commerce or industry.
4. Each current of migration produces a compensating counter-current.
5. The natives of towns are less migratory than those of rural areas.
6. Females are more migratory than males within the county of their birth, but males more frequently migrate further.
7. Most migrants are adults: families rarely migrate outside their county of birth.
8. Large towns grow more by migration than by natural increase.
9. Migration increases in volume as industries and commerce develop and transport improves.
10. The major direction of migration is from agricultural areas to centres of industry and commerce.
11. The major causes of migration are economic.

Ravenstein's was a macro-scale approach, based on data with severe limitations, which emphasized the economic causes of migration. Some of his hypotheses have been substantiated for the nineteenth century. Others, such as the importance of rural–urban movement and the greater propensity of women to migrate, are place and period specific. The tendency for women to migrate more than men probably reflected the lack of employment opportunities in rural areas in the later nineteenth century and the high demand for female domestic servants in the towns. On the other hand, the suggestions that large towns tend to grow by immigration rather than natural increase and that for every current of migration there was a counter-current provide valuable insights for preindustrial times.

Ravenstein's ideas were refined by Lee (1969) in a series of hypotheses relating to the volume of migration, migration flows and the characteristics of migrants, both in the past and in modern times. These may be summarized as follows:

Volume of Migration

1. The volume of migration within a given territory varies with the degree of diversity of areas included in that territory.
2. The volume of migration varies with the diversity of people.
3. The volume of migration is related to the difficulty of surmounting

intervening obstacles.

4. The volume of migration varies with fluctuations in the economy.
5. Unless severe checks are imposed, both volume and rate of migration tend to increase with time.
6. The volume and rate of migration vary with the state of progress in a country or area.

Stream and Counterstream

1. Migration tends to take place largely within well-defined streams.
2. For every major migration stream, a counterstream develops
3. The efficiency of the stream (ratio of stream to counterstream or the net redistribution of population effected by the opposite flows) is high if the major factors in the development of a migration stream were minus factors at origin.
4. The efficiency of stream and counterstream tends to be low if areas of origin and destination are similar.
5. The efficiency of migration streams will be high if the intervening obstacles are great.
6. The efficiency of a migration stream varies with economic conditions, being high in prosperous times and low in times of depression.

Characteristics of Migrants

1. Migration is selective.
2. Migrants responding primarily to plus factors at destination tend to be positively selected.
3. Migrants responding primarily to minus factors at origin tend to be negatively selected.
4. Taking all migrants together, selection tends to be bimodal.
5. The degree of positive selection increases with the difficulty of the intervening obstacles.
6. The heightened propensity to migrate at certain stages of the life-cycle is important in the selection of migrants
7. The characteristics of migrants tend to be intermediate between the characteristics of the population at origin and the population at destination.

Given that he was following Ravenstein, Lee derived his hypotheses from migration in the past as well as the present so that many of his ideas have direct relevance for studying population movement in preindustrial times.

Zelinsky (1971) produced a model of **mobility transition** representing a fusion of spatial and temporal patterns. It was the equivalent for migration of the Demographic Transition model, and was based on the belief that there were clear patterns in the growth of personal mobility through time and across space in recent history, and that these formed an essential component of the process of modernization. He suggested, following Ravenstein, that the volume of migration increased with the development of industry and commerce, not in a simple, linear way, but rather in an S-shaped curve, with a rapid increase in mobility during the transition to industrialization being followed by slower growth in rates of mobility in mature industrial economies. In the first of five phases, 'pre-modern traditional societies', there was little migration. Phase 2, 'early transitional society', saw a great shake-out of migrants from the countryside, with massive rural to urban migration as well as the colonization of internal frontiers and large-scale emigration. In Phase 3, 'late transitional society', migration was still predominantly rural to urban, but on a reduced scale as population growth slowed. Zelinsky placed the transition from Phase 1 to Phase 2 in England during the seventeenth century, and from Phase 2 to Phase 3 during the 1820s and 1830s. Although Zelinsky's model has been widely accepted, he was writing at a time when relatively little had been published on the volume of migration in preindustrial British society, especially during the early stages of industrialization. In a British context, the model understates the importance of migration in preindustrial times and exaggerates the changes that occurred with the transition to an industrialized society. Zelinsky paid too little attention to the relationship between mobility and socioeconomic changes, or to the motives and characteristics of the migrants. Nevertheless, the mobility transition model provides valuable hypotheses for further testing and has been used as the basis for more recent theoretical work (Jones, 1986; Pooley and Turnbull, 1998).

Quantitative modelling of migration follows Ravenstein's approach of summarizing large bodies of numerical data to produce generalizations about patterns of migration flows. Simple gravity models were first formulated in the 1930s and 1940s to study the roles of population size and distance in determining levels of migration. They are based on the principle that migration between two places was positively related to the size of their populations and negatively to the distance between them. Thus volumes of migration tend to fall off with increasing distance; the **distance decay** effect, but migration fields were wider for large population centres than for smaller ones. It was later appreciated that the impact of distance on migration flows was usually far from uniform. Stouffer (1960) suggested that in studying the interaction between two places, one had to consider not only distance and population, but also the number of intervening opportunities that existed and which provided alternative destinations for migrants. The distance and direction of migration flows is also likely to be constrained by intervening obstacles. Gravity models are better at identifying patterns than explaining them. They also ignore the behavioural contexts within which migration decisions were made. In the 1960s and 1970s gravity models using increasingly sophisticated techniques of multiple regression were developed. However, they required large sets of uniform, standardized data, which limited their applicability to the pre-census period. Lovett et al. (1985) used poisson regression analysis to examine the migration field of apprentices moving to Edinburgh in the seventeenth and eighteenth centuries, and Kitch (1986) undertook a comparable exercise for London. However, heavily quantitative analysis of large data sets tends to produce an impersonal, dehumanized approach in which flows replace people, and motives for migration are assumed rather than proved, often being interpreted in simplistic, generalized ways.

A very different set of approaches to the quantitative analysis of large bodies of data are those which focus on the motives behind the movement – or lack of movement – of individuals. Essentially, migration occurred because people believed that their needs and desires would be better served somewhere else. Within any population people exhibited a range of potential for mobility, varying between the chronic mover and the confirmed stayer. A person's propensity to migrate depended in part on their social status, occupation and life-cycle stage. In sixteenth- and seventeenth-century England, yeomen farmers were usually the group least likely to move. Leasehold tenants were more mobile, and especially tradesmen, labourers and servants. The decision to migrate was based on how people perceived their world to be, not how it really was. The information available to prospective migrants was usually partial and imperfect. Economic explanations for migration based on the identification of wage differentials between areas can only be partial ones if they ignore the perceptions of migrants and the nature of the information available to them. It may not have mattered whether wages were actually higher and opportunities greater in London than in a remote rural parish. The fact that people believed such differences existed was what counted. In relation to people's information gathering, a distinction has been made between their **activity space**, where information was obtained by direct contact, and **indirect contact space**, where information came from sources such as emigrant letters, newspapers and word of mouth.

The use of a systems framework for modern migration studies was pioneered by Mabogunje (1970). Relatively little use has been made of this technique, but Wrigley's (1967) model of the influence of London on the economy and society of England 1650–1750, incorporating migration, is notable, as is Skipp's (1978) ecological analysis of change in rural Warwickshire.

A good deal of effort has been directed at categorizing preindustrial migration and migrants. Clark and Souden (1987) have divided migration in Early-Modern England into four distinct but interlocking categories, distinguished by the distance involved and their 'definitiveness', or degree of divorce from place of origin. They distinguished; firstly, **local migration** which involved movement within local labour, agricultural and marriage markets. Secondly, **chain migration,** where an initial migratory move established a link between a particular source and destination, generating further migration. **Circular migration** often operated on a seasonal basis, but at various scales, encompassing the movement of labour from wood-pasture areas to neighbouring champion regions and the transatlantic seasonal operations of Cornish fishermen. The fourth category, **career migration**, involved moves which took people out of their home environment into another milieu, including the migration from rural areas of young men starting urban apprenticeships. None of these categories is watertight and all necessitate some qualification. An individual might combine elements from more than one category in a single move or at different stages in their life cycle. Career mobility did not necessarily involve geographical mobility: a young man might become an apprentice in the same town or even the same street in which he was already living. Some kinds of migration, such as the long-distance subsistence movement of poor people in the late sixteenth and early seventeenth centuries, do not fit well into this scheme

Clark (1972) divided migration in Early-Modern England, especially in the late sixteenth and early seventeenth centuries, into two groups, **subsistence** and **betterment**, in some respects an elaboration of the old notion of push and pull influences on migration. Subsistence migrants characteristically moved over longer distances more frequently, and were often older than betterment migrants with a stronger urban orientation. They were drawn to the towns by the possibility of higher wages, charity or poor relief, and a lack of social control, but they were also driven to move because of a lack of opportunities at home or by major subsistence crises. Betterment migrants were, potentially at least, upwardly mobile, moving in search of career opportunities, typified by young men starting apprenticeships. They tended to move less frequently than subsistence migrants over shorter distances, often making only one major move (e.g. from country to town) during their lifetimes, using family links and business contacts. Subsistence migration was largely a new phenomenon in the sixteenth century. Betterment migration was well established, but may have increased during the sixteenth century with growing social mobility. Clark accepts that the motives involved in migration were complex and that relatively few migrants would have conformed to the stereotype outlined here. Most people moved for a combination of motives ranged along a continuum between the two extremes.

Measuring and Mapping Migration

An important distinction in migration studies is between net and gross migration. Net migration for any place is the difference between the numbers of immigrants and emigrants. Gross migration measures the total size of the flows in each direction. Both measures are useful as they highlight different aspects of movement. Net migration indicates the overall migration balance, while gross figures give an idea of the total volume of interaction between places. As almost all migration seems to have involved return flows, gross migration may be several times larger than net migration. Where substantial levels of in- and out-migration almost cancel each other out, net migration can hide a considerable amount of gross movement (White and Woods, 1980).

Two basic features of migration fields which influence patterns of movement into a place are distance and the population of the source areas. Migration flows are usually related negatively to increasing distance from the centre and positively to the size of the population of the place of origin. Thus, in relation to migration to a city, a small nearby village and a large but distant town might contribute comparable numbers of migrants. One of the commonest ways of summarizing the characteristics of a migration field, and how it changed over time, is by calculating the mean distance migrated. The advantage of using mean distances is that they are readily comparable and provide concise summaries of large bodies of data. They may, however, be misleading: means are liable to be influenced by extreme values, so that a handful of long-distance migrants can pull the mean for a sample upwards (Whyte and Whyte, 1987). Even worse, where a migration field was dominated by two distinct groups, one moving short distances, the other a long-distance one, the mean might describe the experience of hardly any migrants. In such cases medians or modal figures may be more useful. Distance-decay graphs, where the proportion of migrants coming from within particular distance bands is shown, are commonly used to pick out this kind of variation within a migration field. Unfortunately, there is no standardization in the distance bands used so that detailed comparison between different studies is frequently difficult.

Mean migration distances and distance-decay graphs do not indicate directional biases within migration fields. These can be shown simply by mapping the origins of migrants and showing the sizes of flows using lines or arrows of varying thickness (Withers, 1985). This can, however, be visually confusing. In addition, while such maps may convey something of the influence of distance on migration flows, they do not introduce any weighting for variations in population density within the migration field. Estimates of population for counties, towns and parishes can often be calculated for the seventeenth, and even the sixteenth centuries, using various listings produced for taxation and religious purposes. Relating migrants to the population levels of their source areas can be done in terms of numbers of migrants per 1000 inhabitants over a given period (Patten, 1976). More sophisticated gravity models can build in both the variables of distance and population, assess their importance and pick out residuals, or anomalies, from the general pattern – areas contributing significantly more or fewer migrants in relation to their populations and distances from the destination under study.

Sources of Data on Migration

Before considering the detailed features of migration in preindustrial Britain, it is important to look first at some of the sources which are available for studying population movement and the problems involved in interpreting them. An ever-increasing range of sources has been exploited to shed light on different groups of migrants and different facets of migration. Developments in data handling, especially the advent of computerized database systems, have aided analysis (Pooley and Turnbull, 1998). Inevitably, research on migration in the past must begin with careful evaluation of appropriate sources, virtually none of which were designed to record migration and which shed light on the process incidentally and incompletely. Similar kinds of sources tend to occur throughout Britain; for example registers of baptisms and marriages, local population listings, apprenticeship registers and emigration data. However, differences in the legal systems of England and Scotland produced variations in the kinds of records kept. In addition the quality of record keeping and document survival before the nineteenth century has generally been much poorer in Ireland and Scotland than in England and Wales.

Contemporary comments on migration and assessments of its impact are uncommon. Movement was such a normal part of the lives of ordinary people that it rarely caused comment. It was generally only when population movement posed a threat to the social order or economic prosperity that the authorities became interested, as with vagrancy in Tudor and Stuart England or worries that emigration from the Highlands in the later eighteenth century might lead to a serious loss of manpower. Such sources thus tend to highlight the unusual rather than the everyday, and are rarely objective or accurate.

Too often, though perhaps inevitably, the availability of suitable data dictates the kind of migration problems which are studied. Migration was often only recorded when people changed their residence across a civil or ecclesiastical boundary. But these were arbitrary divisions and there may be problems of comparability between units like parishes and counties, as migration rates were strongly influenced by variations in their size, shape and populations. Thus population turnover rates and levels of marriage endogamy between a small parish in lowland England and a large one in northern England or Scotland, or between a small city-centre parish and a large suburban one, may not be comparable (Finlay, 1981; Bolton, 1987). Moreover, even the most detailed sources, such as church court depositions, rarely record all migratory moves. Apparently 'immobile' people may often have been those who did not move outside their parish of birth, which is not quite the same thing, for such movements could be significant. For example, in 1799 William Wordsworth and his sister Dorothy went to live in the parish of Grasmere. They remained there for the rest of their lives. Nevertheless, they also made a number of moves: from Dove Cottage to Allan Banks in 1808; to the parsonage in 1811; and, finally, to Rydal Mount in 1813. Although over very short distances, these moves were important: they reflected the needs of William's growing family and also his rising income as his reputation grew. The move from a cramped cottage to a succession of larger dwellings also symbolized his changing political and social alignment as the young revolutionary gradually became a pillar of the establishment.

The quality of source material varies over time. The general tendency for record keeping to improve from the sixteenth century to the nineteenth century does not always apply. Thus, for England, sources relating to migration are better, overall, for the late sixteenth and early seventeenth centuries than for the eighteenth when many of the most informative types of document: church court depositions, apprenticeship records and marriage registers fade out or become less representative. Migration during the early phases of industrialization is especially poorly recorded. Throughout our period, sources for migration are heavily biased towards recording men rather than women, though women may often have formed more than half of those on the move (Stapleton, 1988).

Sources for studying migration in preindustrial Britain can be classified in various ways. One group comprises those which provide information on the origins and destinations of specific groups of people, such as apprenticeship and freemen's registers, church court depositions, marriage registers, settlement records, servants' indentures, hiring-fair records, farm leases, and documents relating to vagrancy and emigrant lists. A problem with these is that they cover particular groups whose migration patterns were not necessarily representative of the population as a whole, or even significant sectors of it. Data from apprenticeship registers have been claimed to be representative of the movement of young betterment migrants into preindustrial towns (Patten, 1976). However, research on migration of indentured servants to London has shown different contemporary patterns of geographical origin for a broadly comparable group

(Wareing, 1981). People who acted as witnesses in civil and criminal cases heard before church courts may have covered a more representative spectrum of contemporary society, but even this group was not free from bias (Clark, 1987). Marriage registers provide information on one particular element of mobility for a substantial proportion of the population; but not every adult got married. Most sources either record a single movement undertaken at a particular period in a person's life – at marriage for instance – without providing information on earlier or subsequent moves, or they indicate a person's place of birth and current residence without giving data on their intermediate travels.

Another category of sources includes various population listings. When drawn up for ecclesiastical purposes, such documents often only include communicants over the age of about 16. Where more than one listing occurs for a particular parish, especially when drawn up a few years apart by the same person for the same purpose, they are valuable in providing measures of population turnover (Laslett, 1977). Such lists indicate who moved into or out of a community between two points in time, but not normally where they came from or went to. Other forms of listings which allow movements into and out of a community to be monitored include medieval manorial records such as lists of frankpledge (Schofield, 1994) and estate rentals listing tenants (Whyte and Whyte, 1985). Listings drawn up for taxation or ecclesiastical purposes may be wider in their coverage, allowing studies of net migration at a broader scale (Pickles, 1996), as do private censuses such as the ones for Scotland produced by Alexander Webster in 1755 and Sir John Sinclair in the 1790s (Devine, 1994; Kyd, 1952; Sinclair, 1791–99). The first official census of Britain was taken in 1801, but detailed information relating to birthplace and current residence is not available, either in summary form or from surviving enumerators' books, before 1841.

Particularly valuable are sources which provide migration biographies charting all, or at least some, of the moves made by people during their lifetimes. Church court depositions and settlement examinations often provide potted migration biographies, though rarely, one suspects, complete ones. Much rarer are diaries and autobiographies which contain information not only on migration, but the motives involved (Pooley and D'Cruz, 1995). People who kept diaries and wrote autobiographies in preindustrial times were clearly not representative of society as a whole. However, the scope for amalgamating genealogical information for the eighteenth and early nineteenth centuries to allow national-scale aggregative studies of migration patterns has recently been demonstrated (Pooley and Turnbull, 1988). Diaries like that of Ralph Josselin, vicar of Earl's Colne, Essex, (Macfarlane, 1970) and Richard Gough's incomparable history of Myddle in Shropshire (Hey, 1981) provide information on movement into and out of a few select communities.

The keeping of registers of baptisms, marriages and burials was first required in England in 1538, although few survive from this early date. Many more parish registers are more or less continuous from Elizabethan times. Marriage registers have been used most for studying migration (Chapter 2), but sometimes baptism entries may contain information on the origin of parents, and even grandparents (Holderness, 1967–70; Pickles, 1996). Family reconstitution, the linking of data on baptisms, marriages and burials for particular individuals provides, by default, information on those who moved into and out of a parish, though the interpretation of such data is not straightforward (Souden, 1984). In Scotland parish registers were authorized in the mid-sixteenth century, but surviving registers from even the early seventeenth century are rare and the quality of record keeping was poorer than south of the Border. As a result, scope for reconstitution studies in Scotland is limited. Recording baptisms, marriages and burials in Ireland was complicated by the fact that the Anglican church had only a minority following, though the records of other religious groups, like Quakers, have been analysed (Houston, 1992). In England marriage registers suffer from under-registration due to the increase of clandestine and dissenting marriages in the eighteenth century. In Scotland many registers only record the calling of banns, which was not always followed by marriage.

During the later sixteenth and seventeenth centuries, witnesses in civil and criminal cases heard by diocesan courts were required to preface their depositions by brief autobiographies which, as well as providing information on age, occupation and status, also give place of birth and, frequently, details of subsequent moves, with length of residence in different places. The people who acted as witnesses were often of some standing in their community, but before the mid-seventeenth century a reasonable proportion of poor people were asked to testify. Some diocesan courts never recovered from the upheavals of the mid-seventeenth century though others, notably Norwich, functioned for longer. There may have been a bias in the choice of witnesses against women and younger or poorer people and in favour of longer-term residents, so that the data may under-represent migration. Nevertheless, on account of the numbers of depositions available, their fairly standardized format and wide geographical coverage, and the fact that they provide information on multiple (though probably rarely all) movements, they form perhaps the most important source of information on migration in England down to the early eighteenth century (Clark, 1987). Although not directly comparable, testaments of good moral conduct issued by Scottish kirk sessions contain information of movements into and out of parishes, and sometimes also allow some migration histories to be reconstructed (Houston, 1985)

Apprenticeship and freemen's records provide an often voluminous, but fairly standardized source of information on migrants to Early-Modern towns. However, many apprentices entering poorer trades were not registered and systems of apprenticeship declined during the seventeenth century in England and the eighteenth century in Scotland. Apprenticeship records have been used to define the migration fields of preindustrial British towns at various periods from the fifteenth century to the eighteenth, and to show how they evolved through time. Freemen's registers tend to contain less information than apprenticeship records and their value is increasingly undermined from the later seventeenth century by the practice of creating large numbers of new freemen for electoral purposes.

Documents relating to eligibility for poor relief, generated by the Acts of Parliament of 1662, 1697 and later, concerning settlement, provide a considerable volume of information on the movements of poor migrants in England from the later seventeenth century to the early nineteenth. Records are widely scattered among the collections of parishes and in the papers of courts of petty and quarter sessions. They include settlement certificates, records of examinations before magistrates which were used to decide a person's parish of settlement and orders for removing them to that parish. Certificates are the most detailed settlement documents, sometimes giving potted biographies of the people under investigation, including previous migratory moves. Settlement examinations are likely to survive in the parish in which a person was living, but removal orders in the parish of settlement to which they were sent back. Settlement records are full of family crises and a wide variety of human experience, but as Taylor (1989) has suggested, they are a poor place to search for statistical norms, chronicling failure and tragedy rather than success.

Records relating to emigration may also be valuable in highlighting patterns of internal migration. Nicholas and Shergold (1987) have used the records of criminals transported to the new colony in Australia between 1818 and 1839 to study migration within Britain, measured by the distance between the criminals' county of birth and county of arrest. The biographical information on the criminals, sentenced mostly for petty crimes, suggested that they were little different from the rest of the working population. Servants' indentures can be used in a similar way. Wareing (1981) has studied a sample of indentured servants leaving London for the New World between 1683 and 1775 whose origins lay outside the capital. At best they give the name, age, origin, destination, period of service. They cover the period when apprenticeship and feemen's records become less useful, and relate to a more representative group of migrants. The data may under-represent female migrants and people from the hinterlands of ports like Bristol and Liverpool, but otherwise are likely to reflect general patterns of migration to London.

Much migration research has been static, providing cross-sections rather than dynamic views of an evolving process. This is an inevitable result of temporal variability in the quality of the sources. Physical mobility has been studied more than the extent to which migration disseminated new ideas, attitudes and skills such as literacy. New sources relating to migration are still being discovered and more sophisticated ways of analysing established ones developed.

2

MOBILITY AND MIGRATION IN THE COUNTRYSIDE

Richard Gough's history of Myddle in Shropshire, written in 1701 but reaching far back into the seventeenth century, provides fascinating insights into the mental horizons of a rather remote English parish 256km from London (Hey, 1981). The community of Myddle had a distinct identity, but it interacted with others in a circuit of neighbouring parishes, as well as with nearby market towns including the county centre of Shrewsbury. The inhabitants of Myddle saw themselves as being different from their Welsh neighbours, but English people from beyond Shropshire were also described as 'foreigners'. This emphasizes the localism that one might expect from preindustrial society. More surprising, perhaps, is evidence for long-distance contacts and a knowledge of events occurring on a wider stage. Nineteen of the 90 or so families in Myddle in the late seventeenth century had at least one son or daughter living in London. Some families had several members there and many other individuals had visited the capital on shorter trips. During the Civil Wars 20 men left Myddle to fight on the royalist side; most were of humble origins, the sons of craftsmen and labourers. Thirteen were killed in action. As in the later poems of Housman's 'Shropshire Lad', enlisting as a soldier was one way of getting out of a local rut and seeing the world: one man from Myddle ended up in the garrison at Tangier, under Charles II temporarily an English colony

Migration among Britain's rural dwellers, who comprised most of the population throughout our period, was a normal feature of life. Most, though by no means all, of this movement operated over short distances. The contacts maintained by people living in any community were predominantly with a circuit of neighbouring parishes, whose extent can be gauged by contacts such as the choice of marriage partners, patterns of debt and credit, property ownership and trading links with market centres (Hey, 1974; Wrightson and Levine, 1979). Most links of this kind operated within a radius of 16–19km. Rural people might move considerable distances during their lifetimes, often in a succession of short stages, but frequently in a circuit rather than a straight line so that they often ended up close to where they had been born.

High levels of mobility were not a new feature of rural society in sixteenth-century Britain. Considerable population turnover has been identified in late-medieval times. Within any community there were mobile and immobile elements. Migration was extremely age-specific, with a concentration of movement amongst adolescents and young adults. The frequent turnover of agricultural servants accounted for much of the mobility. More prosperous farming families often provided communities with a stable core, anchored by land ownership, although such families were also a source of mobile younger sons. Hoskins (1957) showed that in the Leicestershire village of Wigston Magna, 44 per cent of the families listed in the late-seventeenth-century hearth-tax lists had been in the village for over 100 years, 20 per cent for 200. Labourers showed a rapid rate of turnover pre-1620, but by the end of the seventeenth century they were nearly as stable as craftsmen and husbandmen. However, even freeholding families were not totally immobile; there was an active land market and the deep attachment to specific plots of land, characteristic of peasant societies in many parts of Europe, was not a feature of preindustrial England (Kitch, 1992). Small farmers, vulnerable to fluctuations in harvest quality and prices, were quite mobile. In England, from the sixteenth to the eighteenth centuries, they were squeezed out in many rural communities as their holdings were absorbed by larger, more successful neighbours or by commercially minded landowners. This produced increasing polarization in many communities, with new mobility patterns. Families of craftsmen, and especially labourers, were more mobile in the sixteenth and early seventeenth centuries, though from the later seventeenth century they tended to become more rooted in particular parishes.

Rates of population turnover can be established for a few parishes by comparing successive listings of inhabitants. More generally, there were important differences over time in levels of mobility and the average distance people moved. The peak of mobility in the English countryside coincided with the most rapid phase of population growth in the later sixteenth and early seventeenth centuries. There is widespread evidence that mobility diminished in the later seventeenth and early eighteenth centuries. One likely influence was the impact of the Settlement Laws and better provision of parish poor relief, but other factors, such as the slow down in population growth after the mid-seventeenth century, the expansion of agricultural production and the spread of industrial by-employments, may have reduced pressure to move (Kitch, 1992). There were significant differences in levels of mobility at various scales between upland and lowland zones, arable and wood-pasture districts within the lowlands and, more locally, between parishes with different landholding and social structures. At an inter-regional scale, the development of industry may have helped stem the outflow of population from many upland areas, especially in the north, during the later seventeenth and eighteenth centuries. Migration at marriage was another component of mobility. At lower levels of society, the wanderings of the vagrant poor were a source of concern to central and local authorities. The development of the system of poor relief in seventeenth-century England and the application of increasing controls on settlement had an impact on mobility and migration, the nature of which is still keenly debated. Rural societies in Wales and Lowland Scotland shared the characteristics of mobility identified for England, due in part to broadly comparable social structures. Less is known about migration in the Scottish Highlands or Ireland, but there are indications that here too population was far from static (Whyte, 1989).

The frequency of migration but the prevalence of short-distance movement has generated the idea that most rural dwellers spent their lives within a 'local country', in which their activities were structured by a number of networks, such as kinship, occupation and religion, which operated at a wider level than those of the individual community. A local country might equal the distance easily walked in a day, an area over which information about landholding or job opportunities would circulate easily by word of mouth. Within a local country people might have had access to larger pools of kin than in any individual community (King, 1997).

The ubiquity, yet at the same time the local nature, of so much of the movement within the countryside could be taken as implying that immigrants into new communities were easily assimilated. However, this has been assumed rather than proved. King (1997), studying the textile-manufacturing community of Calverley in West Yorkshire, has argued that the assimilation of migrants, even of those who had come only from neighbouring townships and who had kin living in the communities to which they moved, was slow and that first-generation migrants did not settle easily. The possession of kin in the community and a shared occupational tradition was not enough to ensure that migrants were warmly received. Many do not appear to have been accepted and were either forced to move on or were condemned to a marginalized existence, economically and geographically. Immigrant families were more likely to receive poor relief than established families, whose members could draw upon local networks of credit which were denied to strangers. The fact that migrant families suffered higher rates of infant and child mortality than native families may reflect their exclusion from such forms of assistance. Upward social mobility in Calverley was relatively rare among first-generation migrants and was more a feature of their children, who tended to marry into longer-established families within the community.

This leads to the question of how important kinship was in enabling migrants to fit into new communities. Kinship links were probably very significant, though they are not easy to detect. Razi (1980) indicated that many of the peasants moving into the Midlands arable parish of Halesowen in the late fourteenth and fifteenth centuries were related to families already established in the community. That this helped them to be accepted was shown by the way in which an increasing number of them were appointed to offices within the manor or parish soon after arrival. For Early-Modern England, though, it has been widely believed that kinship recognition and ties beyond the immediate nuclear family were of limited and declining importance (Wrightson, 1981), especially below the level of the gentry. The same suggestion has been made for Lowland Scotland (Houston and Whyte, 1989). As a result, it has been considered that effective kinship densities were low, so that even a short-distance move might cut a migrant off from family help. However, the correspondence of seventeenth-century emigrants to New England suggests that even distant kin could be called upon to provide help for emigrants and open doors for them (Cressey, 1986). It has long been accepted that betterment migrants to large towns, especially London, often used family links as well as business contacts to find places and ease their assimilation into urban society (Chapter 3). As most rural migrants moved short distances, then wider recognition of kin may often have helped them.

Mobility in Medieval Times

The migration of peasants was a common feature of medieval England, even before the Black Death, with or without their lords' permission (Field, 1983; Raftis, 1964). Analysis of tithing lists in Essex shows that by the 1320s and 1330s, communities had levels of population turnover comparable with levels 300 years later (Poos, 1991). This was the outcome of a markedly stratified rural society with a significant component of landless, wage-dependent workers. Attempts by manors to ban or expel outsiders may reflect pressure as medieval population levels reached their maximum, possibly associated with high levels of vagrancy, as occurred during the sixteenth century (Poos, 1991). Villeinage did not necessarily tie peasants to particular communities. The manorial economy and the services required by the lord of the manor might cause peasants to travel to other communities as much as 32–48km away (Raftis, 1964). Family ties were frequently extended by marriage to partners from outside the community.

Nevertheless, there is widespread agreement that there was an increase in population mobility, a sharp one in some areas, in the later fourteenth and early fifteenth centuries. The Black Death, and later plague outbreaks, increased the demand for labour and encouraged a loosening of seigneurial bonds (Raftis, 1964; Razi, 1980). On the manors of Ramsey Abbey increasing numbers of villagers began to leave their homes with the permission of their lords in the 1390s, but from around 1400 there was a flood of illegal emigrants. Peasant farmers moved to obtain land on better terms, labourers to gain higher wages (Raftis, 1964). Few returned and some at least moved to London. The basic features of population mobility in late-medieval England were similar to those of Early-Modern times. Migration was closely related to life-cycle stage, with movement concentrated among people in their late teens and early 20s. Most movement occurred within a radius of 16–24km. People often moved to communities in which they already had kin whose presence allowed easier assimilation (Razi, 1980). A good deal of mobility was due to the movement of male and female servants, who often changed employers annually. Labourers were also mobile, craftsmen and farmers less so.

McClure's (1979) study of the 1327 subsidy rolls, focusing on Nottinghamshire, used place-name surnames as an index of lifetime migration at a time when non-hereditary surnames were still common. Even at this early date a good deal of mobility was evident. As in later times, most migration operated over short distances; 61 per cent within a radius of 16km. Movement into towns like Nottingham and Leicester was over slightly greater distances than migration between villages. Over 15 per cent of migrants had moved over distances ranging from 55–241km, indicating a significant long-distance component to migration.

Table 2.1 Rural Immigration in Early-Fourteenth-Century Nottinghamshire (After McClure, 1979)

Distance (km)	% of migrants (place-name surnames)
<8	40.7
9–16	20.4
17–24	10.6
25–32	4.6
33–40	4.2
41–48	3.2
49–54	0.5
55–241	15.7

Medieval sources hint at the existence of local variations in social structure and of labour requirements between communities, which generated mobility among servants and labourers, in areas like Essex, the Midlands and Devon (Fox, 1995; Poos, 1991). For Devon, Fox (1995) has discerned local socioeconomic contrasts reminiscent of the 'open' and 'close' parishes of eighteenth- and nineteenth-century England (see below). Seasonal labour from outside the community was an important feature of the workforce on some medieval manors (Raftis, 1964). The late medieval period, with falling population, scarce labour, low food prices, and a trend towards pastoral farming, ought to have favoured the employment of large numbers of mobile servants (Fox, 1995) and there are some indications that they were at least as prominent in rural society as in the sixteenth century (Poos, 1991).

Population Turnover

A basic measure of the volume of migration is the level of population turnover within a community. This involves establishing how many of the people who were resident in a community at a particular date were no longer there a number of years later, and how many new people had arrived. Subtracting those who are known to have been buried from those who had disappeared provides a measure of out-migration, while the number of new appearances, other than those who had been baptized, provides an indication of in-migration. Unfortunately, turnover can only occasionally be calculated because it depends on the existence of two or more listings of a parish's population, ideally produced by the same person for the same purpose, a number of years apart; a rare occurrence.

The classic study of population turnover, which clearly demonstrated the amount of mobility in preindustrial England, was by Laslett (1977) on the parishes of Clayworth, in Nottinghamshire, between 1676 and 1688, and Cogenhoe, in Northamptonshire, between 1618 and 1628 (Table 2.2). At Clayworth 61 per cent of the population present in 1676 had vanished by 1688. At Cogenhoe 52 per cent of the inhabitants of 1618 were no longer there ten years later. The annual rates of turnover for the two communities – around 5 per cent each year or one person in 20 – were fairly similar. About 40 per cent of the missing people had died; the remainder had moved away. Apart from the biological causes of birth and death, turnover could be broken down into movements related to the entry and exit of servants, marriage, the movement of households and families, and the migration of other individuals. Young servants were the most mobile group in both communities. They accounted for only 16–17 per cent of the population, but accounted for 42 per cent of movements in Clayworth and 45 per cent in Cogenhoe. In Cogenhoe three-quarters of the servants mentioned in one listing had left two years later. Virtually all had gone within a decade. The movement of marriage partners in and out of the two parishes played only a small role in migration; 8 per cent of movements in Clayworth and 6 per cent in Cogenhoe. This is interesting considering how much attention has been devoted to marriage migration (see below). The entry and exit of families and households accounted for about a third of movements; change of residence after marriage was more significant in population turnover than migration at marriage. In Cogenhoe between 1618 and 1620 five out of 33 families moved out of the village, something which must have had a significant effect on the social structure of the community, especially as the family at the manor house was one of them, but movement of landholders on this scale may have been exceptional. Most families on the move in Clayworth were those of husbandmen and labourers.

Table 2.2 Population Turnover (per cent) in Clayworth and Cogenhoe (After Laslett, 1977)

	Clayworth 1676–88	**Cogenhoe 1618–28**
Exits from Parish		
Died	37.7	16.1
Married	2.5	c.5.1
Household members migrating	18.4	*c*.40.4
Movement of servants	21.7	18.2
Unaccounted for	19.7	*c*.21.2
Entries to Parish		
Born	36.2	31.0
Married	7.1	*c*.3.0
Household members migrating	22.7	*c* 15.
Movement of servants	23.5	27.0
Unaccounted for	0	*c*.24.0
Children of marriage partners	6.3	?
Lodgers, kin, etc.	4.3	?

Findings for other communities from the sixteenth to the eighteenth centuries have confirmed the pattern of turnover established at Clayworth and Cogenhoe, while identifying interesting differences in detail. Some levels of turnover were particularly high. Towcester, in Northamptonshire, recorded turnover levels of 17 per cent in one year in the mid-sixteenth century, but evidence from late-sixteenth-century muster rolls produces rates of around 5 per cent per annum for other communities, more comparable with Laslett's findings (Kitch, 1992).

High turnover rates were also a feature of the eighteenth century. Schofield (1987) has studied a listing of 1782 for the arable farming community of Cardington, Bedfordshire, which showed that around 70 per cent of the population had been born elsewhere. However, movement within Cardington was almost as frequent as it was into and out of the parish. In 1782 seven families moved within the parish, compared to four moving in from other parishes and five moving out. The listing provided details of children, including those who were not resident with their families. All children under ten, and most between ten and 14, were still living at home. For boys between 15 and 19, however, only 22 per cent were still at home. The rest had gone into service. Girls went into service a little later; 71 per cent aged 15–19 were at home, but only 48 per cent aged 20–24.

Escott's (1988) study of Binfield, Berkshire, based on a series of listings and tax records between 1779 and 1801, provides some interesting contrasts with Clayworth and Cogenhoe. There 76 per cent of households within the parish persisted for over a decade and 36 per cent persisted between 1780 and 1801, a rate which, although applying to households rather than individuals, implies slower turnover, something which may relate to the impact of the Settlement Laws (see below). The lists allowed movements of families within the parish to be charted and show that 18 per cent of household turnover was due to movements within the parish as opposed to 15 per cent due to out-migration, emphasizing the importance of small-scale local moves and the artificiality imposed by the use of parish boundaries. Tinley and Mills (1994) examined turnover in the Lincolnshire parish of Swinderby using listings dated 1771 and 1791. Of 224 inhabitants in 1771, only 23 per cent were still there 20 years later. About 57 per cent of the turnover was due to migration. The annual turnover rate, just under 4 per cent, was on the low side in relation to Kitch's (1992) suggested figure of 4–6 per cent for English village populations as a whole. Cruder measures of turnover have used the persistence of surnames within communities. Turner's (1995) study of Nidderdale in Yorkshire identified groups of incoming surnames in the lower part of the valley in the late seventeenth century, associated with an influx of lead miners from Derbyshire and other areas.

Many of these surnames disappeared around 1730 when production in the mines fell. By contrast, the more remote dale head had a high persistence of established surnames suggesting a more stable population.

Parish population turnover has also been examined using family reconstitution to differentiate between 'movers' and 'stayers'. Because family reconstitution is undertaken for substantial time periods it offers the prospect of identifying temporal variations in turnover, as well as providing comparisons between parishes, though it has the disadvantage of failing to cover movements of servants who, being young and single, did not appear in marriage and baptism records and were the least likely group to figure in burial registers. Even linking baptisms and marriages can enhance the picture of mobility produced by marriage registers alone. In Terling, Essex, of people marrying and then staying in the parish long enough to have at least their first child baptized, only a little over a quarter of men and a third of women had themselves been baptized in the parish (Wrightson and Levine, 1979). While the figure for women remained steady from the late sixteenth century to the end of the seventeenth, the percentage of men marrying in the parish and having their first child baptized there, who had themselves been baptized in the parish, rose from 19 per cent in 1580–1619 to 40 per cent in 1660–1699, suggesting that there was a reduction in male in-migration.

All family reconstitution forms can provide information on mobility, not just those for the 'reconstitutable minority' (Wrigley, 1994), because data missing from such forms may indicate migration. Souden (1984) used reconstitution data on married couples to determine whether or not residence was continuous from baptism, through marriage and the baptisms of their children, to their deaths. Gaps in such a sequence were interpreted as evidence of movement into and out of a parish. An increasing proportion of people being registered at all points of their life cycles would suggest decreasing mobility. Conversely, a rising proportion of people recorded only at the mid points of their lives would indicate increasing turnover. Souden admitted the possibility that people might have left a parish and returned between the dates at which their residence was pinpointed, particularly during the long period between the end of childbearing and death. He used reconstitution data for 16 parishes, making allowance for variations due to differences in their population sizes. He found that in a number of southern agricultural parishes, turnover fell during the seventeenth century, comparable with findings derived from sources such as church court depositions (Clark, 1987). Trends during the eighteenth century varied. In some parishes mobility appeared to increase; in others it fell, this being associated with strong landlord control.

Snell (1984) has criticized Souden for assuming that people were necessarily living in the parish in which they were registered for baptisms, marriages and burials. He pointed out that Souden's trends in mobility levels were small so that even slight changes in the factors influencing registration could have seriously affected his results. Snell suggested that it was common for mothers to deliver children, especially their firstborn, in their parents' parish. After baptism children were taken to the mother's parish of residence. Marriage often took place in the wife's or her father's parish of residence: under Souden's system a wife would become a migrant merely by moving away temporarily from her parish of birth or residence in order to get married. Burial information could also be misleading. Old people often insisted on being buried in a particular parish, perhaps beside their spouse, either moving there in old age or leaving instructions to be buried there. If someone died in their parish of baptism but requested to be buried elsewhere, then by Souden's method the corpse became a migrant. Snell suggested that the movement in this way of elderly people before death might help explain the greater continuity of parish registration from the later seventeenth century – through reasons which had nothing to do with labour mobility. After the settlement legislation of 1662, and especially 1685 (see below), elderly people became removable to their parish of settlement when they became chargeable or seemed likely to become so. As settlement in a parish was usually gained when young, this might often involve removal to the parish in which a person had been married. This would explain the apparent decline in out-migration from many of Souden's parishes from the late seventeenth century. Snell claimed that Souden's method emphasized the movement of economically inactive elements within the population; baptized infants, pregnant women, the aged and the dead. Snell believed that most of the apparent temporal changes in turnover identified by Souden were due to variations in parochial registration in response to changes in the settlement and poor law system. The debate emphasizes the importance for migration studies of a full understanding of the social, economic and legal context of the sources employed.

Temporal and Geographical Variations in Migration

In England before *c*.1640 migration was a normal experience. Much of it involved local movements of servants, apprentices, marriage partners and others trying to better themselves, though there was also a significant element of long-distance subsistence migration (Clark, 1987). Wrightson and Levine (1979) have suggested that between the mid-sixteenth and mid-seventeenth centuries, there was a significant weakening of localism in English rural society, with increasing economic specialization within an emerging national economy, and local loyalties giving way to increased participation in the political and cultural life of a wider community. Associated with this was increasing social differentiation in many rural communities, with a growing split between rich and poor. Such changes were gradual rather than catastrophic, selective rather than all-embracing: many aspects of life remained little changed. Many of the changes reflected, and were a response to, population growth. Migration was important not just as a response to socioeconomic change but as one of its prime causes.

Court depositions from the later seventeenth and early eighteenth centuries suggest that population turnover remained high, but operated over more limited distances than in the early seventeenth century. Lack of population growth with fewer people being squeezed out of local society is one possible reason for this change, along with a decline in vagrancy (see below). The long-distance, north–south, west–east movement which was so evident before *c*.1640 declined markedly. Migration outside county of birth was more common among townspeople than country dwellers. About half the people who moved travelled 16km or less; only around 10 per cent travelled over 64km, under 5 per cent over 160km. Professional people moved furthest on average, yeomen and husbandmen least. Even poorer migrants moved mostly over short distances. Levels of mobility seem to have been greatest in eastern England, less in the west, possibly due to differences in the quality of communications and levels of urbanization (Clark, 1987). Before 1640 higher-status people had tended to migrate over short distances. In the late seventeenth and early eighteenth centuries gentlemen and professional men moved over longer distances, increasingly for leisure purposes. Nevertheless, local-scale migration remained the most striking feature of English demography and society into Victorian times. That there was more short-distance movement does not necessarily imply a reduction in the actual volume of migration though. Snell (1984) has cast doubts on the idea that labour mobility decreased from the later seventeenth century, citing Kussmaul's (1981) evidence that this was the period in which farm service, with its associated high turnover, was at its peak.

In preindustrial Britain patterns of population movement can be identified: at a large scale between contrasting zones, especially upland and lowland; at a medium scale between different types of farming regions; and at a local scale between parishes with different socioeconomic characteristics. It has been customary to present certain areas as ones of net in-migration or outward movement. In reality migration patterns were more complex. Not only did counter-currents of movement exist. Regions which in most years were characterized by net in-migration, including wood-pasture districts with substantial reserves of woodland and waste, like the West Midlands, or the uplands of northern England, might experience heavy short-term outflows due to harvest failures or industrial slumps. At a large scale, the most consistent patterns were movements of people from northern and western areas of England towards the south and east, often coinciding with migration to a town, especially London. However, despite the pull of the capital, there may also have been reverse movements from the lowlands of south-eastern England towards the north and west (Skipp, 1978).

Agricultural historians have identified patterns of farming regions in Early-Modern England and Wales, which changed through time as the agrarian economy became more commercialized (Thirsk, 1987). Particular farming systems had different labour requirements, which tended either to attract people into an area or send them out. Whether an area drew in migrants or lost population also depended on patterns of holding sizes, social structures, and the presence or absence of non-agricultural employment. Whatever the farming system, immigrants were attracted by the availability of common land or the lack of tight landlord controls on settlement. Areas of immigration included the Fens, especially where land drainage and reclamation was in progress, wood-pasture or forest areas where medieval settlement had been thin, and upland zones. Densely settled arable areas with little waste for colonization tended to be net exporters of people as population rose from the mid-sixteenth century.

A range of communities which experienced immigration during the sixteenth and seventeenth centuries has been examined. Skipp's

(1978) study of parishes in the Forest of Arden identified two waves of immigrants, in the 1570s and in the first decade of the seventeenth century. Some arrived as single adults, their subsequent marriages causing a baby boom; others came as married couples. The amount of available land was limited and most incomers settled as cottagers, some at least with industrial by-employments. The immigrants were associated with a marked expansion of industry in the parish and a growing polarization of society, with a rising proportion of landless families. Their origins are rarely known. Most were probably local, from the more arable areas of Warwickshire, but a few came from Buckinghamshire, Oxfordshire and Northamptonshire further to the south-east. Some in-migration was temporary; a number of families moved out again during years of food shortage in the 1610s and 1620s.

Myddle in Shropshire was another wood-pasture community affected by in-migration (Hey, 1974). Although there had been woodland clearance and enclosure from late medieval times, it was not until the last 20 years of the sixteenth century that the first wave of squatters arrived. Manorial court records show that in 1581 the first of these incomers was presented for erecting a house without permission. Most of the people who followed during the next two decades were labourers, smallholders and cottagers. Another group of immigrants arrived during the mid-seventeenth century. There was plenty of land to spare and the additional revenue was welcomed by the manorial steward. Between 1563 and 1676 the population of Myddle nearly doubled. Some immigrants were Welsh; others came from neighbouring parishes within Shropshire. Unlike the parishes in Arden, immigration at the end of the sixteenth century did not cause an increase in baptisms, which tended to fall rather than rise. The influx of labourers seems only to have balanced those who died during the worst years of harvest shortage. From the 1630s, however, baptisms rose with the arrival of the second, larger wave of immigrant labourers. The incomers had a significant impact on the social structure of Myddle. In the mid-sixteenth century it had been a parish of small pastoral farms and a few large ones supporting minor gentry families. The incomers sharpened social stratification within the parish by broadening the base of society, while the richer yeomen and gentry families engrossed many of the smaller farms.

Another region which drew substantial immigration in the later sixteenth and early seventeenth centuries was the uplands of northern England, including the Pennines and the fringes of the Lake District.

Attractions included huge reserves of unimproved waste, acquiescent landlords who permitted squatting, and the availability of industrial by-employments, especially in textile manufacture. This process has been charted in Rossendale (Tupling, 1927), Bowland (Porter, 1974), the Forest of Inglewood between Penrith and Carlisle (Appleby, 1978), and the Yorkshire Dales (Turner, 1995). Not all population growth in such areas was due to in-migration. The subdivision of medieval vaccaries by landlords, the planned intake of large areas of waste, and customs of partible inheritance among smaller freeholders allowed growing local populations to be absorbed. All these areas did, however, experience squatting by incomers on the margins of the improved land. Little is known about them other than that they were poor. Most probably came from nearby lowlands, but it is possible that rumours of land freely available may have brought some from more distant places.

On the other hand, upland and wood-pasture areas were also, at times, a source of out-migration. The small sizes of their holdings, the marginal nature of agriculture, and their dependence on domestic industries to make ends meet, rendered them particularly vulnerable to the effects of bad harvests and industrial depression. This seems to have occurred on a significant scale in the 1620s and 1630s in Pendle (Swain, 1986). The classic study is Appleby (1978) on Cumbria, where population pressure in a marginal environment brought a major famine in 1623 following a disastrous harvest failure.

Other areas of in-migration included the Fen-edge parishes of Cambridgeshire, which changed from being one of the most lightly occupied zones of the county to one of the most thickly settled (Spufford, 1974), though the scale of immigration compared with natural increase is not clear. Much of the movement was probably local from nearby parishes on the clay plateau. A combination of livestock rearing and dairying made it possible for people to survive with small holdings due to the availability of extensive fen commons, wildfowling and fishing.

Rural industry, as an attraction for migrants, was not confined to pastoral areas. From the mid-seventeenth century it spread into arable farming communities, which were not controlled by single powerful landowners but by smaller freeholders, who saw additional cottages as sources of profit (Thirsk, 1984). The development of framework knitting in Leicestershire is a good example. Wigston Magna had many small farmers, but relatively few labourers in the early sixteenth century. Between 1525 and 1625 the population doubled, some of it at least due to migration into this relatively 'open' community. There was a further inflow of families in the later seventeenth century, perhaps related to enclosure and the conversion of land to pasture in other Leicestershire parishes. This growth of population was associated with the emergence of the poor as a distinct class in village society. In the later seventeenth century framework knitting provided an income for a growing proportion of the poorer inhabitants (Hoskins, 1957).

Coal mining areas also attracted migrants. Levine and Wrightson's (1991) study of Whickham, on the south bank of the Tyne, highlights a community with a very mobile, indeed transient, population. In the hearth-tax lists for the 1670s, only a quarter of the inhabitants had been listed in the parish the previous year, while many newcomers had appeared. Much of the migration seems to have come in a series of waves, the largest probably during the first two decades of the seventeenth century. Some of the workforce came fairly long distances, including from Scotland to judge by the occurrence of surnames like Leslie, Lindsay and Wallace. Others may have moved from upland areas to the west which recorded a surplus of baptisms, but no population growth in the later sixteenth and seventeenth centuries. Most immigrants, however, seem to have been local, from other mining areas on Tyneside and in northern County Durham. Whether the migrants were driven out of their home areas by poverty and unemployment, or were attracted by higher wages, is not clear. Colliery areas often provided temporary accommodation for workers, which may have been one pull factor. Wages, though difficult to determine, do not seem to have been outstandingly high. Some of the turnover was due to dangerous working conditions and a high accident rate. For many young men, mining may have been a temporary life-cycle phase like agricultural service, but much mining on Tyneside was still seasonal due to the impossibility of maintaining shipping links with London in winter. There was thus probably a lot of population movement even in good times.

There is more information about in-migration to communities in the sixteenth and seventeenth centuries than out-migration. Yet every incomer had moved from somewhere else, even if the reasons for their departure are rarely evident. The fifteenth and sixteenth centuries were notable for depopulation associated with the shrinkage or desertion of communities where small-scale mixed farming was replaced by commercial sheep raising, often associated with farm amalgamation and enclosure (Beresford, 1954). Deserted settlements from this period are widespread, but are concentrated in a belt running from west-central England, through the Midlands to Yorkshire, and on to Northumberland. The fate of the displaced population is unknown, though many are likely to have been resettled fairly locally.

Kussmaul (1990) has suggested that increasing specialization within the rural economy occurred in the second half of the seventeenth century, with farming regions becoming more sharply differentiated economically and socially. This is likely to have led to an increase in seasonal labour movements between neighbouring districts with different farming systems. There have been fewer studies of inter-regional migration for the late seventeenth and eighteenth centuries. By the later seventeenth century, wood-pasture areas were becoming sources of seasonal harvest workers for nearby arable districts (Kitch, 1992). Norfolk men migrating from wood-pasture areas tended to move to other wood-pasture districts. Migrants from sheep-corn areas more often went to the towns or to wood-pasture areas than to other sheep-corn districts (Clark, 1987). Pickles (1996) has examined population movements within Yorkshire. With population growth sluggish yet London and many provincial towns growing steadily, she argued that there must have been considerable rural depopulation in some areas. She compared data from the hearth taxes of the 1670s with an ecclesiastical census of 1743 to examine changes in numbers of households, using data from 60 parish registers as a check. Migration was the main determinant of whether parish populations grew or fell. The populations of many agricultural parishes remained static or declined, while many urban and industrial parishes witnessed growth well in excess of feasible rates of natural increase. The population of the East Riding fell by about 17 per cent between the 1670s and 1743, while that of the North Riding grew by around 5 per cent and the West Riding by 38 per cent. Parishes experiencing depopulation were mostly agricultural, both pastoral and arable. Those with county towns, market towns and ports tended to grow, but increase was especially marked in the industrial parishes of the West Riding, where the deanery of Leeds increased its population by 192 per cent, that of Halifax by 215 per cent.

Much of the debate about local movements of labour in later-eighteenth- and nineteenth-century England has centred around the concept of open and close communities. The terms 'open' and 'close' were first applied to parishes in the mid-nineteenth century, referring to vestry meetings which were open to all ratepayers, or closed to all but a handful of them. This often reflected the presence or absence of a single major landowner controlling parish meetings and, more generally, parish affairs, including the settlement of incomers. The term was extended to include control over labour by the squire. Many close parishes were associated with estate villages. They were often found in areas of early depopulation due to enclosure and the conversion of arable land to pasture, as in the north-east Midlands and the East Riding of Yorkshire or the Sussex downlands (Short, 1992). Open parishes, by contrast, were found in areas like the Weald, where settlement was easy for immigrants and small-scale farming could be combined with industrial and craft work. Open and close parishes seem to have existed from at least the seventeenth century (Holderness, 1972; Kitch, 1992) and elements of them have been identified in late medieval times (Fox, 1995).

Open and close parishes have, however, been defined in different ways. Holderness (1972) distinguished them in terms of labour supply. In close parishes all but a bare minimum of wage-earning labourers were excluded from residence, and much of the workforce had to be imported daily from surrounding parishes. Open parishes had a surplus of labour, often with a proliferation of tumbledown cottages let out at high rents. Mills (1980) defined them in terms of landownership, assuming that parishes dominated by a single landowner were automatically close ones. Close parishes were rare in the uplands of the north and west, as well as in old forest and wood-pasture regions. They were most numerous in the light-soil uplands of eastern and Midland England and on the Midland clays. However, as the movements of labour which were required to support them operated at a local scale, the existence of a close parish presupposes that open ones occurred nearby. In practice, it has proved difficult to identify permanent out-migration from close parishes and day-to-day labour mobility into them. Banks's (1988) study of Norfolk failed to pick out such functional linkages between open and close parishes or to find clear relationships between levels of population density, poor law expenditure and the percentage of families engaged in agriculture. Kitch (1992) nevertheless found that close villages in the South Downs had lower median marriage distances than the open villages of the Weald, whose menfolk travelled more outside the parish in search of work.

Agricultural Servants

Much rural population turnover in preindustrial England was linked with the movement of male and female servants. These formed the most mobile social group, and comprised a significant proportion of the population; 13.4 per cent in 63 listings between 1574 and 1821, 17 per cent in Clayworth in the late seventeenth century. Most were agricultural workers rather than domestic servants, accounting for a third to half of the hired agricultural labour in Early-Modern England. Up to 60 per cent of the population in the age group 15–24 spent some time in service (Kussmaul, 1981). The impact of agricultural service on mobility is shown by Schofield's (1987) study of Cardington. In 1792 84 per cent of boys aged 10–14 were still living at home but only 22 per cent aged 15–19: the rest had gone into service.

Numbers of male and female servants were fairly even; in the sample of 63 listings there was only a slight preponderance of men. While some sons of yeomen and prosperous farmers may have gone into service to acquire skills, service was the normal experience for children of husbandmen and labourers. Their mobility set them apart from the rest of society. They were young, unmarried men and women who mostly entered service in their mid-teens and left it at marriage in their mid–late twenties. In Kussmaul's study the median length of service of servants was six years, but nearly a quarter were servants for ten years or longer. Agricultural servants were found throughout England, but were most frequent in northern and western pastoral areas where farms were small. They normally worked on annual contracts, and frequently moved from one master to another at the end of a year in search of more experience, higher wages and better conditions: most agricultural work was age and skill specific. At Tetney, Lincolnshire, between 1780 and 1830 the annual turnover of servants was 68 per cent and in Radley, Berkshire, between 1779 and 1819 it was 80 per cent (Kussmaul, 1981). Only occasionally did servants stay in the same household for a number of years.

It was common for teenagers to enter service first with families in their home communities and then to move further afield (Clark, 1987; Schofield, 1987). Movement from one contract to another generally took place at Michaelmas in the south, and a month after at Martinmas (11 November) in northern England, fitting in with the later harvest. In some western areas and the Fens, May Day was the traditional hiring date. The distances moved by servants were generally short. Moves of over 5–6km seem to have been uncommon and moves over 15km rare (Kussmaul, 1981). At Spalding, in Lincolnshire, between 1767 and 1785, the records of movement of 844 male and 722 female servants at the Statute Sessions indicate that the median distance travelled was 12km for men and 10km for women, the difference being due to a few men travelling relatively great distances (Table 2.3). Only 18 per cent of men and 8 per cent of women travelled 20km or more. Settlement examinations in Hertfordshire and Suffolk suggest a lower median distance of 4–5km. At Cardington in 1782, three-quarters of men aged 20–29 were employed in service outside the parish, but three-quarters of these were within a 16km radius. Girls were even more likely to be working within easy reach of home. A third of them were in domestic service in Bedford, 4km away (Schofield, 1987). On the other hand, long-distance migration of servants did occur. At Romford in Essex in the mid-sixteenth century, one man from Cumbria entered the community, probably as a servant, and stayed eventually to become a yeoman (McIntosh, 1984).

Table 2.3 Distances Travelled by Agricultural Servants between Successive Masters, Spalding, Lincolnshire, 1767–85 (After Kussmaul, 1981)

	Distance (km)						
	0–3	4–7	8–11	12–15	16–19	20–23	24+
Male servants (%)	15	16	18	19	14	10	8
Female servants (%)	15	19	22	22	13	5	3

The rise of hiring fairs from the late seventeenth century, which were advertised in newspapers, may have promoted longer-distance mobility of servants. Where successive moves of servants have been plotted, they have sometimes been shown to focus within particular areas, perhaps to maintain contact with family, friends and potential marriage partners. Detailed biographies of servants are rare, but Kussmaul cites the case of Joseph Mayett, born in 1783, the son of a Buckinghamshire labourer, who moved 11 times as a servant between 1795 and 1802. None of the moves took him more than 15km from his birthplace.

Because of their frequent moves, variation in the proportion of servants in the population form an important index of general rural mobility. Kussmaul has charted the rise and fall of servants in husbandry by examining the seasonality of marriages and the extent to which they clustered in the periods after hiring dates, when servants left their final contracts in order to marry. From a peak in the mid-sixteenth century, she suggests that servant numbers fell to a low point in the mid-seventeenth century, rising to another peak around 1740, then declining again. The influences behind the fall in numbers in the early seventeenth century may have been population growth increasing the supply of poor labourers prepared to work for low wages. Servants increased when population growth was sluggish in the later seventeenth and early eighteenth centuries as farmers needed to ensure a supply of labour. The rise and fall of servants was also related to changes in the cost of living: when food prices were low, the cost of feeding living-in servants was reduced. In the late seventeenth and early eighteenth centuries, low grain prices also encouraged a shift from grain to livestock production which, with more even demands for labour throughout the year, encouraged the employment of servants.

The late seventeenth and early eighteenth centuries were the great age of servants in English agriculture. During the eighteenth century and into the nineteenth, they were increasingly replaced by labourers paid at monthly or weekly rates, who were much more closely tied to particular parishes. In northern England the growth of employment in urban and rural industry forced farmers to continue using servants into the nineteenth century. In the south the shortage of labour during the French wars temporarily increased the demand for servants. Following Waterloo, however, there was a glut of labour and by the mid-nineteenth century, servants had virtually disappeared in southern and eastern England. Concentration on grain production encouraged the employment of labourers on short contracts, increasing the seasonal demand for workers, while the spread of the threshing machine reduced the need for labour in winter. There may also have been growing reluctance to employ servants on annual contracts to prevent them from gaining potential rights to poor relief; farmers in some areas, under pressure from their landlords, resorted to 51-week contracts and other shifts to prevent this from happening.

Agricultural servants were also widespread in Wales and Lowland

Scotland, where they were as mobile as in England, accounting for a high proportion of people moving within the countryside. In the Clydesdale parish of Wiston and Roberton, 65 per cent of people recorded moving out of the parish between 1741 and 1791, and 81 per cent of those moving in, were servants (Houston, 1985). Movement of population between parishes in Lowland Scotland was concentrated around Whitsunday and Martinmas, the traditional hiring dates, with more than 70 per cent of movements of single men and women occurring at these times. Because they were young, unattached and mobile, servants were often viewed by Scottish kirk sessions as troublesome and disruptive (Whyte and Whyte, 1985). Servants do not seem to have been nearly as common in the Scottish Highlands. In upland areas of Aberdeenshire, male farm servants accounted for only 8–9 per cent of recorded adult males in the 1695 poll tax lists against 40 per cent in some parishes in the Lothians and Berwickshire (Whyte, 1979). Nevertheless, they were common in the Northern Isles in the seventeenth century and were also found in the Hebrides (Shaw, 1979), though it is not clear whether systems of hiring and mobility in these areas were comparable with the Lowlands (Whyte, 1985). In Ireland the lack of servants may help explain the lower rates of short-distance mobility, which seem to have been a characteristic feature of Irish society (Cullen, 1981).

Unlike England, the use of long-hire servants continued in Lowland Scotland during the eighteenth century. Farmers there faced a different labour market. While there was a glut of labour in southern England, in Scotland population growth was more sluggish, workers more willing to move to the towns, and there was strong competition for labour from industry. Labour demands were also different on Scottish farms; cereal production was less dominant and mixed farming, with the cultivation of root crops and sown grasses, spread the demand for labour more evenly throughout the year, encouraging the retention of long-hire workers. Mobility at the end of annual contracts, and the circulation of workers through hiring fairs, remained a feature of Scottish rural society through the nineteenth century. This kept levels of population turnover in rural communities high and may have made migration from the countryside to industrial towns easier.

Marriage Mobility

Although, as we have seen, movements at marriage formed only a small component of total mobility, marriage migration has been studied extensively, partly because marriage registers are a widespread and easily analysed, though sometimes misunderstood, source. Marital choice was important in defining groups and communities in the past, as today (Coleman and Haskey, 1986). Marriage usually resulted from everyday contacts, bringing together people of similar ages and social backgrounds living fairly close to each other. The distances between places of residence of brides and grooms at the time of their marriage have been seen as measures of patterns of contact and the extent of the horizons of various social groups. Levels of **endogamy** and **exogamy** – where both partners were resident in the same parish at the time of marriage or where one of them came from another parish – are easy to establish. Given the limited distances over which inter-parish contacts leading to marriage were generally made, the calculation of 'marriage distances', usually a mean or median derived from distances between parish churches, is also straightforward. Levels of endogamy/exogamy have been seen as a measure of the isolation of communities (though the area, population size and location of parishes must be taken into consideration) and changes over time, marking the widening of social horizons, have been sought. Patterns of exogamous marriages show interaction with other communities and the distance, direction and density of contacts can be assessed (Millard, 1982).

Modern studies have shown that the higher the social class, the greater the average marriage distance (Coleman and Haskey, 1986); this was also the case in the past (Whyte and Whyte, 1985; Whyte, 1987). The need to look outside a parish for a marriage partner can be understood when it is appreciated that, even in a community with several hundred inhabitants, the number of potential marriage partners of the appropriate age, sex and social background could be limited (Clark and Souden, 1987). Nevertheless, the value of marriage distances as a surrogate measure of more general levels of contact has often been assumed rather than proved. Perry (1969) believed that they indicated the distances over which courtship was practicable, but this makes assumptions about how courtship was begun and maintained.

Kitch (1992) has suggested that it was normal for 25–40 per cent of marriages to involve a partner drawn from outside a parish. In Myddle (Hey, 1974) the proportion of marriages which were endogamous was 41 per cent in the late sixteenth century, falling to 36 per cent in the early seventeenth, then rising again to 48 per cent in the second half of the century (Table 2.4). In Terling only a little over a quarter of men and a third of women who were married in the parish had been baptized there (Wrightson and Levine, 1979). For women this pattern did not change from the late sixteenth to the late seventeenth century, but for men, while only 19 per cent of those marrying in the parish between 1580 and 1619 had been baptized there, between 1660 and 1699 this figure rose to 40 per cent, suggesting a reduction in male immigration and a drop in mobility, possibly due to the Settlement Laws (see below). Other communities recorded less movement at marriage. At Berrier, in the Cumbrian parish of Greystoke, during the later sixteenth century 34 per cent of marriages had both partners from within the hamlet, and most of the rest came from elsewhere within the (admittedly large) parish (Armstrong, 1994).

Table 2.4 Origins of Marriage Partners (per cent) in Myddle, Shropshire, 1541–1701 (After Hey, 1974)

	1541–99	1600–43	1647–1701
Both Partners from Myddle	41.4	36.1	47.7
Myddle Woman and Shropshire Man	49.9	59.9	31.5
Myddle Woman and Man Outside Shropshire	0	0	0.9
Myddle Man and Shropshire Woman	3.6	3.3	9.0
Myddle Man and Woman Outside Shropshire	0.9	0	0
Neither from Parish	4.5	1.6	10.8

The use of marriage horizons as indicators of mobility has been questioned (Pain and Smith, 1984). Studies of parish registers in Yorkshire and County Durham in which, for a few years in the late eighteenth and early nineteenth centuries, the occupations and residence of the parents of brides and grooms are given, suggests that marriage registers underestimate levels of mobility of both men and women by confusing place of residence with place of origin. Snell (1984) has indicated that marriage migration cannot be fully understood without appreciating the social, economic and legal context of parochial registration. For example, marriage often occurred in the parish of residence of the wife's father (which may or may not have been the parish in which the bride was born) rather than that of the wife's current residence. Information on 'residence' in marriage registers is often haphazard; it may be a mistake to assume that, when no other information is available, the bride can automatically be classified as living in the parish at the time of her marriage. Studies such as Stapleton's (1988) for the parish of Odiham in Hampshire have shown that the recording of the extra-parochial origins of marriage partners can be extremely inconsistent. Given that a wife took her husband's settlement on marriage, there was more incentive for marriage registers to record which parish the husband was 'of' or 'from' so that, if necessary, a case for a poor law settlement could later be established (Snell, 1984). If this practice was widespread, it could lead to the underestimation of the amount of female marriage migration, affecting levels of endogamy/exogamy and marriage distances. Hardwicke's act of 1753 for preventing clandestine marriages required that couples had to be married in a parish in which one of them had lived for at least four weeks. This made residence more closely synonymous to place of marriage and might tend artificially to increase the apparent immobility of population from the mid-eighteenth century.

Constant's (1948) pioneering work on inter-village contacts in Northamptonshire and Huntingdonshire demonstrated a widening of marriage horizons between the mid-eighteenth/early nineteenth centuries and the late nineteenth/early twentieth, linked in part to the coming of the railways. Mean marriage distances were greater for escarpment foot and valley parishes compared with more isolated scarpland communities, while distinct directional flows along major routeways were also evident. Perry's (1969) study of marriage migration in 27 Dorset parishes in the nineteenth and early twentieth centuries, though outside our period, is important for its focus on local mobility rather than longer-distance contacts. He recognized the potential ambiguities of entries in marriage registers, but acknowledged the potential influence of rising levels of literacy in allowing contacts to be maintained over greater distances. He found differences in rural isolation between chalk and vale parishes, and marked directional variations in levels of marriage contact. In the chalklands, contacts up and down valleys were more frequent than those between them. He found little change in rural isolation until the end of the nineteenth century. The achievement of virtually universal literacy, rural depopulation, shorter working hours, higher wages and the increased mobility for agricultural workers provided by the bicycle were seen as significant in widening rural social contacts.

In all studies of marriage distances, most exogamous marriages involved strictly short-distance contacts. Millard's (1982) analysis of marriage migration in Buckinghamshire demonstrated that interaction between places was strongly influenced by distance, but with the distance-decay effect decreasing over time. Within a radius of 20km he found no significant directional bias, but at greater distances a lengthening of contacts along major routeways was evident. His analysis did not, however, incorporate any weighting relating to different parish populations. Kitch's (1992) study of Sussex between the late sixteenth and early nineteenth centuries found that the mean distance travelled by marriage partners was 4.7km, and that 86 per cent of marriage contacts were within 16km. Marriage distances were greater in the Weald than along the foot of the chalk downs. Directional patterns of contact followed the topography, running parallel to the Downs. Wrigley's (1977) research on the origins of brides in Colyton, Devon, in the later eighteenth century, found distinct differences in the numbers of brides originating from different directions within a 16km radius. The long-term persistence of particular directional patterns of marriage contacts is emphasized by MacPherson's (1984) study of the Highland parish of Laggan from 1350 to 1850. Long-distance marriage contacts were channelled down the Spey valley to the lowlands of Moray, probably reflecting economic links associated with the import of grain and the sale of cattle.

Holderness (1967–70) examined mobility in ten mainly agricultural parishes in Yorkshire where for a few years, as a result of a directive from Archbishop Markham in 1777, many parishes recorded the place of residence of the paternal and maternal grandfathers of baptized infants. When these origins lay outside the parish in question, it was assumed that the babies' parents had migrated. Still in the same parish as their fathers were 54 per cent of farmers against 48 per cent of tradesmen, while 15 per cent of farmers had moved more than 16km against 18 per cent of tradesmen. Farmers were a more stable element within society and when they did move, tended to do so over shorter distances. The percentage of women who were living in the same parish as their fathers was significantly lower than that for men, but more migrating women were drawn from within a 16km radius than men. Long and Maltby (1980) used similar data for three West Riding parishes: Skipton, containing a market town; Bolton Abbey, an upland agricultural parish; and Addingham, a centre for woollen manufacture. Industrial parishes in the Dales had higher percentages of migrants from beyond 16km than the lowland parishes studied by Holderness. Longer-distance migrants to the Dales came mainly from established textile areas within Yorkshire. The occupational breakdown of migration was similar with farmers being the most stable element, but with less long-distance migration of farmers than in the more attractive agricultural environment of the lowlands. Skipton attracted more long-distance migrants than the other Dales parishes, drawing people eastwards along the turnpike from as far away as Kendal. Most migrants came from places which had links with Skipton through the woollen industry, but stray long-distance migrants included a woolcomber from Bristol, a whitesmith from Edinburgh, a gardener from Arbroath and a comedian from Westminster. As in the Plain, smaller proportions of women than men were living in the same parish as their fathers, but their migratory patterns were more restricted.

Within communities different social groups had different marriage horizons. Holderness (1967–70) demonstrated that in the plain of York in the late eighteenth and early nineteenth centuries, farmers married brides from a wider geographical area than tradesmen, despite the fact that they were less likely to move out of the community. Kitch (1992) found that in Sussex between the late sixteenth and the early nineteenth centuries, a similar contrast existed between yeomen and labourers, as did Whyte and Whyte's (1985) research on tenants and cottars on the Panmure estates in seventeenth-century Forfarshire.

Poverty and Vagrancy

A significant element of population movement in preindustrial Britain, especially in the sixteenth and seventeenth centuries, was associated with poverty. Late-medieval legislation identified two groups of paupers: the impotent poor comprising mainly the elderly, infirm and young; and the able-bodied poor, not deserving charity, who should have been able to find work. As population grew in the sixteenth century, labour markets became glutted and it became harder for people to obtain employment. Tudor legislation on poverty and vagrancy, however, remained locked in a medieval mindset which did not recognize the reality of unemployment and assumed that able-bodied beggars, 'masterless men', were lazy rather than desperate (Beier 1985). Legislation in 1597 included common labourers who would not work for reasonable wages in its definition of rogues and vagabonds. On this basis anyone travelling in search of work could be threatened with arrest. Under an act of 1589 landlords could be fined for taking such people into their homes or letting empty houses to them (Styles, 1978).

The underlying cause of increased poverty was population growth with its attendant problems of pressure on resources, inflation, increasing reliance on insecure wage labour and falling real wages. Other factors operating at a local scale, such as enclosure and the removal of village communities, or more widely, like the reduction in living-in servants (Kussmaul, 1981), are likely to have generated insecurity and increased the numbers of displaced people. The pauper element in many communities may have doubled between 1560 and 1640 to account for up to a third of the population. Closed villages, where landowners could expel people who were surplus to local labour requirements, had smaller proportions of paupers than woodland and fen areas affected by immigration.

Poverty was worsened in the later sixteenth century by subsistence crises which bankrupted small farmers and set them on the roads, begging. In Scotland conditions were, if anything, worse; a combination of small holdings, inefficient farming systems, lack of integrated markets in basic foodstuffs and more marginal climatic conditions increased the risk of subsistence crises. Little is known about the scale of mortality in sixteenth-century famines, but the one in 1623 was very severe. In that year systems of poor relief were inadequate to cope with the needs of local parish populations, never mind providing aid for vagrants, while conditions were little better during the last major Scottish famine in the later 1690s. The flow of refugees into Edinburgh at this time was so great that the burgh council set up a relief camp for starving vagrants in the Greyfriars churchyard (Flinn, 1976). In the Highlands periodic famine continued to occur throughout the eighteenth century, notably in 1740–41 and in 1782 (Whyte, 1989).

In England and Wales poverty and vagrancy were gradually tackled by the provision of parish poor relief. The system, which developed from Tudor times, was remarkably uniform and comprehensive. All parishes were responsible for providing relief and all men and women were eligible to receive it. Many sixteenth-century parishes already operated their own systems of relief. Tudor legislation codified practices which were already in widespread use and, during the seventeenth century, the system spread throughout England and Wales. Relief in each parish was administered by overseers appointed by local magistrates and responsible to the parish vestry, made up of ratepayers, who controlled the fixing of the poor rates.

Scottish legislation on poverty echoed that of Tudor England in distinguishing between the elderly and infirm – considered deserving of charity – and the able-bodied unemployed, who were seen as a threat to the social order. Efforts were made to introduce a similar system of poor relief. Unfortunately, the Scottish system of administration was unable to cope. In 1597 the Scottish Parliament handed over responsibility for providing poor relief to the kirk sessions, which were assemblies of church elders presided over by parish ministers. Relief was based on voluntary contributions, supplemented by occasional legacies, rather than a regular levy on landholders. As a result, less money was available to help the poor and the efficiency of the system varied markedly between parishes. Relief was less generous than in England, being designed not to provide a basic subsistence, but merely to supplement assistance from family, friends and neighbours (Mitchison, 1974 and 1989). As a result there was no need to pass settlement laws. The operation of the system improved and became more standardized only in the first half of the eighteenth century. Due to the failure of the Protestant church to penetrate much of the Highlands before the eighteenth century, a system of poor relief failed to develop there at all. However, in the Highlands access to land, even if often in tiny amounts of poor quality, was widespread and the obligations inherent in the clan system ensured that chiefs provided support for poorer clansmen. The tightknit structures of clanship may have ensured that while there was a lot of poverty in the Highlands, there was also, before the eighteenth century, relatively little vagrancy. In Ireland, too, widespread access to land, compared with Tudor and Stuart England, may have reduced the vagrant population.

As poverty in England increased more people, unable to find work, took to the roads. A growing proportion of them were classed as vagrants. Vagrancy became a major concern during the later sixteenth and early seventeenth centuries. The term 'vagrant' is difficult to define precisely; nor is it clear at what point a poor migrant's circumstances deteriorated sufficiently for this label to be applied. Not all beggars were vagrants; many were licensed to beg within their own local area. Other authorized beggars wandered further afield, including people bearing special letters, often those who had suffered misfortunes such as fire or shipwreck. There was a growing trade in forged licences and letters.

There was also a problem of vagrancy in Scotland. As in England, the increase in population in the later sixteenth and early seventeenth centuries was probably the root cause, though other factors, such as the meagre level of poor relief, may also have encouraged vagrancy. There may have been more reason than in England for the authorities in Scotland, and the population in general, to fear vagrants. In a country where the rural population was dispersed in small clusters, 'sorning' – begging with menaces – could threaten outlying communities. With so much sparsely settled upland and moorland, beggars could move around and congregate more easily, while the carrying of weapons seems to have been more common than in England during the seventeenth century. In Scotland it may also have been more common for beggars to travel in groups which could sometimes terrorize a whole district, though the band led by James MacPherson, the celebrated gypsy leader who was hanged at Banff in 1700, was probably exceptional. As in England, vagrants were drawn to the towns. The larger towns, especially Edinburgh, carried out periodic purges when beggars who were not classified as 'indwellers' were expelled.

Vagrants were not generally taken to include people like drovers and harvest workers who moved as part of their jobs – though some of them might have resorted to begging on occasion. On the other hand, discharged soldiers and seamen, notionally returning to their homes, were considered as vagrants. So, at times, were students travelling to and from university. There seems to have been a hard core of professional wanderers including pedlars, chapmen and minstrels. Such occupations shaded into less respectable ones like fortune telling and conjuring. Gypsies, mistrusted and singled out for special, severe legislation in England and Wales as well as in Scotland, formed another element in the vagrant population. The Irish, not eligible for poor relief in England, were identified as vagrants from 1572. Such groups attracted attention because of their distinctive dress and sometimes language, but they probably formed only a small proportion of those on the roads. Some of the people who wandered through the countryside or drifted into the towns were the misfits and rejects of society: the sick, the maimed, the blind, the physically and mentally ill, though such afflictions were often feigned. Many people were probably only vagrants for short periods, particularly in their youth, though the ranks of the long-term vagrants undoubtedly swelled considerably during the late sixteenth and early seventeenth centuries.

In England vagrants were blamed for a range of problems including crime and sedition, though only a small proportion of apprehended vagrants was examined for additional offences. National campaigns against them were undertaken periodically, notably in 1569–72 and 1631–9, for political rather than social motives. Vagrancy was seen as a menace to society, a threat to the state and to social order. A colourful 'rogue literature' resulted from this attitude, but also fuelled it with its descriptions of a highly organized vagrant criminal underworld. It is not easy to penetrate the rhetoric and view vagrants objectively. Despite the emphasis in the literature, genuine rogues seem to have formed a minority. It is also difficult to distinguish between vagrants and subsistence migrants searching for work. Poor people were often forced out of their communities and on to the roads by misfortune within their families, such as the death of the major breadwinner. Widows and orphans were particularly vulnerable. Trade slumps might force respectable craftsmen on to the roads, while harvest failures produced waves of displaced, desperate people flocking to the towns in search of charity, but who were sometimes found dead under hedgerows and were buried anonymously.

Vagrants tended to be young but, as economic conditions worsened in the early seventeenth century, their average age rose. A high proportion were male; however, more and more women, many with children, took to the roads. Vagrant women included those who had been deserted by their husbands and unmarried pregnant girls who often moved longer distances in order to have their babies away from home. Large gangs of vagrants were uncommon in England and seem mostly to have comprised Irish and gypsies. Gypsies tended to travel in large groups with acknowledged leaders. Their distinctive language, dress and appearance made them objects of mistrust. The Irish also travelled in large groups at times, possibly because they arrived in boatloads in south-western England and Wales. They came in waves after rebellions such as those in 1569 and 1579–83; following famines, as after 1628; and due to civil war in the 1640s, including thousands of Protestant refugees after the uprising of 1641 (Chapter 4).

Pedlars and chapmen were often little better than beggars, though some were relatively well off. Those selling books and pamphlets might come under suspicion of spreading seditious and heretical material. Tinkers, mending kitchen utensils and doing odd jobs, were, if anything, even lower in status. Numbers of wandering sailors and soldiers increased more rapidly than other vagrants in the late sixteenth and early seventeenth centuries. In London they accounted for 1.5 per cent of vagrant occupations in 1580, but 12 per cent between 1620 and 1640. The discharge of servicemen at the end of a war could flood the country, particularly the south-east, with hardened men trained to use weapons and more prone to violence than other travellers, often leading to bursts of official action against vagrants in general (Beier 1985).

Scottish kirk session registers sometimes recorded in detail the payments made to vagrants, providing insights into their mobility and composition. Most payments seem to have been made to single men and women, though in some cases the men receiving assistance may have been accompanied by wives and children. As in England, women outnumbered men in lists of parish poor relief. Many sets of circumstances might reduce women to poverty; spinsterhood, widowhood, old age, physical or mental infirmity or unexpected pregnancy. It is harder to determine the factors which forced women to leave home and take to the roads. The entries sometimes hint at the reasons underlying vagrancy (Whyte and Whyte, 1985; Whyte, 1988). The most common was blindness or physical deformity, followed by people whose homes had been destroyed by fire (Table 2.5). Some payments were made to people whose distress was only temporary, such as shipwrecked seamen and the victims of robbery. Bankrupt tenants were surprisingly rare, but a distinct category were those who had formerly enjoyed some social status; people designated as gentlemen, gentlewomen, or 'Mr' (indicating a graduate), distressed gentlewomen or the widows of professional men. Kirk session records also chronicle the harsh side of vagrancy, with payments for graves and winding sheets for beggars found dead.

Table 2.5 Payments to Vagrants Recorded in Monikie Parish, Forfarshire, 1660–1710 (After Whyte and Whyte, 1985)

	%
Payments to Men	73
Payments to Women	27
Reasons for Payment	
Blindness or Deformity	40
Illness	5
Loss of House, Possessions, by Fire	11
Temporary Distress (discharged soldiers, shipwrecked seamen)	10
Bankrupt Tenants	6
Payments to People with former Social Status	28

Estimates of numbers of vagrants at any time nationally, regionally or locally are hard to make. They fluctuated dramatically in the short term due to harvest failure and industrial slumps. Changes in the numbers examined by local magistrates, between different places and over time, may also reflect variations in the degree to which legislation was enforced rather than in the volume of people actually travelling. Contemporary estimates of the vagrant population are highly unreliable. Even so, evidence of arrests suggests a substantial increase in numbers during the first 30 years of the seventeenth century, at a rate faster than population growth. A group of Midland parishes recorded a fourfold rise in numbers of poor travellers between the 1620s and the 1630s. In the 1630s each parish relieved between 1000 and 2000 licensed beggars, many of them moving over long distances, an increasing proportion of them as families rather than individuals (Table 2.6). The fall of population in the later seventeenth century, the cessation of subsistence crises, and the spread of poor relief to virtually every parish led to a decline in vagrancy, which became largely confined to distinct groups; the Irish, the Scots, gypsies, pedlars and the military.

Table 2.6 Numbers of Poor Travellers and Vagrants Recorded in Pattingham, English Midlands, 1611–39 (After Kent, 1981)

1611–15	5
1616–20	43
1621–25	120
1626–30	284
1631–35	525
1636–39	741

In Scotland vagrancy in the early–middle seventeenth century may have been reduced by demographic checks, such as the famine of 1623, and by emigration to Ireland. Vagrancy appears to have grown again in the later seventeenth century, but it fell over most of the Lowlands during the eighteenth century. The cessation of major subsistence crises, better provision of parish poor relief, and additional earnings from industrial by-employments may have combined to achieve this. However, vagrancy was not eliminated, as the Statistical Account of the 1790s shows. In particular, an influx of Irish beggars, sometimes moving as families, was reported from many parishes, as well as begging Highlanders, possibly in many cases seasonal workers searching for employment.

Something of the pattern of movement of vagrants in England can be reconstructed from records of their examinations (Beier, 1985; Slack, 1987). Once apprehended, the normal practice was to whip vagrants and return them to their parish of origin, or at least send them off in the appropriate direction, sometimes with a written passport. Slack (1987) has used such material relating to *c*.3,000 vagrants. The data do not generally indicate whether the place of origin given was the vagrant's birthplace or last place of residence, or how long they had been travelling since they left it. In any case vagrants may not necessarily have given correct answers. Some had been on the road for years, moving long distances, and being accustomed to being whipped and expelled. Gangs of vagrants were relatively infrequent; poor people mostly travelled individually or in small groups. Half of those studied were single men, a quarter single women, though married couples and families with children were also found on the roads. Servants moving between contracts and migratory seasonal workers were usually distinguished by local officials from genuine vagrants, although sometimes such people might be asked to move on or risk being treated as such. Many of those who were caught and whipped may merely have had the misfortune to be in the wrong place at a time when local officials had decided to carry out a purge.

The vagrants studied by Slack were more likely to have moved over 64km than apprentices moving to provincial towns, or witnesses in church court depositions. They were also more likely to move between towns rather than within the countryside or from a rural to an urban location. Three-fifths of those studied by Beier (1985) had urban origins, while for those apprehended in London the figure was 90 per cent. Towns were attractive due to the wider availability of charity, casual labour and cheap accommodation. Experience of urban life may in itself have encouraged itchy feet. Vagrancy was reduced in winter, but increased in spring and summer, falling off in autumn with the availability of harvest work. In summer vagrants tended to move into the countryside to find work in agriculture, in winter back into the towns. There was a tendency for them to move towards the south and east, especially London. Even within northern England, the general flow seems to have been southwards towards the lowlands. However, the restriction of study to vagrant origins and places of apprehension, without information on intermediate destinations, may seem to give their movements greater direction and purpose than was actually the case. Within southern and south-western England, there was a current from west to east along the south coast which included Welsh and Irish vagrants. Within Wales there was a drift from north to south as well as towards the English border, and in the north a movement from Cumbria and the Pennines into lowland Lancashire and Cheshire. Some vagrants were long-distance migrants, travelling in a series of short stages. Others operated more locally within a day's travel of home, or at least within specific regions. Long-distance movers, travelling 124km or more from their place of birth or last residence, formed up to a third of some samples (Beier, 1985). Long-distance movement seems to have increased in the early seventeenth century, with vagrants travelling predominantly on foot, but also by carriers' wagons and by river and coastal shipping, staying at inns and ubiquitous alehouses, sleeping in barns and outbuildings and, when necessary, in the open.

Some Scottish vagrants seem to have moved purposefully through a regular circuit of parishes. William Bouack, sometime schoolmaster in Forfar, appeared for several consecutive years in Monikie parish, Forfarshire, payments to him being grouped within a five-week period during September and October. William Lyell was recorded once every summer for several years, generally in July. Such patterns may have been linked to seasonal rhythms in the market for casual labour. Other vagrants appeared less regularly, but with sufficient frequency to suggest that they were operating within a comparatively restricted area (Whyte and Whyte, 1985). This contrasts with Slack's evidence of rural–urban movement, but the smaller Scottish burghs, less anonymous than larger English provincial towns, may have been less attractive to vagrants who could be more easily supervised by officials.

The Settlement Laws and Mobility

An aspect of English poor law administration which affected migration was the question of settlement. The Poor Law Act of 1601 established the responsibility of each township for its own poor. This implied a closer definition of who was eligible to receive relief in any parish and under what circumstances: their **settlement** (Mills, 1959). During the seventeenth century it became accepted that everybody should have a parish of legal settlement in which they were entitled to relief. Growing population movement made it more important to define clearly the criteria which would give an incomer to a parish the right to receive assistance. The original idea of settlement was to identify somewhere to send vagrants if they did not know their parish of birth, but another question became apparent in the early seventeenth century; how long did a non-vagrant stranger have to live in a parish before gaining entitlement to poor relief ?

The 1662 'Act for the Better Releife of the Poore of this Kingdom' marked a new stage in the development of English poor law. The practice of taking securities from migrants to prevent them from becoming a financial burden on the parish to which they had moved, already widespread, was confirmed by statute. From the 1640s, quarter sessions had issued orders for removing people from parishes on the grounds that they might become a charge on the poor rates (Styles, 1978). The 1662 Act made this easier, giving Justices of the Peace rather than quarter sessions jurisdiction over such cases. The seemingly draconian wording of the Act was moderated by the provision that a complaint had to be made by a churchwarden or overseer to the local Justices within 40 days of a person coming to live in a parish. Previously, the time required to gain a settlement had been variously defined under the vagrancy laws; three years' residence in 1504 and 1572, one year in 1597. The 1662 Act aimed to prevent poor people from flocking into parishes when there were woods, commons and waste where they could build cottages, appreciating that such people, even if not a charge on the poor rate, could nevertheless strain the resources of a community. The legislation established rules for determining a person's parish of settlement, and allowed the mobility of poor migrants possessing certificates stating that their parish of settlement would assume responsibility for them should they become destitute (Landau, 1988). The Act provided that a settlement could be claimed on the basis of birth, by renting land at £10 a year or more, by service for a year, by completing an apprenticeship, paying taxes or serving in a parish office for a year. The 40-day rule seemed to make gaining a new settlement relatively easy. In 1685 an amending act was passed which provided that the 40 days could only be counted from the time that a formal written notice was delivered to the overseers or churchwarden, which would, of course, have spurred them into action to remove the applicant.

The 1697 Act 'for Supplying some Defectes in the Laws for the Relief of the Poor' stated that holders of settlement certificates could not be removed from other parishes until they had actually become a charge (Styles, 1978). This made settlement certificates important, legally-binding documents, but there was still no obligation on parishes to issue them. Nevertheless, by granting certificates parish authorities could export unemployed poor to find work elsewhere (Landau, 1990). The 1697 Act also indicated that settlement certificates covered not only the individuals to whom they had been issued, but also their families, generating the idea of 'derived settlements'. It was this Act rather than the one of 1662 which regulated the lives of many poor people during the eighteenth century. An act of 1795 abolished settlement by 40 days' public notice and by the payment of rates. Until 1795 a parish officer could obtain a removal order for any person or family to their parish of settlement, though if an immigrant had a certificate from their parish of settlement, they could not be removed until they requested relief.

How did the Settlement Laws affect mobility? It is hard to generalize about a system whose effects depended so much on local circumstances. In the past it was widely believed that the Settlement Laws reduced population movement in England and Wales. Malthus thought that they restricted labour mobility by discouraging labourers from moving in case they lost rights of settlement in a good parish (Huzel, 1980). Adam Smith agreed, writing that 'There is scarce a poor man in England of 40 years of age ... who has not in some part of his life felt himself most cruelly oppressed by this ill-contrived law of settlements.' Hampson (1926–28) suggested that labourers were inculcated with the idea that to leave their parish in search of work was little short of criminal and that, as a result, they tended to stay put. Wrightson and Levine (1979) attributed the stabilization of mobility in the seventeenth century to the Settlement Laws. Redford (1926) believed that it was not so much the effects of the Settlement Laws, but the generosity of poor relief that reduced mobility. This view has been widely challenged (Styles, 1978). Clark (1987) believed that after 1662 the Settlement Laws did not stop migration, but did inhibit long-distance movement. Holderness (1976) saw the 1662 Act as being ineffective in restraining mobility. Landau (1995) suggests that extensive monitoring of inter-parish movement under the Settlement Laws would not necessarily have stifled or even greatly restricted migration. Snell (1992) also doubts whether people moving in search of work were much restricted by the Settlement Laws; many contemporaries believed that they were, at worst, only a slight obstacle to mobility. Much of the movement which was regulated through the Settlement Laws was probably short distance, as officers might be reluctant to commit their parishes to the expense of removing a man whose parish of settlement was distant. Many parishes, especially in industrial areas, granted casual relief to residents who did not have settlement rights, while others provided relief to nonresidents whose right of settlement in the parish was acknowledged. Casual relief may often have been the cheapest option to help someone on their way and out of the parish. Flexibility of this kind encouraged migration to places which needed labour, especially the industrial areas of northern England.

Often about a third of the inhabitants of a parish had their settlement there, but the figure could vary between around 20 per cent and 55 per cent (Snell, 1985). An annual hiring was probably, after marriage, the commonest means of gaining a settlement, though one which declined rapidly in southern England in the early nineteenth century (Snell, 1985). Each person had only one place of legal settlement, though not everyone was clear where that was. The acquisition of a later settlement – such as a person's last year as a farm servant – cancelled out previous ones. Women took their husbands' parish of settlement on marriage – though they may never have lived in or even visited the parish. With the decline of agricultural service as a way of gaining a settlement, an increasing proportion of people took their father's, or even grandfather's, settlement. Derived settlement had been provided for in the seventeenth-century legislation in the unlikely event of someone not having gained a settlement by other means, but the changed economic and social conditions from the later eighteenth century meant that this way of gaining a settlement assumed major importance. This may well have reduced rural mobility in southern England. Snell (1985) has calculated from samples of settlement examinations that when examined, the distance of people from their place of settlement, was 34km for men who had gained their own settlement against only 16km for those who had taken their father's settlement (Snell, 1985). By the later eighteenth century it was becoming harder for sojourners (people living out of their parish of settlement) to acquire settlements, as various loopholes in the laws were closed. Parish officials also grew more efficient in ensuring that migrants were not allowed to fulfil the criteria which would give them a settlement, using measures such as 11-month contracts for servants, refusing to appoint incomers to parish offices, and fixing rents at just under £10

Landau (1995) has argued that under the Settlement Laws, migration was monitored thoroughly by parish officials. She believes that most men were examined by local petty sessions without any intention to remove them, but as part of the monitoring process because they had recently moved into a parish rather than because they were destitute. This argues for a higher level of efficiency in parish administration than has been considered likely in the past. Snell (1991,1992), on the other hand, believes that migrants were only examined if they became destitute. Landau has calculated that at Sittingbourne in Kent just under 4 per cent of families in rural parishes were brought before the justices each year because they had moved from one parish to another, a figure close to what she believed to be the total proportion of families migrating. In Kent perhaps 6–9 per cent of families who were not living in their parish of settlement might be examined by the petty sessions each year. She considered that parish officials ensured that each year, most of the newly arrived men in a parish renting for under £10 would be examined, especially married men whose families posed a bigger threat to the poor rates. By the later eighteenth century parish officers seem to have been confining their attentions to the poorest levels of society, especially labourers migrating short distances. Officials in the towns operated a more relaxed system of monitoring than their rural counterparts (Landau, 1990). This regulation of immigration ceased after 1795, when the legal basis for parish officers doing this was abolished.

Snell (1991,1992) disagrees with Landau that the purpose of the Settlement Laws, and the way in which they were implemented, was to regulate migration, something that he considers was at variance with the idea that society in eighteenth-century England was highly mobile with an active labour market. He considers that most settlement examinations, and all removals, related to people who were unemployed at the time and searching for work, and that most examinations were generated by applications for poor relief. He assumed that in the search for work, priority would have gone to those settled in a parish. For those whose settlement lay elsewhere, presentation of a certificate might be a prerequisite for obtaining work or housing, but he rejects the idea that the Settlement Laws were used as a monitoring device. On the other hand, Landau (1991) has suggested that the seasonal patterns of examination identified by Snell are exaggerated by the legal requirement to have examinations signed by two justices, who were not necessarily resident in the parish, and that examinations were often saved up and sent to them in batches

The representativeness of surviving settlement documentation is questionable. Appeals against removal orders went to quarter sessions, generating large collections of information which formed the basis of much early work on mobility related to the Settlement Laws. However, the number of removals from any parish which went to the quarter sessions on appeal was very small; only a handful each year in some shires, the numbers tending to fall during the eighteenth century. The petty sessions' minute books, relating to the monthly meetings of Justices of the Peace, covering petty sessional divisions comprising groups of between a dozen and 30 parishes, provide information on a much greater proportion of settlement cases. These records suggest that removals under the Settlement Laws were more frequent than the quarter sessions material implies. Removals often seem to have been instituted to force the parish of settlement to issue a certificate, and were not necessarily associated with destitution. It is not clear how representative the details of mobility from settlement documents are of the movements of rural workers overall. They concern only those who moved – there was no need to examine those who stayed in their parish of settlement – so that they may exaggerate the amount of mobility among farm workers.

The emphasis of recent research has been on the uniformity rather than the diversity of experience under the Poor Law. In addition, much work has focused on south-east England, where assistance was relatively generous and, for many, their main means of support. But in many northern and western parishes poor relief was less generous and did not necessarily provide enough to live on, implying that other strategies, such as unofficial charity from family and friends, borrowing or pawning must have been more important. Such mechanisms were heavily dependent on people's ability to use local networks and here immigrants were at a clear disadvantage. King's (1997) study of Calverley in the West Riding shows that immigrants, most of them from neighbouring parishes, were more frequently dependent on relief than natives.

* * * * *

Although short-distance mobility within the countryside accounted for the vast majority of population movements throughout our period, migration from the countryside to the towns, often over longer distances, was of particular importance in demographic, economic and social terms, and it is this theme that we consider in the next chapter.

3

MIGRATION TO THE TOWNS

Introduction

Migration to the towns was an important component of population movement in Early-Modern Britain for several reasons. Urban in-migration reduced population pressure in rural areas. High mortality rates among urban immigrants served as a safety valve, reducing national population growth. For much of the seventeenth century, English towns absorbed around 40 per cent of the natural growth of population, converting slow growth into absolute decline towards the end of the century. While urban mortality rates were particularly severe in London, there is no reason to believe that they were much lower in larger regional centres like Bristol and Norwich (Patten, 1973). The towns and cities of Early-Modern Britain could not have sustained their populations, far less grown in the way that they did, without a steady influx of migrants. Urbanization was important among the economic and social changes which led to industrialization, and urbanization would have been impossible without migration. Immigration to the towns facilitated structural changes within the economy and promoted social mobility. It brought large numbers of young, upwardly-mobile men and women into environments which have been seen as 'engines of growth' and change in preindustrial Britain (Wrigley, 1967). Towns were places of opportunity, epitomized by the story of Dick Whittington. They were also places of danger for the unwary migrant, as emphasized by Hogarth's series of illustrations, entitled 'The Harlot's Progress', which begins with an innocent country girl alighting from a carrier's waggon in London and being accosted by a brothel keeper (Bailyn, 1986). Urban in-migration also precipitated further moves. A common finding from the analysis of samples of urban and rural migrants in church court depositions is that the inhabitants of towns were more likely to migrate than those of rural areas (Clark, 1972). A move to a town, even a local one, might precipitate further migration up the urban hierarchy, or even abroad (Chapter 4). The assimilation of large numbers of incomers created problems for urban society and urban authorities. Movement was not all one-way though: the return flow of people to the countryside was important for the transfer of ideas and innovations.

In the later fourteenth and fifteenth centuries towns throughout Britain were stagnant, even in decline, their populations often smaller than in the later thirteenth century. While a few towns experienced growth, it was generally at the expense of others. Nevertheless, although migration to British towns increased during the sixteenth century, it did so within well-established patterns which were distinct from mobility within the countryside. In the early fourteenth century migration to Leicester and Nottingham operated over longer distances than migration within rural areas. Of migrants within rural Nottinghamshire, 48 per cent had moved 11km or less, but the comparable figure was 31 per cent for those moving to Leicester and 20 per cent to Nottingham. Norwich and York drew migrants from even wider areas, with York showing a marked expansion of its catchment in the late fourteenth century, possibly due to population growth (McClure, 1979).

London's migration field was wider still. The pattern of long-distance movement to London which was evident in the sixteenth century had already developed by the early fourteenth century, at which time 52 per cent of migrants came over 64km against 30 per cent for York, 25 per cent for Nottingham and 18 per cent for Leicester (McClure, 1979). Not all late-medieval towns drew in long-distance immigrants though. Warwick was not attractive to migrants, perhaps due to economic problems; only a quarter of the recorded population came from elsewhere, contrasting with Stratford, Coventry and Bristol where the figure was a third to a half (Beier, 1981). In the later sixteenth century in England and Scotland widespread urban growth, fuelled by in-migration, began once more. While individual towns, or even whole levels of the urban hierarchy, experienced decline at certain periods between the late sixteenth and the early nineteenth centuries, the overall trend was one of continued urban growth throughout our period.

Early-Modern Urbanization

In late-medieval Britain most towns were small and levels of urbanization were low. In 1500 only 3.1 per cent of the population of England lived in towns with more than 10 000 inhabitants. For Scotland the figure was a mere 1.6 per cent, while no Irish town had yet reached this size. By 1600 (Table 3.1) the percentage of the population of England and Wales living in towns with over 10 000 inhabitants had risen markedly. Towns with over 5000 inhabitants (excluding London) probably accounted for about 5 per cent of England's population in 1540, 8 per cent in 1600 and 14 per cent by 1650. The rise continued during the seventeenth and eighteenth centuries with Scotland catching up rapidly, especially during the eighteenth century. By 1800 Scotland was, on this measure, nearly as urbanized as England and Wales. Ireland, after rapid urban growth in the later seventeenth and early eighteenth centuries due mainly to the expansion of Dublin, lagged well behind (De Vries, 1984). However, cities with over 10 000 inhabitants, while important, formed only part of the urban population, a substantial proportion of whom lived in smaller centres.

Table 3.1 Proportions of the Population (per cent) Living in Towns with Over 10 000 Inhabitants (After De Vries, 1984)

	1500	1550	1600	1650	1700	1750	1800
England and Wales	3.1	3.5	5.8	8.8	13.3	16.7	20.3
Scotland	1.6	1.4	3.0	3.5	5.3	9.2	17.3
Ireland	0	0	0	0.9	3.4	5.0	7.0

These were generated by some remarkable rates of growth in particular towns. Of these London was probably the most dramatic (Table 3.2). In the mid-sixteenth century London ranked only sixth among European cities in terms of size. By 1600 it was third after Naples and Paris; by the end of the seventeenth century it was the largest city in Europe, accommodating over 10 per cent of England's population, developing from a medium-rank city, with an economy largely tied to the export of cloth, to a major metropolis.

Table 3.2 The Growth of London

1500	40 000
1550	75 000
1580	100 000
1600	200 000
1650	400 000
1700	575 000
1750	600–675 000
1801	900 000

Other cities also grew rapidly (Table 3.3). Growth of smaller towns was more prominent in the late sixteenth and early seventeenth centuries. In the seventeenth century growth was especially evident in new industrial centres like Birmingham and Manchester, ports such as Liverpool and leisure centres like Bath. Although during the sixteenth and seventeenth centuries, no provincial town matched the x10 growth rate of the capital, in the eighteenth century Sheffield grew by x15 and Bath by x12. Between 1700 and 1800 the proportion of the population living in provincial towns with 10 000–20 000 inhabitants, especially in those with over 20 000, increased significantly more than the proportion in smaller towns (Corfield, 1982). There was also an important geographical shift in the distribution of urban population towards the North and the Midlands. Not all towns grew equally fast, or even grew at all though; some long-established centres stagnated or declined. English towns became more specialized, with distinct groups such as manufacturing centres, ports, dockyard towns and spas often eclipsing traditional market centres.

Scotland shared the pattern of rapid urban growth in the late sixteenth and early seventeenth centuries. The 1640s and 1650s witnessed a decline of population in towns like Aberdeen and Dundee due to war, economic dislocation and plague. The later seventeenth century was a period of relative stagnation with only Edinburgh and Glasgow growing markedly. Towns lower down the hierarchy which increased their population were balanced by ones which declined. The eighteenth century saw renewed growth, especially among smaller urban centres with the rise of many small textile centres and the first factory communities such as New Lanark (Whyte, 1989; Lynch, 1992).

Table 3.3 The Growth of Some Major British Cities (After De Vries, 1984)

	1500	**1550**	**1600**	**1650**	**1700**	**1750**	**1800**
Birmingham		1000	2000	4000	7000	24 000	69 000
Liverpool					6000	22 000	78 000
Manchester				5000	9000	18 000	70 000
Edinburgh		12 000	30 000	35 000	50 000	57 000	82 000
Glasgow	3000	4500	7000	12 000	18 000	24 000	77 000
Cork			2000	2000	25 000	58 000	75 000
Dublin		5000	5000	17 000	60 000	90 000	168 000

Urban Migration Fields

Urban growth was widespread for most of our period and much of it was generated by in-migration. However, patterns of migration, the people who made up the migration streams, and the impact of their movement on the towns to which they moved was complex and varied over time, as is shown by the characteristics of urban migration fields. Information on urban migration fields is invariably partial and incomplete. No source lists all the people migrating into towns at any period. Some groups, such as apprentices and freemen, are well recorded, though most of London's freemen's registers have been destroyed. However, while apprentices formed a significant proportion of urban immigrants in the late sixteenth and early seventeenth centuries, and may thus have been representative, at least, of the more upwardly-mobile elements in the migration stream, the decline of apprenticeship systems makes studying apprenticeship migration less useful thereafter. We know very little about the geographical and social origins of the large numbers of poor migrants who flocked to the towns. Some are recorded in lists of vagrants who were apprehended and expelled but many, especially women, including female domestic servants, are poorly documented. The focus on apprenticeship records has sidelined questions regarding the extent and methods of female recruitment to the towns. For England, church court depositions probably provide the best indication of urban in-migration fields in the sixteenth and early seventeenth centuries, but these fade out from the later seventeenth century. In the eighteenth century settlement documents become more prominent. Marriage registers for urban parishes may give the places of origin of immigrant spouses, but have received little attention (Whyte and Whyte, 1988). Far more information is available relating to people migrating into towns than for those moving out of them.

Nevertheless, enough research has been undertaken for some general features of urban migration fields to emerge. At all periods the size of the area from which people were recruited was directly related to the population of the towns to which they moved. The interest generated by long-distance migrants tends to obscure the fact that most preindustrial towns attracted high proportions of immigrants from their immediate hinterlands, within a radius of perhaps 32km. Only London, and to a lesser extent Edinburgh and Dublin, had truly national migration fields throughout the period, though towns like Bristol and Norwich recruited at least a few people from every English county (Patten, 1973). Short-distance movement to local market towns which were already familiar through previous regular contacts may have been nothing out of the ordinary for many migrants, but a long-distance move from the countryside to a major city is likely to have involved greater adjustment.

Urban immigration provided the context within which Clark (1972) developed his ideas of 'betterment' and 'subsistence' migration, suggesting that betterment migration was characteristically rural to urban, operating over short distances while subsistence migration was longer-range and more likely to be inter-urban (Chapter 1). However, as Patten (1973) has noted, these ideas developed from the analysis of migration to three relatively small Kentish towns, none of which had any really significant local manufactures which would have attracted large numbers of long-distance migrants. London, for instance, clearly received many betterment migrants from distant origins as well as subsistence migrants from close at hand, as did Edinburgh, Norwich and other larger provincial towns.

Nevertheless, the later sixteenth and early seventeenth centuries were characterized by the relative importance of long-distance migration, both betterment (as with apprenticeship migration) and subsistence. Southern English towns like London and Norwich received many immigrants from the north of England. From the 1640s this long-range component declined, causing a contraction of urban migration fields. Likely reasons included an overall reduction in population growth in northern England plus increased opportunities for migrants in northern towns. It is important to appreciate, however, that the contraction of urban migration fields does not necessarily indicate any reduction in the numbers of people moving into the towns – only that they were recruited from more restricted hinterlands. In fact, the number of migrants must have continued to rise in order to have sustained the urban growth which occurred.

Migration fields changed gradually, but were also subject to short-term perturbations. Urban epidemics, which might kill a quarter of the population of a town in a single season, created large numbers of vacancies, encouraging surges of migration from surrounding rural areas. Urban authorities, concerned to keep out poor migrants during years of food shortage, might suddenly be forced to relax entry conditions to guilds after an epidemic in order to encourage immigrants, as with Aberdeen after the plague outbreak of 1647 (Desbrisay, 1991). Population losses were often made up within two or three years. In London in the three years after the influenza epidemic of 1557–59, the average number of apprentices enrolled was 66 per cent above that for the previous five years. After the plague outbreak of 1603, it was 74 per cent above average (Rappaport, 1984). Apprentices were especially at risk from the plague as more men than women died of it and younger people were particularly susceptible. The plague of 1665 and the Great Fire in 1666 killed up to 100 000 people in London, but again there was a rapid recovery (Wareing, 1981). The pattern was similar for smaller towns such as Colchester and York (Goose, 1986). Waves of in-migration continued even after bubonic plague had disappeared. In Stratford upon Avon in the late 1720s smallpox and fever epidemics killed over 800 people within six years, but there was an influx of immigrants in the early 1730s and twice as many marriages as in previous years (Martin, 1978). On the other hand, famine in the countryside drove starving refugees into the towns. In the 1590s large numbers of near-destitute labourers and smallholders flocked into English towns. The decline of rural industry in depression years may have worsened the problem (Clark, 1985). Such refugees, poorly fed, were especially vulnerable to urban diseases such as plague and smallpox. In Scotland the famine of 1623 caused a flood of desperate migrants into towns such as Dunfermline and Kelso. The massive rise in burials recorded in their registers were probably mainly of recently arrived outsiders (Flinn, 1976).

These circumstances represent the extremes of pull and push factors encouraging movement to the towns. Other positive forces prompting urban immigration included higher wages. Wage rates are difficult to calculate and compare, but there is little doubt that urban wages, especially in London, were often considerably higher than in rural areas. Workers in London were better paid than in provincial towns. Seventeenth-century London was a high-wage area *par excellence*, especially for building workers, who got twice the wages of those in northern towns, though against this must be set the higher cost of living in the capital (Boulton, 1996). Later-seventeenth-century average wages for 300 days' work were £25 in London, but £17 in the west of England and £11.10s in the north (Kitch, 1986). There were also intra-regional differences in wage rates, which may also have influenced migration. Northern towns had split into two groups by the end of the seventeenth century in terms of the wages paid to building craftsmen. High-wage towns included Beverley, Hull, Newcastle and York, low-wage ones Carlisle, Chester, Durham, Kendal and Lincoln (Woodward, 1994). The relationships between migration, labour supply, economic demand and wages were complex, but it is significant that York, Newcastle and Hull at least had more active economies than some of the low-wage towns.

Other urban attractions were the possibility of acquiring skills which might enhance income and social mobility, and the chance of finding a suitable marriage partner. Conversely, the possession of certain skills may have predisposed people to migrate to the towns. The high levels of literacy of London's population in Early-Modern times has been commented upon. But as most people moved to the capital in their late teens or early 20s, they must have learned to read and write before migrating. It is therefore likely that London creamed off a significant proportion of young, literate, ambitious people from the provinces. Analysis of migrants to various towns in the late seventeenth century, using data from church court depositions, has shown that literate men moved over greater distances than illiterate ones; 10.5 per cent of literate men moved 100km or more against 5.3 per cent of illiterate ones (Souden, 1987). For migrants such as runaway criminals or pregnant girls, large towns and cities may have offered anonymity. Towns were also seen as offering cheap accommodation, more generous handouts and a wider range of ways to scrape a living than was possible in the countryside.

Migration to London

Throughout our period London consistently attracted more immigrants, drawn from wider areas, than any other British city, but our knowledge of patterns of migration to London is patchy. Apprenticeship migration has been studied in detail, but very little is known of the social origins of most people moving to the capital or how these changed over time. Various estimates have been made of London's in-migration stream. In 1550, when London's population was *c*.70 000, it has been calculated that about 700 immigrants a year were needed just to maintain population levels. In fact, at this time London received around 1250 immigrant apprentices a year and several hundred domestic servants (Rappaport, 1989). In 1552 there were *c*.37 600 males in London, *c*.19 700 of them over 26. Around 657 of them would have died in any year so *c*.854 men were needed to replace them and allow for 1 per cent growth. In 1600, with a population of *c*.150 000, *c*.3750 new migrants were required each year to maintain population and allow for growth; gross migration would have been much higher.

The population of London grew by *c*.3300 per annum between 1550 and 1650. Assuming that the death rate exceeded the birth rate by around 10 per 1000, there would have been a shortfall of *c*.2500 a year on average. A net immigration of 6000 people a year was needed to maintain growth. These 6000 represented the survivors of a cohort of some 9000 at birth so that *c*.9000 births a year were needed for London to grow at the rate it did. At the start of the seventeenth century the population of England was about four million, with an annual surplus of births of perhaps 20 000. London must have been absorbing the natural increase of some two million people – or about half the population of England (Finlay, 1981). Again, these are only net figures; assuming that significant movement out of London also occurred, the gross numbers of annual immigrants would have been substantially greater. Overall it is thought that around a million people migrated to London between 1550 and 1750 (Wareing, 1981).

Most Londoners, then, were born outside the city. Only 13 per cent of a sample of people living in East London between 1580 and 1640 had been born in the capital and a larger sample from church court depositions from the same period gave a figure of 22 per cent (Brodsky-Elliot, 1981). Given this, much of the social structure of London must have been influenced by the family backgrounds of the immigrants. The high levels of immigration, balanced in part by movement out of the city, meant that between one in eight and one in six adults in England had lived in London at some time in their lives (Finlay, 1981), plus an unknown proportion who had visited the capital more briefly.

Apprenticeship migration to London was particularly important, especially during the sixteenth and early seventeenth centuries, and apprentices formed the largest group whose migration patterns can be easily studied (Kitch, 1986). In the early seventeenth century apprentices accounted for a third to half of the total immigrants to London (Boulton, 1987). In 1600, 4000–5000 apprentices were registered each year in London and 28 000–35 000 were already at work so that there were 32 000–40 000 in all, about 15 per cent of the total population. By 1700 there were only *c*.27 200–32 640 apprentices among a much larger population, only around 5 per cent of whom were apprentices (Finlay, 1981). The decline, especially in immigrant apprentices, continued into the eighteenth century (Landers, 1993).

For a brief period in the early 1550s data on apprenticeship migration are supplemented by information on the origins of London freemen (Ramsay, 1978), provided by the 1088 who were admitted between 1551 and 1553. Under a quarter came from within the city; 99 came from Yorkshire, Lancashire and Cheshire, 21 from Wales and 15 from Ireland. The preponderance of north-country origins was already evident. In the later sixteenth and early seventeenth centuries migrant apprentices moving to London came from throughout England, with a significant component originating in the north and west. In the 1550s apprentices migrated on average 185km; a third came from the six northern counties. Subsequently, the migration field contracted as apprenticeship declined, with a marked reduction in the percentage of apprentices moving over longer distances. Changes in the pattern of apprenticeship migration to London have been highlighted by Wareing (1980). By the early fourteenth century, London was already drawing migrants from throughout England. In the late fifteenth century 61 per cent of migrant apprentices to the Skinners' and Tailors' companies came from north of a line from the Dee to the Wash.

Between the late fifteenth and mid-eighteenth centuries the apprentice migration field contracted. The proportion of apprentices who came from London itself was only 14.3 per cent in the late fifteenth century, but had risen to 57.2 per cent by the mid-eighteenth. The percentage of apprentices drawn from northern England fell from 61.2 per cent in the late fifteenth century to 10.9 per cent over the same period. The average distance migrated by apprentices fell from 212km in the late fifteenth century, to 111km (Table 3.4). Despite this, London continued to attract higher percentages of apprentices from over 50km than any provincial town. Apprenticeship migration patterns in the later seventeenth century were influenced by coastal and river transport; there were more migrant apprentices than expected from Berwick, Newcastle, Reading and Oxford, places linked to London through the capital's market for food. At this time 32 per cent of immigrant apprentices came from market towns, emphasizing the importance of trade contacts; but only 6 per cent came from the 16 largest towns (Kitch, 1986). The cut off of apprentices from northern England in the later seventeenth century was linked to the rise of rural industry and a more prosperous agriculture, as well as a reduction in population growth.

Table 3.4 The Contraction of London's Recruitment Field for Freemen and Apprentices (After Wareing, 1980)

Period	Group	Mean Distance Migrated (km)
1486–1500	Tailors' and skinners' apprentices	212
1551–53	Freemen	197
1573–94	Carpenters' apprentices	182
1562–1600	Stationers' apprentices	178
1601–40	.. ..	161
1654–74	Carpenters' apprentices	126
1676–94	.. ..	122
1690	Freemen	139
1710–20	Fishmongers' and grocers' apprentices	127
1740–50	.. ..	111

During the later sixteenth and early seventeenth centuries the sons of gentlemen, and especially yeomen and husbandmen, accounted for two-thirds of London's immigrant apprentices. Most apprentices moving to London probably already had arrangements made for them, as so many people would have had a friend or relative there. Apprentices whose families lived in London started younger; on average 17.7 years against 19.5 for immigrants. Many immigrant apprentices came from farming backgrounds and may have been needed at home until they were older.

During the seventeenth century the percentage of apprentices from gentry origins rose, while the percentage from more modest origins such as husbandmen fell. Their literacy levels were very high; literacy was a formal requirement for apprenticeship in some companies.

Wareing (1981) believed that the trends in apprenticeship migration mirrored London's migration field as a whole, but in a more extreme way. This is suggested by patterns of migration of indentured servants to London between 1683 and 1775 (Table 3.5). Indentured servants came from a range of social backgrounds and were considered to be more representative of migrants than apprentices, though migrants from the hinterlands of ports like Bristol and Liverpool were under-represented, as were women. Wareing argued that most of them moved in a two-stage process; first to London, then emigrating to the New World rather than moving to London in order to emigrate.

Table 3.5 Origins of 7666 Indentured Servants (per cent) Bound in London, 1683–1775 (After Wareing, 1981)

	1683–86	1718–29	1730–39	1749–59	1773–75	1693–1775
London	40.8	34.6	40.9	26.9	60.7	48.0
Home Counties	11.2	12.3	11.9	12.3	10.5	11.3
South and West	10.0	13.3	9.4	15.0	6.8	9.2
Midlands	14.1	14.5	11.7	16.9	7.8	11.0
Eastern Counties	4.0	6.2	4.7	1.9	2.8	4.0
Northern Counties	11.5	10.9	11.9	11.5	6.1	9.1
Wales	1.3	1.6	1.9	1.5	0.2	1.0
Others	7.2	6.7	7.7	13.8	5.1	6.5

The migration field for people moving to London who subsequently became indentured servants covered every county in England and Wales. Between 1676 and 1750 13.8 per cent of migrant apprentices came from the northern counties against 19.9 per cent of indentured servants. Large towns, such as Bristol, York, Norwich and Exeter, were particularly significant in the migration of indentured servants; they formed 7 per cent of the population of England and Wales outside London, but provided 21 per cent of the migrants. Twelve per cent of migrating servants came from outside England and Wales between 1486 and 1750 against only 1 per cent of migrant apprentices. This suggests that apprenticeship data underestimate movement from Ireland and

Scotland to England.

Another important, but less well-recorded group of urban immigrants were female domestic servants. As early as the 1550s several hundred young women a year moved to London to enter domestic service. They often had previous experience, leaving home in their late teens or early 20s, working for a year or two with a country family or in a market town, then moving to the capital. Many stayed with relatives there until they found a place. They were often mobile within the capital. The median time spent by servants in one place was about a year in late-seventeenth- and early-eighteenth-century London. Unlike apprentices, there is little indication of a contraction in the migration field for female domestic servants in late-seventeenth-century London (Table 3.6). A small decrease in migrants from the north of England was compensated for by a rise in female migrants from Scotland and Ireland. A further indication of London's continuing attraction for long-distance migrants, notwithstanding the decline of apprenticeship migration, is shown by a study of the birthplaces of 3236 married people attending the Westminster General Dispensary between 1774 and 1781 (Landers, 1993): 25.5 per cent were born in London and 57.7 per cent elsewhere in England and Wales, but 6.5 per cent came from Scotland and 8.7 per cent from Ireland.

Table 3.6. Origins of a Sample of 2121 Women Commissary Court Witnesses in London, 1665–1725 (After Earle, 1989)

Region of Origin	Percentage of Migrants
London	30.6
Home Counties	18.9
South Midlands	14.4
North Midlands	10.6
Western England	16.8
Eastern England	6.1
Southern England	3.8
North East England	7.0
North West England	10.0
Wales	3.3
Scotland and Ireland	5.7
Abroad	2.4
Total	**100.0**

As well as betterment migrants, London also attracted large numbers of poor incomers. Their numbers rose markedly in the late sixteenth century. London's Bridewell Court recorded a rise of three times in numbers of vagrants dealt with between 1578 and 1601. The proportion of poor among London's population has been put as high as a third, but Rappaport (1989) casts doubts on the extent of dire poverty in London; suggesting that probably only about 10 per cent were indigent in the difficult decade of the 1590s. London's vagrants in the sixteenth and early seventeenth centuries resembled apprentices in that they were predominantly young and male, and had mostly originated outside the city. East Anglia, Yorkshire, a belt of country between London and Bristol, and after 1600 Ireland, sent large contingents, but as the seventeenth century wore on, a greater proportion originated from London and its suburbs. Before 1580 vagrants claiming to have been born, or last resident, in the London area accounted for 20–30 per cent of the total, from the south-east around 40 per cent. After 1600 around 50 per cent were from the city and another 10 per cent from the south-east (Beier, 1981). Wood-pasture areas were prominent among vagrant origins in London. They loitered in alehouses, begged in the streets, dossed down on the pavements and rented rooms in slum tenements.

This pattern continued into the late eighteenth century. A survey of 2000 adult beggars in London in the 1790s showed that only 38 per cent had come from parishes within a 16km radius of the city. Of those who had come further, only 17 per cent came from other parts of England against 34 per cent from Ireland and 3 per cent from Scotland (Corfield, 1982). The similarities between the profiles of apprentices and vagrants suggest that vagrants were not a group apart, as portrayed in the 'rogue' literature (Chapter 2). Many had probably not arrived in the capital as vagrants, but had become destitute due to the social and economic conditions that they found there. Almost three-quarters of vagrants with London origins who were apprehended between 1597 and 1608 had been apprentices or servants. Partly, this was due to the significance of these groups in the labour force, but even so they were disproportionately represented among the vagrant population. Apprentices were liable to be laid off suddenly if their masters died or if they had a dispute with their employer.

Migration to English Provincial Towns

The patterns which have been identified for London were repeated on a smaller scale, with more limited catchment areas, for English provincial towns. These patterns probably originated at least as early as the late fifteenth and early sixteenth centuries, when population growth recommenced. Once they had been generated, they were often self-reinforcing with continuity often persisting into the eighteenth century. Lack of suitable sources makes it hard to compare migration patterns for towns below the level of major regional centres; a problem highlighted by Patten (1973), but not yet addressed, is the extent to which the migration fields of smaller towns varied with their economic and social structures – between manufacturing or marketing centres, for instance.

As with London, the best-recorded, most easily isolated group of migrants were apprentices. One of the most frequently quoted studies has been Patten's (1976) study of apprenticeship migration into Norwich, Ipswich and Yarmouth. He analysed *c.*6000 apprentices registered in Norwich from the mid-sixteenth to the mid-seventeenth centuries, 500 in Yarmouth from the 1560s to the 1660s, and 370 in Ipswich from 1596 to 1651. A third of the Norwich apprentices were migrants, about half in Yarmouth and Ipswich. A feature of migration to Norwich was that relatively few apprentices were drawn from areas close to the town, something also noted by Clark (1972) for Canterbury. Patten suggested that in such areas, there may have been opportunities as outworkers for urban manufacturers and in specialist dairying and market gardening. Most migrant apprentices came from beyond 32km of Norwich. There was a marked decline in migrant apprentices during the seventeenth century, along with a drop in the proportion who came long distances. There were marked directional differences in the migration field within East Anglia; fewer apprentices came from the direction of Yarmouth, more from areas to the north-east of the city where there were links through local textile industries. Long-distance migrants came from almost every English county. There were strong links with other textile areas such as Yorkshire, Lancashire and Cumbria. The rise and fall at any one time in numbers of apprentices migrating to Norwich was related to the prosperity of the textile industry. For Yarmouth, the migration field was smaller; most apprentices came from within a 32km radius and for Ipswich 26km. The migration field for Yarmouth was more coastal, with fewer apprentices from inland areas.

The pattern of most apprentices originating from a local region, but with a significant proportion moving over long distances was repeated for other provincial towns. In Oxford in the 1560s, a third of migrant apprentices came from the West Midlands and the North. In the mid-sixteenth century Bristol recruited around 9 per cent of its apprentices from northern and western counties, excluding Wales. Only about half the apprentices came from the city itself and an immediate area comprising Gloucestershire and Somerset. There was a substantially higher proportion of immigrants than for Norwich (Patten, 1973). Only a quarter of those becoming freemen in York during the sixteenth century came from the city itself (Palliser, 1985). Of the rest, half came from Yorkshire. Beyond this was a marked migration flow from the north-west; from Swaledale, Wensleydale and Westmorland. Relatively few came from the East Riding, where Hull acted as the local magnet, or from the West Riding, whose textile industries provided local opportunities. Smaller towns tended to recruit migrants from more restricted areas. Nevertheless, some long-distance linkages existed. Ipswich had clear links with Newcastle, doubtless through the coal trade (Patten, 1973), while Canterbury attracted immigrants from Cheshire, Lancashire and Yorkshire (Clark, 1977).

Large numbers of immigrants before *c.*1640 were poor subsistence migrants who often travelled over long distances (Clark, 1981). In Warwick, of 113 vagrants arrested between 1580 and 1587, most had come from within an 80km radius, but some had travelled over longer distances from the Highland zone (Beier, 1981). In Salisbury, out of over 600 vagrants expelled between 1598 and 1638, about a fifth had come over 160km. For Kentish towns, the 1590s were the worst period for migration pressure, but problems continued into the seventeenth century. From a sample of late-sixteenth-century church court depositions relating to Canterbury, only 21.5 per cent of male witnesses had been born there and never moved. Long-distance migrants to Kentish towns came from northern England, from Cheshire, Lancashire and Yorkshire; from East Anglia via London or direct by sea; from the Thames valley and along the south coast as far as Devon, many people probably coming by ship (Clark, 1972). The immigrants were predominantly from rural backgrounds, but long-distance migration was more closely linked to urban origins. People who moved from Canterbury, Maidstone and Faversham having been born there, tended to settle in other towns. The extent of migration fields was related directly to the size of the towns. Canterbury drew migrants from a radius of 18–24km, but the smaller centres of Maidstone and Faversham only up to 18km. Gentry and yeomen moved the shortest distances, while long-distance migration was more marked for servants. An immigrant servant coming to Canterbury was three times more likely to have come from outside the county as an immigrant gentleman.

In a sample of 861 church court depositions for Cambridge between 1580 and 1600, over 80 per cent of witnesses were migrants: 17 per cent had been born in Cambridge; and a further 18 per cent within the county (Sirault, 1981); 24 per cent came from adjacent counties; but 21 per cent were from the North; 53 per cent had travelled over 64km. Some deponents recorded up to six or seven moves. Many Cambridge-born witnesses had subsequently moved out of the town. Only 3 per cent had never moved at all. Most migrants had rural origins, but a third had been born in other towns. About 30 per cent had moved more than once. Sirault suggested that some of the long-distance migration was due to recommendations by Cambridge-trained clergy. People from the same place sometimes moved together; five men and a woman in the sample had come from Sedbergh in west Yorkshire. Migrants who prospered encouraged younger family members to join them.

In Gloucester, from a sample of church court deponents between 1595 and 1640, only 27 per cent of men and 19 per cent of women had never moved, and over a quarter of both sexes had come from outside the county. A significant number of the immigrants were betterment migrants, but there were also many subsistence migrants forced onto the roads by rural overpopulation, especially in pastoral areas like the Vale of Tewkesbury and the Cotswolds, where conditions were aggravated by depopulation associated with enclosure (Clark, 1990).

The patterns of migration to English towns outlined above continued to the outbreak of the Civil Wars in 1642. In the later seventeenth century there was a marked change, with a decline in long-distance subsistence migration to towns paralleling similar trends within the countryside (Chapter 2). Easing of demographic pressure, rising agricultural production, lower food prices, the spread of rural industry, the more widespread availability of poor relief and possibly the impact of the Settlement Laws (Chapter 2) are likely to have been important influences. Church court depositions capture the differences from the pre-1640 period, as well as identifying variations between regions and social groups. Souden (1984) examined 2262 depositions for Exeter, Bath, Wells, Salisbury, Oxford, Leicester and Norwich. There was a higher percentage of immobile men and women in western England than in the east. In Exeter 51 per cent of women had never moved, but in Norwich only 33 per cent. Larger towns had lower percentages claiming not to have moved than smaller ones. Craftsmen, textile and clothing workers were the least mobile groups, those in food and drink more mobile. Men moved an average distance of 48km to the larger towns, women 44km. Distances moved to smaller towns were significantly less. A high percentage of migrants were in their teens and early 20s. Professional men and retailers moved on average 60km to large towns and 50km to small ones, workers in wood, metal and the building trades only 35km and 22km respectively. Immigrants from other towns tended to travel further than those from the countryside. Larger cities still had a fair percentage of long-distance migrants; over a third of male and female migrants to them had travelled over 50km, twice the proportion moving to smaller towns. In the later seventeenth century the average distances travelled by men fell, but there was little change for women. By this time, a higher percentage of women than men were migrating and they were doing so over greater distances than earlier in the seventeenth century.

Although long-distance movement to the towns fell during the later seventeenth century, the aggregate level of migration remained high. Another important feature was a shift in the sex ratio of migrants. In the late sixteenth and early seventeenth centuries men had been in a significant majority. By the end of the seventeenth century, however, more women than men were moving to the towns due to the decline of apprenticeships and the expansion of opportunities for women as servants and in the service sector generally (Clark 1984). In the wealthy inner parishes of late-seventeenth-century Bristol, 25–30 per cent of the population were servants, five out of every eight of them women.

There seems to have been a good deal of stability in the migration patterns of industrial towns during the eighteenth century. For Sheffield, the proportion of migrant apprentices to the cutlers' company coming from over 64km was 6 per cent for the period 1625–49. It fell to 3 per cent for 1675–99, but rose to 7 per cent for 1750–74 and 8 per cent for 1775–99. The stability in the second half of the eighteenth century was striking (Buckatzsch, 1949–50). Overall, two-thirds came from within 32km, but those within 8km were not included in the study. For Birmingham, a register containing 736 settlement certificates between 1726 and 1757 shows that most migrants came from within 24km. Few came more than 96km. There was a directional bias towards the North West, including the Black Country and Wolverhampton (Parton, 1987).

There is more information about people who moved permanently to Early-Modern towns than short-term ones, whether visiting gentry or itinerant poor. Between the two categories were 'temporary residents' renting accommodation, but never acquiring their own household. In Ludlow such sojourners formed 8–10 per cent of the adult population (Wright, 1990). In any year *c*.25 people moved as sojourners to Ludlow, a town with a total population of *c*.2500–3000 in the 1750s. London had long acted as a magnet for landed society, but provincial towns also began to serve as social, cultural and leisure centres. Elements of this can be seen from the later sixteenth century, with towns like Canterbury already providing facilities for visiting gentry, but this trend became more marked from the late seventeenth century with the development of spas, and in the later eighteenth century with the rise of seaside resorts. Traditional regional centres, such as Preston or Shrewsbury, had by the early eighteenth century established lively social seasons in addition to their market and administrative functions, but there was also a growing number of specialist centres catering specifically for tourism and leisure. Visitors to centres like Bath usually only came for a few weeks and were not strictly migrants. However, such towns acted as magnets to more permanent residents who serviced the needs of the short-term visitors, especially doctors and lawyers, people in the luxury trades and entertainers. In Ludlow rural gentry were drawn as sojourners and temporary lodgers by fairs, races, theatres and balls. Wealthy widows might prefer to live in Ludlow rather than on their estates. Ludlow's social role also attracted lawyers, dressmakers, wigmakers, writing masters and musicians (Wright, 1990).

Scottish Urban Migration Fields

Urban migration fields north of the Border were similar in many respects to those in England. However, the frequency of subsistence crises down to the end of the seventeenth century, the limited poor relief and the lack of settlement laws meant that there was a constant flow of subsistence migrants into the towns, rising to flood levels in major crises such as the later 1690s. Despite the generally poorer quality of Scottish sources, some quantitative modelling of migration flows to preindustrial towns has been attempted. Lovett et al. (1985) analysed the migration of apprentices to Edinburgh in the seventeenth and eighteenth centuries, using poisson regression analysis. Numbers of migrant apprentices from counties and burghs were related to the populations of their source areas and their distance from Edinburgh. The mean distance migrated by apprentices rose from 41km in the late sixteenth century to 18–24km for most of the seventeenth and early eighteenth centuries, before falling to 28km at the end of the eighteenth century. The analysis showed, however, that although population and distance accounted for a substantial proportion of the variation in numbers of apprentices, the migration field was far from uniform in any of the three periods studied. In the late seventeenth century numbers of apprentices from western Scotland were surprisingly high given the area's comparative remoteness. Despite steady growth during the later seventeenth century, Glasgow did not affect Edinburgh's recruitment of apprentices from this area. However, there was a sharp contraction of the capital's migration field in western Scotland during the eighteenth century as Glasgow, and satellite towns like Greenock and Paisley, expanded rapidly, providing local opportunities for prospective apprentices (Figure 3.1, p. 65).

Edinburgh consistently received more migrants than predicted from many counties in south-eastern Scotland. Nevertheless, a weakening of the migration field in parts of southern Scotland is evident in the eighteenth century, possibly due to increasing contact with England, especially the attraction of Tyneside. The more urbanized counties of Fife and Angus had lower levels of movement to Edinburgh in relation to their populations and distance from the city, probably due to the availability of local opportunities, while the north-east sent more apprentices than predicted, perhaps due to contacts generated through coastal trade.

By the mid-eighteenth century Edinburgh was attracting more apprentices from Highland counties such as Inverness-shire and Ross-shire. The stability of the mean distance migrated by apprentices moving to Edinburgh between the mid-seventeenth and mid-eighteenth centuries masks a marked change in their origins, with a decline in numbers coming from the western lowlands being offset by greater numbers from the Highlands. A study of the migration of apprentices to Edinburgh from other towns showed similar results to the county data. The pattern of apprenticeship migration to Edinburgh resembles that of London, with nationwide recruitment and a contraction of the migration field through time. Edinburgh's apprenticeship migration field contained clearly defined migration flows from particular areas, once the effects of distance and population had been taken into account, some of which persisted over long periods. Superimposed on these were important changes in the apprenticeship migration field caused by the growth of other towns during the eighteenth century, especially Glasgow, which provided more local opportunities.

The format of some Scottish marriage registers allows the study of the migration of women into certain towns before, as well as at, marriage. Those for eighteenth-century Edinburgh, which are particularly detailed, provided information on over 30 000 female migrants (Whyte and Whyte, 1988). Where the marriage registers record a woman as living in Edinburgh when the banns were proclaimed and her father as living elsewhere, then a migratory move between her original home and the city had probably been made. In some cases the move may have been made shortly before marriage, but in others probably at an earlier date for the purposes of employment. While the registers do not usually differentiate between first and subsequent marriages, it can be assumed that a substantial proportion of the women involved were young and that many had moved to Edinburgh to enter domestic service. One cannot assume that a single move between home and city had always been made or that a father's parish of residence was always that of his daughter's birth. Nevertheless, given that most mobility within the Scottish countryside was very localized (Houston, 1985), in a high proportion of cases this is likely to have been a close approximation to the truth.

Where a woman's residence was recorded as being with her father outside Edinburgh, then migration presumably occurred at, rather than before, marriage. In such cases contact leading to marriage may have arisen in various ways. The groom may have originally come from the bride's place of residence and kept in touch after moving to the capital. The bride may have lived in Edinburgh for a period, met her future marriage partner and returned home prior to marriage. These two sets of circumstances would tend to produce patterns of migration similar to that of women migrating to Edinburgh before marriage.

Fig 3.1 Poisson regression analysis of apprentices migrating to Edinburgh (*Source*: Lovett, Whyte and Whyte, 1985)

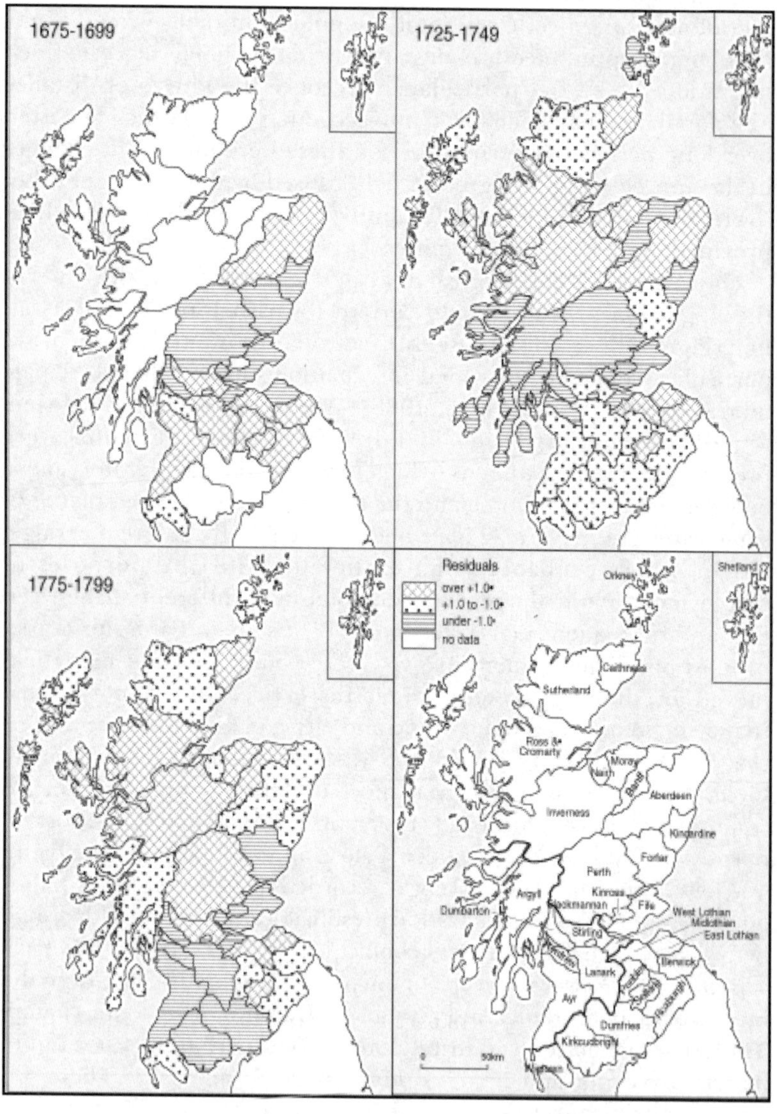

A third possibility is that initial contact between bride and groom was made during regular trips into or out of the city by one or both partners. Such contacts would involve a more local field of interaction between the capital and its immediate hinterland, corresponding to the marriage distances considered in Chapter 2. The influence of such purely local marriage contacts should reduce the average distances migrated by women at marriage compared with those migrating before marriage.

Table 3.7 shows the average distances migrated by women into eighteenth-century Edinburgh. There was a clear difference between distances migrated by women before and at marriage, the latter moving, as expected, over shorter average distances. Mean distances for all groups are surprisingly high, even in the early eighteenth century. Women moving to Edinburgh before marriage, many of them probably as domestic servants, tended to come from further afield than apprentices. In addition, their migration field widened during the eighteenth century, in contrast to the contraction of that for apprentices.

Table 3.7 The Migration of Women to Edinburgh in the Eighteenth Century (After Whyte and Whyte, 1988)

	Women migrating to Edin. before marriage	**Women migrating to Edin. at marriage**	**Women migrating from Edin. at marriage**	**Men migrating to Edin.**
	Average Distance (km)			
1701–10	54.9	41.8	49.1	77.8
1711–20	64.7	39.8	32.9	62.0
1721–30	60.0	46.4	40.7	71.8
1731–40	61.4	41.9	40.6	86.2
1741–50	68.3	40.8	38.2	75.9
1751–60	67.7	42.9	47.2	95.6
1761–70	66.2	47.5	44.2	97.4
1771–80	67.7	56.5	50.3	82.1
1781–90	77.8	48.0	46.0	100.4
1791–1800	62.9	61.2	56.5	74.0

Table 3.8 shows the changing regional pattern of migration of women to Edinburgh. There was a local region, including the Lothians, Fife and the Borders, from which a high, fairly stable proportion of the sample was drawn throughout the century. By contrast, the proportion of migrants from the western Lowlands fell over time. Given that the population of this region increased rapidly during the eighteenth century, this represents a marked relative decline. The growth of Glasgow and other industrial towns in west-central Scotland must have diverted prospective female migrants away from Edinburgh. The most remarkable feature, however, is the steady rise in the proportion of women drawn from Highland counties; 1.2 per cent in the first decade of the eighteenth century, but 11.6 per cent in 1781–90. This reflects the growing integration of the Highlands with the rest of Scotland, particularly after the 1745 Rebellion. The Highlands may have been a source of cheap domestic labour, while Edinburgh was also an important assembly point for Highland girls who came to help with the Lothian harvest.

Table 3.8 Migration of Women to Edinburgh before Marriage by Region (per cent per decade) (After Whyte and Whyte, 1988)

	1701 –10	**1711 –20**	**1721 –30**	**1731 –40**	**1741 –50**	**1751 –60**	**1761 –70**	**1771 –80**	**1781 –90**	**1791 –1800**
Lothians	37.0	35.0	37.7	38.3	33.7	35.0	36.7	37.1	33.6	38.1
Borders	10.6	9.0	8.2	8.9	8.1	6.5	7.5	6.8	6.8	8.2
Fife	18.7	14.8	15.1	18.5	16.3	14.5	15.5	15.5	17.1	19.8
Tayside	6.8	11.5	9.8	10.0	13.2	13.7	14.2	14.4	11.5	6.7
North East	4.9	5.0	5.6	6.4	7.2	8.2	5.2	4.9	2.8	3.0
South West	3.4	3.0	2.5	2.0	2.4	3.4	2.7	2.4	1.7	2.4
West-Cent	12.5	14.5	15.8	9.6	10.2	9.0	8.2	7.3	9.3	10.6
Highlands	1.2	2.4	3.4	3.3	5.8	5.8	5.9	7.0	11.6	7.3
N. Isles	0.9	1.6	0.3	1.2	1.0	1.5	1.5	0.6	1.0	0.6
Northumber-land	0.4	0.2	1.1	0.5	0.6	1.0	1.2	1.3	1.6	1.5
London	0	0	0.3	0.7	0.4	0.4	0.7	0.7	1.2	1.1
England	0.4	0.4	1.5	1.7	1.5	2.2	2.5	4.0	4.6	4.1

Another feature of Table 3.8 is the increasing proportion of women originating from south of the Border. The percentage of women moving from England increased 11 times between the first decade of the century and the 1780s. Growing contact with England in the decades following the Union of 1707 must have been an influence. The two most significant origins south of the Border were Northumberland, including Newcastle where many Scots were employed as keelmen, and London. The surnames of many of the women moving from England to Edinburgh suggest that they were the daughters of expatriate Scots.

Poisson regression analysis of migration origins within Scotland at county level emphasizes the under-representation of Highland women in the migration stream at the start of the century. Much of eastern Scotland, from Shetland to Roxburghshire, supplied more migrants than predicted, similar to the pattern for apprenticeship movements, highlighting the importance of contacts by sea between Leith and other east-coast ports. There were also higher than predicted levels of migration from some counties in central, western and south-western Scotland. Negative residuals for Dumbartonshire, Lanarkshire and Renfrewshire suggest the localized pull of Glasgow. The negative residual for Fife may reflect the attraction of Perth and Dundee, as well as the many smaller burghs within the county. By the mid-eighteenth century migration from Ayrshire and some Border counties was declining, as with apprentices. This was more than counter-balanced by a growing flow of women to Edinburgh from the north, especially the Highlands. By the end of the century the pattern of movement was markedly different from the opening decades. A core area around the Firth of Forth still supplied more migrants than predicted, but for almost all of the remainder of southern Scotland, levels of migration were lower than expected, reflecting the growth of other industrial towns and, in the Borders, possibly the pull of Tyneside. On the other hand, virtually the whole of the Highlands and northern Scotland, from Perthshire to Caithness and the Northern Isles, were providing more migrants than predicted.

The increase in the mean distance migrated by women to Edinburgh during the eighteenth century is explicable in terms of the changing origins of migrants, with a decline in the proportions of women drawn from the western and southern Lowlands being more than offset by an increase in those coming from more distant Highland and northern counties. The data suggest that apprentices were, as in late seventeenth century England, an increasingly unrepresentative group. The marriage registers also allow the migration of a large sample of men, from a wide range of social origins, to be analysed.

They tended to come over longer distances, on average, than women moving to Edinburgh before marriage. The average distances migrated by this group, as with women, rose through the eighteenth century when the hinterland for apprenticeship recruitment was shrinking sharply.

Migration from Towns

It would be easy to imagine that larger towns in Early-Modern Britain were purely parasitic, sucking migrants in from rural areas and killing off a substantial proportion of them. This is an oversimplification which ignores the fact that we are far better informed about migration into towns than out from them. Figures quoted for annual movements into London and other cities are for net migration. In fact, the gross totals must usually have been far greater, being balanced by a substantial movement of people from towns to other urban centres and back to the countryside. Aside from vagrants who were apprehended and returned to their place of origin, much of the information on this outward movement is indirect and its scale is hard to estimate. Rappaport (1983) has suggested that emigration from London in the late sixteenth century may have been around 10 per 1000 inhabitants per year. Alldridge's (1996) study of the population fluctuations of Chester from the mid-sixteenth to the early eighteenth century shows that outward surges of population were as frequent as inward ones and comparable in scale. Some, such as the 11 per cent per annum outflow between 1644 and 1646, can be related to particular circumstances; in this case the impact of the Civil Wars. In other instances, however, substantial net out-migration seems to have occurred for no clear reason and may have related to economic fluctuations in the town and its hinterland.

There must also have been a lot of temporary movement out of towns. In London labouring in the docks, which employed a significant proportion of the city's male workforce, was markedly seasonal, shutting down dramatically in winter. Reliance on casual labour was also a feature of major provincial ports like Bristol. The building industry was also highly seasonal in its activity. To what extent this caused temporary movement out of the city rather than just underemployment within it is not clear. The harvest drew large numbers of workers out of towns for a few weeks in the autumn. Many subsistence migrants were probably attracted out of London into the armed forces during wartime (Landers 1993). Outbreaks of plague caused substantial temporary outflows of the wealthier sectors of urban society in the sixteenth and seventeenth centuries. The wet nursing of urban children in surrounding rural areas was a highly specialized form of movement from cities like London and Edinburgh (Marshall, 1984). Indentured servants emigrating to the New World formed another group of temporary urban residents in the seventeenth and eighteenth centuries. Over 1000 indentured servants left London each year in the 1680s, a high proportion of whom had originated outside the capital (Wareing, 1981).

Another component of return migration was apprentices who failed to finish their training. The proportion completing their apprenticeships and becoming freemen was often quite small. Only 17–25 per cent of apprentices completed their apprenticeships and became freemen in late sixteenth- and seventeenth-century Norwich; some may have been unable to set up businesses on their own, but many must have moved on (Patten, 1976). The deaths of masters in plagues put apprentices out of work. The apparent mortality of apprentices in epidemics was probably inflated by runaways (Rappaport, 1989). In Salisbury in the 1610s only 21 per cent became freemen. In Bristol only about a third of sixteenth- and seventeenth-century apprentices became citizens (Ben Amos, 1991). The situation was similar in London, where few immigrant apprentices settled permanently and only 41 per cent finished their terms (Boulton, 1996). Some died, but many probably returned home, with several years of training, to set up businesses there. It has been suggested that in the mid-sixteenth century about 700 apprentices left London each year (Ben-Amos, 1991). In Bristol the percentage of apprentices who failed to become freemen was not significantly influenced by their trade or family background. Rising costs of rents and housing in Bristol in the later seventeenth century may have made it harder for finished apprentices to set up in business. By the mid-seventeenth century many Bristol apprentices emigrated as indentured servants. Some former apprentices ended up as vagrants. Of the vagrants arrested in Warwick in the late sixteenth century, a quarter of those who stated occupations had been apprentices or servants (Beier, 1981).

The out-migration of apprentices who had completed all or part of their training, often returning to their home areas, can be viewed as a positive process which diffused urban skills from London and the main regional centres to rural areas and small towns. Return migration was also important in spreading new fashions and tastes – such as drinking tea and coffee – to the provinces. Contemporary writers noted the insidious diffusion of urban culture into rural areas, some of it undoubtedly spread by everyday contacts within localized hinterlands, but a good deal of it probably the result of return migration (Corfield, 1982). During the eighteenth century the numbers of domestic servants employed in towns increased: servants were notorious for aping their employers' dress and manners; they sent news of urban fashions and lifestyles, as well as money, back to their families in the countryside; and they may also have helped reinforce existing migration links. Norwich developed special links with the area of north-west Yorkshire around Dent, which sent a disproportionate number of young men to the city's textile and clothing trades. The parish registers of Dent and Sedbergh indicate the return of at least some of them, and it may be that such links were instrumental in providing the skills which allowed the Dent area to develop as a textile manufacturing centre in the later seventeenth and eighteenth centuries (Patten, 1973). In Scotland the four largest towns; Edinburgh, Glasgow, Dundee and Aberdeen, may have provided employment for *c.*12 000 female domestic servants in the 1690s, a high proportion of them immigrants. As many as one in ten Scottish women in their late teens and early 20s is likely to have been in service in these four towns at any time. Many of them probably returned home to marry, bringing their savings from urban employment with them.

Migration and Urban Demography

The migration of large numbers of people from the countryside to the towns inevitably had a significant demographic impact on their destinations and their places of origin, the former theme having been studied in more detail than the latter. The impact of immigration on urban demography can be seen in a range of variables including mortality, fertility, and the age and sex structures of urban populations. In terms of age structure, migrants to towns were heavily concentrated in their 20s. Earle (1989) has suggested that there were proportionally fewer teenagers in London than elsewhere because so many migrants arrived in their early 20s.

The most notable demographic aspect of urban migration was that a steady influx of people was needed in order to allow towns and cities to maintain their populations, far less grow at the rate which they did. Indeed, it has been suggested that until urban natural increase became more common in the late eighteenth/early nineteenth centuries, urban growth was largely an index of net migration (Souden, 1984). The idea that without migration towns would have experienced net population decline due to high mortality goes back to seventeenth-century commentators such as Graunt and has frequently been restated (Finlay 1981).

Levels of mortality within towns varied considerable between different social areas. In wealthy areas of seventeenth-century London, though not in the poorer ones, population may have been able to replace itself (Boulton, 1987), but, for the city overall, Finlay estimates that the death rate exceeded the birth rate by around 10 per cent in the early seventeenth century. On the other hand, Sharlin (1978) has turned this argument on its head by claiming that it was the high rates of immigration that caused the natural decrease of population and not vice versa. He believed that as most migrants were young and single, they made a negligible contribution to urban fertility, but a significant contribution to mortality (Galley, 1995). Finlay's (1981) reconstitution of four London parishes suggested that not enough native-born children survived to the age where they could marry and replace themselves, but neither he nor Sharlin had enough data to prove their case conclusively.

Landers (1993) suggests that immigrants had restricted immunity and were subject to high levels of mortality from infectious diseases. If London children all caught smallpox before their teens, then deaths in this and older age groups were probably mainly those of immigrants. Of Manchester it was written in 1795 that: 'A lodger fresh from the countryside often lies down in a bed, filled by infection from its last tenant, or from which the corpse of a victim to fever has only been removed a few hours before' (Corfield, 1982). Under such circumstances the vulnerability of immigrants is hardly surprising.

More recently, evidence has been presented for natural increase having been more common in Early-Modern towns than has been previously accepted. Towns such as Cambridge, Exeter, Ipswich, Hull, Reading and Worcester appear to have had natural increases of population for at least part of the sixteenth and seventeenth centuries. Indeed, Galley (1995) has claimed that much of the evidence for urban natural decrease has actually come from the 'long eighteenth century', and may not have been an inevitable feature of earlier periods. In York there was a natural increase of population between 1561 and 1603. From 1605 to 1640 population was roughly in balance, and it was only from 1650 onwards that natural decrease occurred. What caused this change? Mortality seems to have been stable so there must have been a change in fertility, possibly due to a fall in the percentage of the urban population who got married. Galley believes that this was due to a balanced migration flow changing to one with a female bias. As migrants were mainly in their 20s, most of the imbalance was concentrated in the 20–30 age group. As a consequence, marriage opportunities for some female migrants must have become more limited. Natural increase was probably only possible in Early-Modern towns under favourable circumstances: the key factor was the percentage who married; together with balanced sex ratios, an expanding economy and higher nuptiality.

Goose (1994) also supports the idea that English towns did not always have net surpluses of burials over baptisms, even if some had higher mortality levels than the surrounding countryside. London did have a substantial net deficit throughout the period until the later eighteenth century, but this was not the case for all provincial towns. Baptism was probably more under-recorded than burials; so net growth may have been more common than parish registers imply. It would be ironic if natural decrease was a feature of the late-seventeenth–eighteenth-century 'English urban renaissance', and natural increase a characteristic of the 'crisis period' of the late sixteenth and early seventeenth centuries.

The surplus of deaths in London reflected in part the nature of the migration stream; many young single adults moving to the capital died before they could marry and have children. Immigrants were also vulnerable to diseases which were present in the capital, but not in their home areas. However, the most significant cause of the consistent surplus of deaths over births in London was not the susceptibility of young migrants to disease, but high mortality among infants and children (Wrigley and Schofield, 1981). London's mortality regime worsened in the seventeenth century, particularly because the city became large enough for some diseases, like smallpox, to become endemic. The burial surplus of London reinforced England's 'low pressure' demographic regime, preventing excess population growth. In the second half of the seventeenth century immigration to London, along with emigration, turned a small surplus of births in the rest of England into a deficit (Boulton, 1987), causing a fall in total population. By the end of the eighteenth century, however, the annual totals of baptisms in many large towns, such as Leeds and Nottingham, often surpassed those of burials (Corfield, 1982). The influx of young immigrants, no longer tied to years of celibacy in apprenticeships, produced relatively high birth rates.

From the later seventeenth century the expansion of demand for women as domestic servants, and an ever-widening range of jobs in the service sector, led to increased female in-migration. Little is known about the massive influx of women to London which occurred at this time, but it must have had considerable impact on demographic patterns, notably on sex ratios. Rappaport (1989) has indicated that in late-sixteenth-century London, the birth rate was low due to there being fewer women than men in the population. The surplus of males in London was largely due to the high number of apprentices in the workforce. As the apprenticeship system declined, sex ratios changed to favour women (Bolton, 1987). Numbers of male migrants may have fallen off in the later seventeenth century due to slackening of population pressure in the countryside. An increase in the demand for male labour in arable areas may have led to more rural young women looking to the towns for employment (Barry, 1990). By the late seventeenth century the sex ratio nationally was approximately 96 men per 100 women, but for London it was 77 (Wareing, 1981). This pattern persisted throughout the eighteenth century and the 1801 census shows that all large British towns had surpluses of females. This was also a feature of small towns. In Ludlow during the 1720s, among sojourners in lodging and boarding houses, there were ten women for every seven men; the same ratio as the overall adult population of the town (Wright, 1990). By the 1740s female domination was even more marked. The 1695 Marriage Duty Act census shows that there were more females than males, even in poorer suburban parishes where servants were fewer (Souden, 1984). This imbalance must have contributed to the late-seventeenth-century fall in population through its effects on fertility.

Migration and Urban Society

Large-scale immigration also affected urban society. Traditionally, this has been seen as volatile and unstable, due to high levels of in-migration with rapid population turnover, little sense of community and widespread anomy. Although the fact that substantial urban in-migration occurring over relatively short distances must have done much to ease the transition to urban society, the scale of culture shock experienced by immigrants to the towns must often have been considerable. When William Hutton first moved to Birmingham in 1741, aged 18, he was amazed at the contrast between urban and rural society: 'I had been among Dreamers, but now I saw Men awake.' On the other hand, a town could be a dangerous place for the unwary and the gullible. London was described in *The Tricks of the Town Laid Open* (1699) as 'A Kind of large Forest of Wild Beasts' (Corfield, 1982); *The Countryman's Guide to London, or, Villany Detected* (1780) painted an alarming picture of the potential dangers awaiting young men and women who were new to the city. The shock for a Gaelic-speaking Highlander arriving in Edinburgh or Glasgow, never previously having experienced anything bigger than a local market centre, must have been even greater.

An important aspect of urban society is the effect of high levels of in- and out-migration, as well as intra-urban movements, on population turnover. One might expect that population turnover within towns was even greater than in the countryside. This has been confirmed from studies, such as Finlay (1981), for three parishes in the City of London. The persistence of population in each was 28 per cent, 28 per cent and 34 per cent remaining after ten years, against 50 per cent in some rural parishes. It has been suggested that this produced an anonymous, impersonal environment. More recently, however, it has been suggested that the stability of population has been underestimated, especially in small, central urban parishes. In the Boroughside district of St Saviours, Southwark, an analysis of communicants' lists of heads of households has shown that after a year 79 per cent of the households in the sample were still living in the same dwelling, and after 10 years 24 per cent: 91 per cent of richer households were still in the same house after a year, 29 per cent after ten years, against 74 and 14 per cent respectively for poorer households (Bolton 1987). About 35 per cent of the total turnover was due to in- and out-migration. There was also considerable residential mobility within Boroughside itself.

However, these figures give a misleading picture of movement into and out of the community because many moves were over very short distances within streets, or even alleys (Boulton, 1987). There was considerable stability in Boroughside and overall levels of persistence were not much lower than in rural areas. In addition, many people moving out of Boroughside may not have gone far. Persistence levels for Boroughside were higher than for the three central parishes studied by Finlay, but these were smaller in area. High levels of short-distance mobility within urban communities were encouraged by the nature of the housing market. By the early seventeenth century few householders in Boroughside owned the freeholds of their dwellings; most of them rented property. A mixed rented-housing stock allowed people to adjust their lifestyles without leaving an area. Persistence within Boroughside, rather than in the same house, was influenced less by wealth: the poor moved more often than the rich, but mostly within the same area. Short-distance mobility was the means by which urban areas achieved a measure of social stability. Studies of eighteenth- and nineteenth-century cities suggest that personal whim, the death of children, life-cycle phase, and a desire to change business premises were likely motives for moving house (Pooley, 1979). Reasons for moving were probably similar in Early-Modern times.

Despite high turnover, the geographical horizons of seventeenth-century Londoners may have been restricted by poor intra-city communications. Marriage horizons were certainly limited. Marriages in St Saviours between 1655 and 1666 showed that 83 per cent of partners came from within the parish, a further 9 per cent from within London. In Stepney in the early seventeenth century over three-quarters of people getting married found their spouses locally, with only 6 per cent coming from more than 80km away (Patten, 1973). High population turnover was also characteristic of smaller towns. In Warwick between 1582 and 1587 there was a nearly 50 per cent turnover of poor families (Beier, 1981). However, Finlay (1981) has emphasized that the mobile elements within the urban population were quite specific, notably groups like apprentices and domestic servants, and that other elements within urban society were far more stable.

Immigration affected all areas of preindustrial cities. Larger towns and cities had social structures in which the richer districts were concentrated in the central area and the poor more often lived in the suburbs, although at a local scale there was often a great range of wealth and status within individual streets and alleys (Boulton, 1987). Poorer immigrants crowded into suburbs which were often less subject to control by urban authorities than inner-urban areas. In these poorer districts people were more willing to take in lodgers and accommodation, whether in inns, alehouses or lodgings in private houses, was often cheaper (Beier, 1981). On the other hand, domestic servants and apprentices were more frequently located in wealthier town-centre districts. Within preindustrial towns intra-urban mobility followed clear patterns. In Canterbury in the early seventeenth century there was a movement of population from poor outer parishes to wealthier inner ones of apprentices and servants, but also in the opposite direction as a counter-current of men and women left service and returned to the suburbs to set up on their own (Clark, 1972).

The Assimilation of Urban Immigrants

Rural migrants could face problems of assimilation even when they moved short distances within the countryside (King, 1997). Their problems were potentially greater when they moved into larger towns and cities because of the numbers of migrants involved and the greater difficulty of adapting to urban society and working conditions. In the later sixteenth and early seventeenth centuries the large numbers of immigrants to towns, and the inability of urban economies and societies to cope with the influx, led to attempts to control and prevent immigration. Migrants from outside England may have found it even harder to adapt to urban society, especially in London. However, a range of formal and informal mechanisms existed to assist them. Apprenticeship and domestic service helped many to assimilate and allowed towns to absorb the stream of immigrants without being swamped (Rappaport, 1989). On the other hand, the high proportion of vagrants in early-seventeenth-century London who were former apprentices or servants showed that such systems did not always work (Beier, 1981)

The traditional view of migration to the towns in the late sixteenth century is that floods of poor immigrants threatened disorder, caused social tension, increased overcrowding, poverty and the threat of plague, and led to more oligarchic rule as a response. It has often been claimed that around a third of urban populations at this time were living on or below the poverty line. More recently it has been suggested that this picture is exaggerated and that the poor usually accounted for little more than 5 per cent of the population. The idea of urban societies and economies being swamped by an influx of poor migrants is not always borne out by the evidence. For example, Beier

(1981) has shown that arrests of vagrants in London rose from 69 in 1560–61 to 555 in 1600–01. While Beier considered this a massive increase, it was nevertheless still only 0.1–0.2 per cent of the total population. This does not support the idea that the streets of London and other large towns were filled with young vagrants. There is very little evidence of instability and riots in sixteenth-century London (Rappaport, 1980). Remarkably, the flood of immigrants caused little open conflict with existing inhabitants. In London and other south-eastern towns, like Canterbury and Colchester, popular agitation was mainly directed against refugees from France and the Low Countries rather than incomers from surrounding rural districts.

That is not to say, however, that problems did not sometimes arise. In Winchester the decline in the cloth trade during the sixteenth century meant that immigrants could no longer be as easily absorbed. Tensions arose between residents and incomers over competition for employment and poor relief. Native craftsmen complained of competition from immigrants working in inns and alehouses (Rosen, 1981). In London poor immigrants moved into overcrowded, unhealthy housing in suburbs which acted as breeding grounds for disease and crime

Not surprisingly, urban authorities sometimes attempted to control and even check the influx of population, especially, but not exclusively, the poorer immigrants. In Kentish towns efforts were made to discourage respectable immigrants by limiting the numbers of new freemen who could be created and by increasing entry fines. Steps were also taken to expel beggars and vagrants (Clark, 1972). In Warwick in the 1580s the authorities tackled the problem of the poor vigorously, arresting and punishing vagrants (Beier, 1981). The authorities in Ipswich also tried to restrict numbers of immigrants: in 1575 they decreed that no craftsman would be allowed to settle without a licence unless they had been there three years already; this act was repeated in 1578 and 1609; in 1659 letting houses to newcomers was prohibited. The regulations were dropped after 1660 following the easing of population pressure (Reed, 1981). In late-sixteenth-century Winchester the pressure of immigrants caused competition with the townspeople, who adopted increasingly hostile policies towards outsiders with bans on people taking in lodgers (Rosen, 1981). Poor immigrants were driven out of Shrewsbury in 1597. In Lincoln in 1586 no poor incomers were allowed to settle without the mayor's permission. Special beadles arrested people at the gates and in the streets. Those arrested were likely to be kept in one of the houses of correction, which most towns had built by the 1590s, before being sent back to their places of origin (Clark, 1985). In Kendal the corporation tried fairly successfully to control immigration through control of letting of rooms to poor tenants. Migration into Kendal in the seventeenth century was restricted and this was reflected by the lack of growth of the town's population (Phillips, 1984).

After the mid-sixteenth century a growing number of towns insisted that newcomers had to get the magistrates' permission to settle. There were increasing controls on renting property to poor incomers (Clark, 1987). In Scotland the authorities in Edinburgh conducted periodic expulsions of vagrant beggars throughout the seventeenth century, though the frequency with which the measures were repeated suggests that any success was strictly short-lived. In seventeenth-century Aberdeen birth or seven years' residence was required to establish the status of an 'indweller', who could not be summarily expelled from the town and who might be entitled to poor relief (Desbrisay, 1989).

While some migrants arrived in London and other towns without any contacts to help them, it is likely that many used family, friends and business contacts to provide them with accommodation, find them a position, and ease their adaptation to urban life. Of a sample of 604 immigrant women who moved to London between the 1590s and 1619, 37 per cent had kin in city, over 20 per cent were living with relatives. Masters also commonly engaged apprentices with the same surname (Brodsky Elliot, 1981). Many female domestic servants stayed with relatives in London until they got their first place (Earle, 1989). For long-distance migrants with strong cultural identities, like the Scots and Irish, help from fellow countrymen already resident in the town must often have been available, and this also applied to migrants from particular English counties.

In-migration to larger cities sometimes produced distinctive communities within the urban area. In late-sixteenth-century London, German immigrants were concentrated in three acres in the Steelyards, French hatters in Southwark, French silk weavers in Shoreditch and Spitalfields, and Dutch printers in Clerkenwell, localities which were mainly villages outside the walls. Jewish immigrants were divided between the longer-established Sephardim (Portuguese) and more recent, poor refugees from central Europe, the Ashkenazim. The two groups became increasingly united by their religion, commercial specialization and residential concentration, especially around Petticoat Lane.

In London some aliens became denizens, which allowed them to buy land and have other privileges. Only a few became fully naturalized though; only 42 between 1509 and 1602 (Rappaport, 1989). From the 1520s, increasing restrictions were imposed upon aliens. In 1523 all strangers were banned from engaging anyone not born in England as an apprentice. In 1529 no aliens (except denizens) were to operate businesses in London. In 1572, following the St Bartholomew's Day massacre in France, thousands of Protestant refugees fled to England. Many Londoners resented them, but most sympathized with their plight, though there was concern over competition for work. In more prosperous periods aliens were seen as less of a threat. In eighteenth-century London the largest group were the Irish – over 23 000 of them by the 1780s – concentrated in the eastern, riverside parishes. London's Jewish community, located mainly in the East End, numbered 15 000–20 000 by the end of the eighteenth century, having grown from *c.*5000 in the mid-eighteenth century. These two groups had supplanted the Huguenots. The revocation of the Edict of Nantes in 1685 caused an influx of *c.*40 000–50 000 Huguenots, who settled mainly in London and other south-eastern towns. On their arrival they formed distinct communities, but their Protestant religion and skills made it easy for them to assimilate, and they rapidly integrated with the rest of the populations of the centres in which they settled (Gwynn, 1983). A large number of them had settled in the East End in the later seventeenth century; Spitalfields and Bethnal Green, with a smaller, better-off community in Soho. Over time, however, their cohesion was eroded by rapid assimilation. Recent poorer immigrants were concentrated in extramural parishes in Southwark (Landers, 1993) and the East End, which sheltered successively German, Irish and Jewish groups (Clark, 1984)

Welsh migration to English towns, including places like Chester and Shrewsbury but also London, was of long standing, but was encouraged by the Union of 1536. In seventeenth-century Shrewsbury poor Welsh immigrants were concentrated in an area near the Severn known as the Welsh Bridge (Clark, 1987). There was a large influx of Welshmen to London in Tudor times (Jones 1980–81) with a wide range of occupations and status. In a survey of London in 1638 at least 1079 Welsh surnames were identified, suggesting a total population of around 6000. The Welsh at this time were evenly spread throughout the city and its suburbs, with no sign of clustering. They were slightly poorer than average, but not markedly so. A survey of 1695 disclosed 4343 Welsh names, the holders of which, with their families, would have comprised around 7.5 per cent of London's population. Their geographical distribution was just as widespread as in 1638. They may have been more concentrated in the eighteenth century around Welsh schools in Clerkenwell. The Honourable Society of Ancient Britons was established in London in 1715; among other activities it supported the apprenticeship of poor Welsh boys in the city; the Cwmmrodorian Society, founded in 1751, also promoted Welsh cultural activities. Bristol and Birmingham had Welsh societies too.

The Scots formed another distinctive group in English towns. Kentish towns in the late sixteenth and early seventeenth centuries accommodated Scottish migrants, encouraged by the coal trade and the movement of mercenaries (Clark, 1972). Scots rarely appear as apprentices or freemen in English towns. Of 1088 London freemen admitted between 1561 and 1563, there was only one Scot (Ramsay, 1978). They were, however, more prominent among other immigrant groups. In Wareing's (1981) sample of indentured servants leaving London in the later seventeenth and eighteenth centuries, the majority of servants from outside England and Wales were Scots coming from all parts of Scotland, though a quarter came from Edinburgh and Glasgow. They made up 6 per cent of indentured servants, accounting for 4 per cent between 1683 and 1686, 10 per cent from 1748–59 and 9 per cent from 1774–81. The attraction of London for the Scots undoubtedly increased after the Union of 1707. There was a steady influx of them, especially of professional men, to London in the eighteenth century and, on a smaller scale, to the industrial towns of Lancashire (Corfield, 1982). There is evidence of a concentration of Scots in London in the early eighteenth century in the western suburbs close to the city walls, such as St Martins, the Strand and Holborn. Favoured trades were tailoring and hairdressing. Robert Kirk, writing in the 1680s, mentioned a club of Scottish Presbyterian schoolmasters in London whose members found jobs for educated newcomers from Scotland. From 1665 a charitable society, the Scottish Corporation, provided relief for poor Scots in London. Other Scots societies were established during the eighteenth century, including the Highland Society from 1778. Similar societies began to appear in English regional centres at the same period. Norwich had a Scots society by 1775 (Clark, 1987).

The Scots were never as conspicuous a group in English towns as the Irish, who appeared in increasing numbers from the late sixteenth century. In the sample of London freemen only 15 admissions out of 1088 between 1561 and 1563 were from Ireland (Ramsay, 1978). In Kentish towns the Irish also appear mainly after the last years of the sixteenth century (Clark, 1987). Some were *en route* for the Continent to fight as mercenaries, but others stayed. There was a great increase in Irish immigrants to English towns after the poor harvests of 1620s. The Irish accounted for 4 per cent of indentured servants leaving London during the later seventeenth and eighteenth centuries, a similar proportion to the Scots. However, by the 1770s they formed a far greater percentage (Wareing 1981). The Irish were more strongly clustered in London than the Scots or the Welsh. In the early nineteenth century they were concentrated in the riverside parishes of East London and in St Giles, with the emergence of Irish lodging houses, pubs, clubs, schools, chapels, masonic societies. The degree of geographical concentration may have been increased by antipathy to them. In London in 1738 there were riots over cheap Irish labour. London had its Irish societies as well as those for Scots and the Welsh, including the Irish Charitable Society (1704) and the Benevolent Society of St Patrick (1784).

Another distinctive group of urban immigrants in the eighteenth century were Gaelic-speaking Highlanders moving to Scottish towns, especially Edinburgh and Glasgow. Highlanders had started to settle in Lowland towns during the seventeenth century. In Edinburgh many of them did unskilled work as porters or sedan-chair men, or served in the town guard. They often picked up English slowly and imperfectly. Some Highlanders, though, were professional men and merchants. The first evidence of them acting as a coherent group was in Edinburgh in 1705, when they petitioned for a Gaelic-speaking minister to preach to them. Glasgow's first Gaelic chapel was opened in 1770 and others followed. They organized assistance for distressed Highlanders, while the Glasgow Highland Society (1727) and the Gaelic Society of Glasgow (1780) provided foci for Gaelic language and culture, at the same time encouraging assimilation with the rest of urban society (Withers, 1985).

Regional affinities helped the assimilation of English migrants to London (Clark, 1987). From the seventeenth century, if not earlier, inns often served as meeting places for regional groups. In the late seventeenth and eighteenth centuries these gatherings became increasingly formalized into county clubs and societies in London and other towns. While the

Scots, and more particularly the Irish, showed signs of geographical concentration within London, there is no clear evidence that people from different English regions were heavily concentrated within London to the degree that occurred in continental cities.

In the late sixteenth and early seventeenth centuries traditional mechanisms for assimilating migrants into urban communities came increasingly under stress. This emphasized the growing importance of urban alehouses as informal means of assimilation. Their numbers increased greatly as they serviced the needs of subsistence migrants, providing food, accommodation, credit, news of jobs and also some work on premises. After 1660 alehouses became larger and more comfortable, catering for more wealthy customers. Many served particular trades. The later seventeenth and eighteenth centuries also saw a great expansion of voluntary associations, including benefit and friendly societies, and county and regional societies. These also played an important role in the assimilation of newcomers, giving a more institutional focus to the local contacts and solidarity which had traditionally helped migrants in towns. They proliferated in London after 1660. There were up to 20 associations linked to particular English shires, as well as ones for the Scots, Welsh and Irish. The later eighteenth century saw a spate of new philanthropic societies concerned with the immigrant poor. A growing number of registry offices acted as employment agencies for servants and other workers. They began to appear in London from the 1680s and spread to provincial towns after the mid-eighteenth century. With mechanisms such as these, the Hanoverian era managed problems of accommodating urban migrants somewhat better that in Tudor and Stuart times, despite rapid population growth.

* * * * *

Whether it was a short journey to a local market town or a longer one to a major city, the experience of migration to a town, or a movement up the urban hierarchy, often widened the horizons of migrants and encouraged further mobility, sometimes beyond Britain. In other cases moving to a town was a planned preparatory stage on a journey to a new life in the New World. In the next chapter we will look at emigration, first within the British Isles and then abroad, at the background of emigrants and the influences which prompted them to move, and consider whether emigration was merely an extension of internal mobility within Britain or a markedly different process.

4

EMIGRATION

Introduction

Emigration, operating over long distances, sometimes under considerable difficulties and hardships, represents the exotic end of the migration spectrum, and has long attracted the attention of historians. This does not necessarily mean that the process is well understood though. There is remarkable little evidence about why people emigrated or why some moved when others did not (Baines, 1994). It is not clear how potential emigrants weighed up the social and economic benefits of emigration against the costs, to what extent emigration was seen as an alternative to movement within Britain, and whether previous experience of mobility encouraged emigration. For the nineteenth century, economists have focused on differences in income between source areas and destinations, linking emigrant flows with periods of boom and slump in the areas left and those to which the emigrants moved. For earlier periods, these variables are hard to estimate, and quantitative modelling relating rates of emigration to economic and social data for origins and destinations is much more difficult.

Historians have focused more on the information on destinations that was available to prospective travellers and the costs of passage than on emigrant origins. These often appear localized and irregular, suggesting that there was no overall national response to opportunities overseas. Only occasionally can the influences behind such patterns be understood. For example, the emigrant register of

1773–76 analysed by Bailyn (1987) shows a distinct concentration of farmers and their families emigrating from Yorkshire. It is hard to believe that agricultural conditions in Yorkshire at this time were worse than in other parts of northern England so predisposing farmers from this area to emigrate purely due to economic circumstances. Moreover, within Yorkshire, patterns of origins were concentrated among the valleys on the south side of the North York Moors. The problem is partially solved when it is appreciated that agents for land speculators in America were operating from towns in the East Riding, placing advertisements in local newspapers, using local contacts and promising land in Nova Scotia at low rents. Even this does not explain why some families left and others stayed. On the negative side, emigration is often seen as having been precipitated by specific events, like trade depressions or bad harvests, but this also fails to explain the selectivity of emigration. Irish Catholics, for instance, were poorer and more oppressed in the eighteenth century than in the nineteenth, but relatively few emigrated to America in the earlier period, when land was cheaper.

There has been a tendency to study emigration from Britain in isolation from internal population mobility. Often, this has been due to the different perspectives of historians. Many have been American, with interests focusing on the impact of the arrival of emigrants rather than on the effects of their departure on their home areas. These could be considerable; for example, emigration from the Scottish Highlands to America in the later eighteenth and early nineteenth centuries so alarmed Highland landowners, and the government, that attempts were made to promote development and create employment within the region to reduce the outflow. The construction of the Caledonian Canal was a direct outcome of the concern over emigration (Bumstead, 1982). Recent studies, searching for the social origins of emigrants and the motives which promoted them to move, have emphasized the importance of socioeconomic, political and religious conditions at home, and the links which existed between internal mobility and emigration (Bailyn, 1986; Cressey, 1986; Wareing, 1981). Although rates of net emigration from England were never very high, their impact on England's population over 300 years was considerable. For a good deal of the period, net emigration reduced the rates of population growth in England. Between the mid-seventeenth and mid-eighteenth centuries, when natural increase was either very low or at times negative, net emigration was especially important. Between

1656 and 1696, when England's population, on Wrigley and Schofield's (1989) calculations, fell by about 416 000, around 58 per cent of this was due to net emigration (as defined in their back-projection technique), the rest to an excess of deaths over births.

It is generally agreed that emigration was an extension of internal mobility, though the linkages between local mobility, longer-distance migration and emigration are hard to identify. People who migrated once were more likely to move again, and to consider emigration as an option, than first-time movers. It has sometimes been assumed that emigration was more difficult than internal migration, assimilation harder in a distant land than in a nearby locality, but this was not necessarily true. A Gaelic-speaking Highlander would have experienced a greater culture shock in moving to the slums of Glasgow than to a frontier area in North America peopled by settlers from his home district. The motives which encouraged emigration were often complex, the paths which led to the quayside tortuous. Bailyn (1986) cites the example of John Harrower, who was unusual only in that he kept a diary which has survived. A shopkeeper and petty tradesmen from Lerwick, he was literate and ambitious, but poor. He left Shetland in December 1773 with a desire to better himself, but with almost no money and only £3-worth of trading goods on his back. Initially, he had no intention of emigrating to America, considering the Netherlands the most promising destination. He travelled down the east coast of Scotland to Dundee, where he failed to find a ship bound for the Netherlands. He embarked for Newcastle, where he was equally unsuccessful in obtaining a passage to the Low Countries. He walked to Sunderland and got a free berth on a ship supposedly bound for London or the Netherlands. In fact, it ended up in Portsmouth, from where he walked the 130km to London. After some weeks there, trying desperately to gain employment but with no local contacts, he signed up as an indentured servant for four years to work as a schoolmaster in America.

Sources

The migration of people between the nations comprising the British Isles is often poorly recorded before the mid-nineteenth century censuses. There are also problems regarding the documentation of emigration. At no time within our period were full records kept of numbers of people embarking, or arriving in other countries. Even the detailed register of emigrants from England and Scotland to North America which was kept between 1773 and 1776 is incomplete (Bailyn, 1987). Passenger lists survive for some emigrant ships. Groups like transported convicts or indentured servants were better recorded because they generated official documentation. Information on motives for emigration, the importance of family links in encouraging chain migration, and the nature of information flows can be obtained from correspondence between emigrants and their friends and relations back home. More generally, motives for emigration have been inferred from indirect evidence such as age, occupation, marital status, and the social and economic characteristics of areas of origin (Baines, 1994)

Other approaches can be used to estimate emigration. Wrigley and Schofield (1989) have employed back projection to calculate English net migration totals for each quinquennium between 1541 and 1871. Total numbers of net emigrants were around 20 000 per quinquennium in the later sixteenth century, rising to over 60 000 in the mid-seventeenth century. In the late seventeenth and much of the eighteenth centuries the figures fluctuated at *c.*20 000–25 000, rising to over 90 000 in the quinquennium beginning in 1831. The rate of migration, as a proportion of the population, peaked in the 1650s and was higher in the early seventeenth century than the early nineteenth. Annual net emigration from England was only 1.0–1.8 per 1000 people for most of the period. This technique, however, treats deaths in battle abroad and losses of life at sea as 'emigration'. These elements were particularly significant during periods such as the Napoleonic Wars, artificially increasing the numbers of 'emigrants'. On the other hand, for much of the Early-Modern period it is likely that more Welsh, Scots and Irish migrated to England than English did to other parts of the British Isles. So substantial emigration from England to North America could have occurred in years when net migration was modest. Nevertheless, the calculated balance of migration for England was always outwards.

Migration Within the British Isles

Migration flows within the British Isles are often difficult to identify. There were probably net movements from poorer peripheral regions towards cores centred on Edinburgh, Dublin and, especially, London. However, counter-currents from core to periphery also existed, as from east-central Scotland to the Northern Isles following their pledging to Scotland by Denmark in the fifteenth century (Donaldson, 1966). The English plantations in Ireland in the late sixteenth and early seventeenth centuries were another example of movement from centre to periphery. There were also flows between peripheral areas, such as the colonization of Ulster from south-western Scotland in the early seventeenth century. At most periods movement was probably in both directions; while English and Scots settlers were colonizing Ireland in the early seventeenth century, Irish vagrants were travelling in the opposite direction in search of opportunities in England.

The Welsh had been migrating to England long before the Battle of Bosworth brought the Tudors to power. The flow increased with the accession of Henry VII and as a result of the union with England under Henry VIII, which gave the Welsh equality of status with the English. The Welsh had an impact on Tudor and Stuart England out of all proportion to their numbers. Girls from the Border areas moved to towns like Bristol, Chester and Shrewsbury as domestic servants, men as apprentices and craftsmen. Over 12 per cent of Bristol apprentices between 1532 and 1542 came from Wales. Many moved as students, especially to Oxford and the Inns of Court. Welsh immigrants in England were readily identified by their accents and problems with English pronunciation. Taffy was a well-known stage and literary stereotype; impulsive, eloquent, warmhearted and quick-tempered, but the caricature Welshman was a more sympathetic figure than Sawney or Teague, the comic Scotsman and Irishman, suggesting that Welsh migrants were assimilated more readily into the English population (Williams, 1987).

Numbers of Scottish migrants to England are difficult to estimate, but are likely to have been small before the seventeenth century. In 1571 there were only 33 Scots in London out of 4287 aliens. The southward move of James VI in 1603 to take the throne of England encouraged some Scottish nobles and gentry to follow, and perhaps people of lower status too. By the late seventeenth century there was a distinctive Scottish trading and business community in London. Elsewhere, Scots were probably few in number, except on Tyneside where a high proportion of keelmen were Scots-born. After the Union of 1707, the Scots moved south in greater numbers (Whyte and Whyte, 1988). Although Irish vagrants are recorded in England during the late sixteenth century, their numbers increased dramatically in the early seventeenth century, following harvest failures at home (Chapter 2). Seasonal migration from Ireland to Britain was established by the 1720s and, by the 1780s, was increasingly leading to permanent migration. From the mid-eighteenth century, Irish communities were developing not only in London, but in towns like Bristol and Liverpool.

English migration to Wales, and Scotland undoubtedly occurred, but it was probably a trickle compared with the flow in the reverse direction. Even so, at a local scale it could be significant. Between the mid-sixteenth and late seventeenth centuries over 2000 English families are estimated to have migrated into Denbigh, Flint and Montgomeryshire, affecting the linguistic boundaries between Welsh and English (Williams, 1987). Movement of people from England to Scotland was probably more limited. In the later seventeenth century there was a fashion among the Scottish nobility and wealthier gentry for having English servants, but the numbers involved must have been small (Marshall, 1973). After the Union of 1707, some Englishmen moved to Scotland as skilled workers, especially in association with new industrial ventures such as the Strontian lead mines and the ironworks at Bonawe. The mines at Leadhills, in upper Clydesdale, attracted English miners from Alston Moor and the Lake District (Smout, 1967).

The Irish Plantations

Far more significant in scale and impact was English migration to Ireland, a movement which, during the seventeenth century, was comparable with emigration to America and which had no parallel in Europe. Sixteenth-century Ireland, especially after the devastation of the Tudor campaigns, was thinly populated with perhaps 0.75 million inhabitants in 1600. From the viewpoint of the English government, colonization was undertaken primarily to provide a buffer against Gaelic society, the Catholic religion, and potential invasion from France or Spain. This contrasted with America, where economic motives were paramount in colonization. However, for the actual migrants, the attractions were primarily economic, in the form of cheap land and the possibility of greater social mobility than at home (Robinson, 1984).

Canny (1985) estimates that *c*.70 000 English and Welsh had moved to Ireland by 1641, the majority during the 1610s and 1620s. Sir William Petty reckoned in 1672 that *c*.100 000 English and Welsh settled in Ireland during the Cromwellian period, giving a total of *c*.170 000 immigrants overall, though some returned to England following the rising of 1641. Numbers of immigrants from Scotland were also substantial. After 1641 the role of landlords in sponsoring immigration was reduced; much of the settlement in the later seventeenth century was done on an individual basis, with the main migration flow being from Scotland to Ulster, especially in the 1650s, late 1670s and in the 1690s. By 1672 there were *c*.100 000 Scots in Ulster. Another *c*.50 000 arrived in the 15 years after 1690, causing a dramatic social change, turning the immigrant population from a minority into a large majority in many areas. Government-sponsored surveys probably overestimate population on the official plantations (Canny, 1985), but historians have tended to ignore the extensive penetration of individual English and Scottish settlers to other parts of Ireland. Overall, the scale of British migration to Ireland in the early seventeenth century has probably been underestimated rather than exaggerated.

In the first 40 years of the seventeenth century migration from Britain to Ireland probably averaged *c*.1000 a year, but at its peaks in the 1650s and 1690s the annual rate may have been over 8000. Pre-1641 migration, though smaller in scale than in the later seventeenth century, determined later patterns of British settlement in Ireland. In 1600 the proportion of Ireland's population with English or Scottish blood was only around 2 per cent. By 1660 it had risen to 18 per cent, and by 1733 it was about 27 per cent. Immigration on this scale had profound effects on Ireland's society and economy, altering the landscape, increasing the pace of commercialization, causing growing social stratification, changing Irish culture, and causing the Irish language to fade more rapidly than any other Celtic language in modern times. The establishment of Protestant English and Presbyterian Scottish settlers, often on land from which the native occupants had been dispossessed, inevitably led to unrest, with sensitive frontier zones creating a legacy of social tensions and political problems which survives to the present. Having uprooted themselves once in moving to Ulster, many Scots, in particular, remained mobile within Ireland, while their descendants were especially prone to emigrate to America during the eighteenth century.

Migration from England and Scotland to Ireland in the first half of the seventeenth century has often been considered narrowly, without an appreciation of its wider context, including its relationship to transatlantic emigration. The close links between south-west England and the Munster plantations may help explain why this region did not figure prominently in the early settlement of North America. Migration to Ulster occurred from areas which were relatively remote from London and Bristol, whose hinterlands furnished so many of the early emigrants to America; the two migration streams may thus have been complementary. Prosperity among settlers in Ireland, despite the setback of the 1641 Catholic uprising, probably outstripped that of most migrants to North America and the West Indies.

The different streams of migrants to Ireland created markedly contrasting societies. Munster was settled principally from south-west England, while east Ulster was an extension of south-west Scotland. The plantations involved a merging of social and economic traits between natives and immigrants. The incomers promoted the English language, but some also learned Gaelic. They brought with them new crops and cultivation techniques, but integrated them into the traditional Irish pastoral economy. There was hostility between native and immigrant, which erupted particularly in 1641, but the degree of tension may have been exaggerated (Bailyn and Morgan, 1991)

Sixteenth-century English plantations in Ireland had the character of garrisons more than open agricultural communities. Tudor plantations affected only limited areas of south-western, eastern and northern Ireland. An attempt was made by the government under Mary Tudor to plant the counties of Leix and Offaly in order to extend the Pale. Two forts, established in the 1540s, were designed to form the nuclei of towns. Success was limited and costs to the government high. The plantation in Munster between 1586 and 1598 was more carefully planned and involved a major migration. It was initiated by the forfeiture in 1583 of *c.*300 000 acres belonging to the Earl of Desmond. In 1586 the lands were divided into 12 000-acre seignories, with subdivisions on which fixed numbers of families at social levels ranging from freeholders to cottagers were to be settled. The plantation was controlled and organized by the government. Recruitment was carried out mainly in western England, as well as in Lancashire and Cheshire, but interest came mainly from Devon and Somerset, areas with established trading contacts with southern Ireland. Migration to Ireland from this region would have involved less change than a move to the north of England (McCarthy-Morrogh,

1986). The undertakers who received patents in 1587 included gentlemen, merchants, royal officials and soldiers. By 1598 a settler population of *c*.4000 was established in Munster, substantially altering society in the areas affected. In that year rebellion broke out; the settlers were driven off and some were killed. By 1611 the English population may have been restored to around 5000, while a survey of 1627 suggests *c*.14 000 colonists, *c*.15 000–22 000 by 1641. Some may have emigrated in the hope of finding Irish society more tolerant of Catholics and Puritans alike, but betterment was probably a more significant factor, with good-quality land available at low rents. As well as farmers, the Munster plantations attracted artisans and skilled industrial workers. Most migrants were deliberately recruited by landowners. They included farmers and craftsmen, who settled in nucleated villages and planned towns, as well as more isolated settlements.

The largest of the Irish plantations, and in many ways the most successful, was in Ulster. Efforts to colonize Ulster began in the late sixteenth century, but achievements were limited. The position changed with the accession of James I. James had developed a hatred of Gaelic society in dealing with the Scottish Highlands. He had encouraged colonizing ventures by Lowland Scots in Kintyre and Lewis in an attempt to civilize the inhabitants of the western Highlands and Islands, but the first of these ventures had limited success, even with the support of the local magnate, the Earl of Argyll, while the latter was a complete failure (Donaldson, 1966). Close links between the West Highlands and Ulster, where Scottish MacDonalds had settled among the Antrim glens from the late fifteenth century, were a problem for both Scotland and England in the sixteenth century (Robinson, 1984). The Union of the Crowns in 1603 allowed co-ordinated action to be taken against pan-Gaelic links on both sides of the Irish Sea.

The earliest seventeenth-century plantation in Ulster was a private venture organized by two Scots, Hugh Montgomery and James Hamilton. They received grants of land in 1605 and began to bring in Scottish settlers. By 1609 there was a steady flow of Scots to these areas. The flight and forfeiture of the Earls of Tyrconnel and Tyrone in 1607 provided an opportunity for a larger settlement scheme, financed not by the crown as in Munster, but by private undertakers from England and Scotland. The areas involved included lands in Armagh, Cavan, Donegal, Fermanagh Londonderry and Tyrone. The English undertakers, drawn from a wide area of the Midlands, East

Anglia and the south-east, but not from the south-west, acquired nearly half a million acres. Most of the Scottish undertakers, principally lairds with one or two nobles, came from the west-central Lowlands, Galloway and the Edinburgh area. In 1610 the city of London was persuaded to begin the corporate plantation of the county of Derry. English and Scots undertakers each received about 18 per cent of the land, the London Companies about 8 per cent. The church and state officials acquired about 28 per cent with the remainder, about a fifth, being granted to native Irish. The conditions of grant required 24 adult males – English or Lowland Scots – to be settled for every 1000 acres.

Various surveys allow reasonable estimates of the growth of the new colony to be made. Expansion was slow in the early years with around 1000 adult males by 1611. Faster growth followed with *c*.6000 by 1619, but with little further increase in the 1620s. The pattern of settlement, and the success of the venture, was patchy. Areas on the best soils, with ready access to markets, were quickly settled, but on more remote estates, the undertakers found it hard to recruit or retain tenants. Some colonists were selected by the undertakers; others arrived independently looking for opportunities. The economy of the new plantations was an agricultural one, with a pastoral emphasis, though there was also a substantial export of grain to Scotland in some years. There were relatively few craftsmen and industrial workers among the settlers. While the origins of the undertakers are known, less detail is available regarding the social origins of the ordinary settlers. Many Scots probably came from the western Lowlands, an area which, before the famine of 1623, was experiencing substantial population growth. Those who migrated were not poor; they needed capital to transport themselves and their livestock to Ulster and to establish new farms there. The availability of cheaper lands on secure leases may have attracted many tenants threatened with rent rises at home. In Ulster they replicated the settlement patterns and farming systems which were familiar to them. Sponsored settlement also involved the creation of villages and towns. Eight towns were established in Munster during James I's reign, six in Leitrim and Longford, and 17 in Ulster under James I and Charles I.

The number of English and Scottish male settlers between 16 and 60 in Ulster in the 1630s was estimated at over 13 000. English immigrants to Ireland tended to come from relatively well-developed regions such as western and southern England, where the younger sons of the lesser gentry and richer yeomen were finding it difficult to maintain their social position, but had sufficient capital to set themselves up in Ireland. They often moved with substantial numbers of dependants and followers. In Munster they introduced arable oriented farming and a partiality for orchards derived from south-western England. As the economic development of northern England caught up later in the seventeenth century, and social pressures began to increase, this region became a major source area for Irish immigrants, a flow characterized by artisans and small farmers rather than yeomen and lesser gentry. They tended, like the Scots, to favour pastoral farming and to move individually rather than under the aegis of a sponsor. About half the inflow between 1652 and 1672 came from Scotland, especially tenant farmers from the south-western Lowlands. Scottish tenants who emigrated to Ulster enjoyed better tenurial conditions than they had at home.

The impact of Protestant settlement on society in Ulster was significant, but not, at first, profound. There was no wholesale expulsion of native Irish. Although they were displaced from the best lands and pushed to the margins of settlement, they were still taken on as tenants. Tensions between settlers and natives must have existed at both local and regional levels and, in the early years especially, English and Scottish colonists were living on a frontier as potentially violent as in North America. In 1641 a revolt by Ulster Catholics led to the massacre of British colonists, with many more being forced to seek refuge across the Irish Sea. The disruption proved to be only temporary, and further waves of colonists in the 1650s re-established the British communities (Miller, 1985).

Emigration to Europe

Emigration from England and Wales to Europe in the sixteenth and seventeenth centuries was modest compared with the flows from Scotland and Ireland. High rates of emigration from Scotland at this time may have acted as a demographic safety valve comparable to rural–urban migration south of the Border. The Scots had widespread contacts with Europe through trade, scholarship and military service. In the fifteenth century *c.*10 000 Scots had fought in France. In the sixteenth century Scottish mercenaries were also found in Scandinavia and Eastern Europe. There were Scottish merchant communities in many European ports, including Copenhagen, Danzig, Bruges,

Campveere, Middelburg, Bordeaux, Dieppe, La Rochelle and Rouen. At a less-prosperous level, many Scots travelled through countries like Poland as itinerant packmen. A seventeenth-century estimate suggests that there may have been *c.*30 000 Scottish chapmen in Poland alone (Smout, Landsman and Devine, 1991) .

Emigration from Scotland increased in the early seventeenth century as population peaked, including, as we have seen, the colonization of Ulster. In addition, there was accelerated recruitment of soldiers for service in Europe, especially during the Thirty Years' War. Between 1626 and 1632 warrants were issued for an estimated 58 880 mercenaries to leave Scotland. While some places may not have been filled, this outflow was probably equal to 5 per cent of the adult male population of Scotland. At the peak of the conflict, there may have been as many as 25 000 Scottish soldiers in Scandinavian service alone. Some returned home, but, as disease probably killed off far more than enemy action, military service in Europe was a one-way ticket for many. Between 1600 and 1650 it has been estimated that from 85 000–115 000 people emigrated from Scotland – or around 2000 a year from a population of no more than 1.2 million. About 20 per cent of Scotland's young men may have left the country during this period, a substantial proportion of them permanently. In the second half of the seventeenth century military service in Scandinavia fell off, though Scots were still recruited for war in Holland and France. England is likely to have become a more popular destination, but numbers of Scots crossing the Border are impossible to estimate (Table 4.1). Ulster continued to attract settlers and this period also witnessed the start of Scottish emigration to the New World, however, numbers were small compared with movement to Ireland. Between 1660 and 1707 perhaps 5000 Scots moved to America, especially to the West Indies, but also to New Jersey. Between 1650 and 1700 a total of between 78 000 and 127 000 Scots emigrated, again an average of about 2000 per year from a population of a little over a million (Table 4.1). These rates are substantially in excess of those calculated by Wrigley and Schofield (1989) for England, excepting for a limited period in the mid-seventeenth century.

Irish society in the seventeenth century was unusual in that large-scale emigration as well as immigration occurred. Within Europe only the Netherlands was comparable (Cullen, 1981). Apart from the 1690s, however, when there was a massive influx of Scots, it is likely that the net flow from Ireland was usually outwards. Ireland was an important source of mercenaries for European armies. After Cromwell crushed Catholic resistance, thousands of soldiers and clergymen fled to the continent. There was a further exodus following the failure of the Jacobite campaign in 1691. The outflow of fighting men was perhaps not quite so great as from Scotland, but the Irish provided the officers and most of the men for a number of French regiments. The outflow to the French army alone may have been as high as 1000 a year in the 1720s and 1730s. Soldiering in foreign armies was replaced in the later eighteenth century by recruitment into the British army (Table 4.1).

Table 4.1 Scottish and Irish Annual Emigration, *c*.1650–*c*.1700 (After Canny, 1994)

Destination	Scotland	Ireland
America	*c*.140	*c*.400
Ireland	*c*.2000	–
England	?	*c*.150
Europe	–	*c*.200
Elsewhere	*c*.400	–
Army	–	*c*.700
Total	***c*.2540**	***c*.1450**

Emigration to America

From the early seventeenth century, America began to provide an alternative destination for migrants, at first from England, later from Scotland and Ireland. The socioeconomic character of transatlantic migrants varied with their geographical origins and destinations, as well as over time. Settlers in the first half of the seventeenth century were moving to a hostile frontier and garrison conditions. The people involved in the earliest ventures were often not well suited to the work of colonization. The shipload of 105 settlers who founded Jamestown in 1607 included 35 gentlemen and 40 soldiers, whose lack of practical skills and reluctance to do manual work nearly resulted in the embryo colony dying of starvation during its first winter (Middleton, 1996). Barely a quarter of the 4000 settlers who arrived in Virginia between

1618 and 1622 survived. By the end of our period migrants were moving to a country where there was still an expanding frontier, but also a wider range of opportunities in long-settled agricultural areas and growing towns.

Changing economic conditions at home influenced the size and composition of the migration stream and the social mix of the population in the American colonies. For example, a fall in the numbers of indentured servants emigrating in the later 1660s may have been related to the slackening of demographic growth within England, and the increased demand for labour in London after the Great Plague and Great Fire. The drop in manpower for the Chesapeake tobacco plantations led directly to the large-scale import of Negro slaves (Bailyn, 1986). In the 1680s less than 8 per cent of the population of the Chesapeake colonies were black. By 1710 the figure had reached 25 per cent (Bailyn, 1986).

Emigration to North America has attracted a considerable literature, much of it generated from America rather than Britain. American scholars have appreciated that the character of emigration to the New World was influenced by social, economic, political and religious trends within Britain. English historians have often failed to consider that emigration was a process which affected, as well as reflected, British society (Erickson, 1994), though this is less true for research on Scotland or Ireland. Between 1640 and 1699 it has been estimated that 69 per cent of England's natural increase of population was drawn off by emigration to North America. Between 1695 and 1801 emigration accounted for 20 per cent of England's natural increase (Bailyn, 1986). In many respects transatlantic emigration was an extension of migration within Britain, an additional choice which was available for migrants once they had taken the decision to move outside their own local area.

Total numbers of emigrants from Britain to America in the seventeenth century have been estimated by Gemery (1984) as being within the range of 250 000–500,000 – perhaps around 400 000. Most came from England, with *c.*116 000 moving to the Chesapeake, *c.*39 000 to the northern and mid-Atlantic colonies, *c.*15 500 to New England and *c.*210 000 to the West Indies. Over half emigrated between 1630 and 1660. Migration to North America fell in the later seventeenth century. The total British American population in 1700 was *c.*257 000. Of these, some 91 000 were in New England, *c.*130 000 in mainland colonies further south, just over 3000 in Newfoundland and *c.*35 500 in the Caribbean. Fogelman (1992) suggests that between 1700 and 1775 at least 44 000 emigrants came from England, 29 000 from Wales and 35 000 from Scotland, plus 66 000 from northern Ireland and 42 500 from the south of Ireland.

The 1760s and 1770s saw a surge in emigration to North America, matched with a rapid expansion of the frontiers of settlement. Many of the migrants, especially the Irish and Scots, went direct to frontier areas. Between 1760 and 1775 over 125 000 emigrants left Britain. Around 30 000 were from England, *c.*40 000 from Scotland and *c.*55 000 were Protestant Irish. In the seventeenth century the American colonies were seen as a convenient dumping ground for surplus population. By the later eighteenth century it was considered that, by increasing labour supply and widening the market, population growth actually benefited Britain. The scale of emigration in these years caused fears that some regions, such as the West Highlands, would become depopulated, leading to the widespread expectation that Parliament would impose a ban on emigration to North America. The result of official concern over emigration was the compilation of the most detailed set of data about any large group of emigrants, in the form of a register collated from records submitted by customs officers in England and Scotland between December 1773 and March 1776. It illuminates, as no other source does, the occupational and social characteristics of the most mobile sectors of British society and their motives for emigrating. During the wars with France from 1793, the British government became increasingly opposed to emigration, especially from the Scottish Highlands, due to the threat to military recruitment. While stopping short of a complete ban, in 1803 they introduced controls on the transportation of emigrants, including the amount of space per person, and the provision of medical facilities. This was done supposedly on humanitarian grounds, but, as was intended, it caused a substantial increase in the cost of a transatlantic passage and slowed, though did not stop, emigration. With continuing population growth in the early nineteenth century, the official attitude to emigration became more favourable until, by the end of our period, emigration was actively promoted by the state.

What influenced people to consider emigrating to America? Cressey (1986, 1987) has shown that in the early seventeenth century, especially, information about the New World available to potential emigrants was incomplete, conflicting and often wholly inaccurate. Details about New England, for example, were often produced in pamphlets whose prime function was to help raise money for future colonial ventures. Inevitably, they painted an optimistic picture of a garden rather than a wilderness. In the later seventeenth and eighteenth centuries the information flow improved, with more return migrants providing first-hand accounts and more letters from those who had remained in America. Economic motives have been seen as paramount in encouraging emigration, but social and cultural influences, and individual 'last straw' factors, were also important in explaining variations in emigration between different areas and social groups (Erickson, 1994).

During the seventeenth century, the passage across the Atlantic often took eight to 12 weeks, sometimes more. Most emigrant vessels were converted merchant ships, not designed specifically for carrying passengers. Surprisingly few ships were lost, or passengers drowned, on transatlantic passenger voyages. Far more died from disease. The fact that, at this time, emigrants were mainly drawn from the middling groups of society reduced social distinctions within emigrant parties, while the conditions of the voyage often drew them together into cohesive groups and encouraged the development of friendships and contacts which could prove useful once they arrived in America.

Although the passage was generally only six to eight weeks by the later eighteenth century, problems sometimes still occurred, as with the ill-fated voyage of the *Bachelor*, chartered to transport a party of emigrants from Caithness in 1773. The vessel sailed late in the season due to various delays. Storms forced the ship to take temporary refuge at Stromness in Orkney. A second storm off Lewis drove the ship to Shetland, by which time 11 of the passengers had died. Severely damaged at anchor, the vessel was forced to spend the winter at Lerwick. In April the following year it limped into Leith, where most of the passengers scattered in search of work though some finally made it to America, sailing from Greenock on another vessel (Bailyn, 1987). In other cases, when ships were inadequately provisioned or supplied with bad water, mortality during the crossing could be high.

During the eighteenth century emigration by relatively limited numbers of people changed into a mass movement. The range of options available in America widened as the colonies grew, their economies developed and the frontier expanded. Equally, the influences which encouraged emigration changed as industrialization and urbanization increased in Britain. In most European countries large-scale emigration began before major urban and industrial growth occurred. In Britain, however, it increased rapidly in the early nineteenth century at a time of major industrial expansion and urban growth, provoking questions regarding the relationship between emigration and industrialization. Were emigrants people who were being pressurized by socioeconomic change, who feared industrialization, or were they looking more positively at a range of options which was open to them? It might be considered that urban growth and industrial expansion in Britain should have provided sufficient opportunities at home to discourage emigration. However, the scale of population increase throughout the British Isles must be remembered. Also, industrialization produced casualties, as well as success stories, including hand-loom weavers who were gradually marginalized within the industrial labour force as power-loom weaving expanded, or agricultural labourers in southern England whose wages were being driven downwards. The experience of changing residence, jobs and lifestyle, often from a rural to an urban environment, is also likely to have made people more aware of distant opportunities across the Atlantic and more able to evaluate them effectively. By the 1770s the structure of the emigrant flow suggests that moves across the Atlantic were often carefully calculated to fit into the most suitable part of people's life cycles.

Emigration from England

Until recently, emigration from England has been given less attention than movement from Ireland or Scotland. Research on English emigration to the New World has focused on the early colonial period rather than the later era of mass migration (Erickson, 1994). This reflects the fact that the seventeenth rather than the eighteenth century was the most significant period of English emigration to America. At the opening of the eighteenth century the inhabitants of the mainland colonies of North America were overwhelmingly English in origin. Seventeenth-century English emigration to New England has traditionally been seen as a movement of Puritans impelled by religious reasons rather than social and economic influences. More recently, Cressey (1987) has disputed the importance of religious motives, stressing the significance of economic reasons behind the emigration of *c.*21 000 people in the 1630s and early 1640s, a period in which English population growth neared its seventeenth-century peak. Nevertheless, the 'great migration' to New England in the 1630s involved fewer than 0.5 per cent of the population of England. Far more migrants went to the Chesapeake and the West Indies at this period. Cressey suggests that the forces encouraging emigration were often social and economic rather than religious. The prime significance of religious motives as a spur to migration may have been partly back-fitted by American Puritan historians. Its existence as an influence cannot be seriously doubted, but, as only a handful of the emigrants in the 1630s had actually experienced religious persecution, its importance may have been overemphasized.

Migrants to New England in the 1630s were not poor – considerable resources were needed to afford a passage and set up as a farmer or tradesman in New England – but this does not mean that such people were not concerned about downward socioeconomic mobility in England. Depression in the English textile industry, rising poor rates, plague outbreaks and bad harvests may all have helped to create a mood at home that exacerbated the political and religious stresses which were propelling society towards civil war. The social structure of people moving to New England has been shown by Cressey to have been more varied, their motivations for moving more complex than the 'Puritan fathers' image. Although New England society remained ethnically homogeneous, the product of a single period of emigration from one country, the Puritan character of New England society gradually faded as second- and third-generation colonists looked less towards England as a cultural and social model, and became more American in their concerns (Bailyn, 1986).

Emigration from Scotland

During the later 1690s an ill-conceived and disastrous attempt to establish a Scottish colony on the isthmus of Darien led to the deaths of several hundred Scots, and demonstrated clearly the impracticality of an independent Scotland undertaking large-scale colonial ventures. One effect of the Union of Scotland and England in 1707 was to open England's American colonies up to Scottish settlers. Before 1707 Scots had been barred from them, except as transported prisoners or unauthorized migrants. After the 1715 rising, *c.*600 Jacobites were transported to North America and the Caribbean, *c.*800 after the

1745 rebellion. Scottish involvement with the Caribbean seems to have started after 1713 and by the mid-eighteenth century Scots were numerous in Jamaica. They displayed an ability to adapt, improvise and improve. This was demonstrated in the tobacco trade, where they developed a more effective organization for buying and shipping tobacco than their English rivals. On the eve of the Revolution most of the factors who controlled the Virginia tobacco trade were Scots (Devine, 1975)

During the early eighteenth century emigration from Scotland to the New World was on a relatively small scale. Following the famines of the later 1690s, there was less population pressure at home. Nevertheless, Scottish contact with America increased as the tobacco trade, centred on Glasgow, expanded. The end of the Seven Years' War saw an influx of Scots to America. Between 1700 and 1760 only *c*.30 000 Scots are estimated to have migrated to America, 90 per cent of them Lowlanders. Between 1763 and 1775 over 40 000 flocked to Georgia, the Carolinas, New England and Canada (Bailyn, 1987). Emigration from Scotland in the later eighteenth and early nineteenth centuries was increasingly a by-product of economic modernization and the social changes that accompanied it. In 1771–72 a group of 138 farmers and craftsmen from an area centred on Inchinnan, west of Glasgow, formed the Scots American Company of farmers, an association for buying land in America (Adams and Somerville, 1993). At a time when agricultural improvement was gathering momentum with the rapid growth of the Glasgow market, farms in this area were being amalgamated and small tenants and cottars displaced. Emigration offered an alternative to the expanding textile industries of Paisley and Glasgow. In the early nineteenth century many hand-loom weavers from the western Lowlands emigrated, some with government aid.

A feature of the later eighteenth century was the rise of emigration from the Scottish Highlands. The region had some contact with North America earlier in the century, but emigration from the Highlands amounted to under 3000 between 1700 and 1760, including transported Jacobite prisoners. Nevertheless, these early migrants established the basis for later chain migration. Contact with America was increased by Highlanders, who served in the army there during the Seven Years' War. Between 1760 and 1775 at least 15 000 Highlanders are thought to have emigrated. Numbers fell thereafter and only 2000–3000 are thought to have moved between 1775 and 1801. The American War interrupted links with established emigrant destinations like New York and the Carolinas, and it took time for links with other areas such as Upper Canada, Prince Edward Island and Nova Scotia to be established. Emigration picked up again with *c.*8000 leaving between 1801 and 1815.

Emigration from the Highlands caused concern to local landowners from the 1730s. From the 1760s, it gained a new momentum, involving substantial groups of emigrants who banded together and chartered their own ships. Those who left were seen as the thin end of a wedge by landowners and government officials. There was concern that if emigration increased, it would depopulate large areas, drain the Highlands of capital and threaten military recruitment. The impetus to emigrate, and the leadership of emigrant parties, was often provided by members of the clan gentry or 'tacksmen', whose middlemen role in traditional Highland society was being undermined as the clan system disintegrated under the impact of economic and social changes. Emigrant Highlanders arriving in America tended to move to the frontier and settle in cohesive groups. Unlike contemporary migrants from England or Lowland Scotland, Highland emigrants often travelled in large parties of closely inter-related people from particular districts. They tried to replicate their traditional society and culture, complete with Highland dress and the Gaelic language, in areas like North Carolina, the upper Hudson valley and, later in the century, Nova Scotia and Prince Edward Island. They retained the joint working of the land and settlement patterns which replicated Highland clachans (Ommer, 1986). As Samuel Johnson commented, the Highland emigrant's departure was: 'no longer exile ... He sits down in a better climate surrounded by his kindred and friends ... they change nothing but the place of their abode ... this is the real effect of emigration, if those that go away together settle on the same spot and preserve their ancient union.' As these colonies developed, correspondence with family and friends in Scotland encouraged others to follow.

Highland emigration has been viewed largely as a consequence of the clearance of the inhabitants to make way for commercial sheep farming, as a movement of desperate and impoverished peasants. However, this kind of migration was essentially a feature of the early nineteenth century. In the eighteenth century Highland landlords generally opposed emigration. It was in their interest to keep tenants on their estates when labour-intensive activities like kelp burning were generating a substantial income. Bumstead (1982) has claimed that emigration in the later eighteenth century was undertaken for positive reasons by farmers who could afford the cost of their passage without assistance and, indeed, often in the face of government opposition. On the other hand, Ommer (1986) has pointed out that while these emigrants were able to afford to migrate, this does not necessarily mean that they went voluntarily. Population pressure, land hunger, rising rents, and the threat of poverty and famine were undoubtedly important background influences encouraging emigration. They were not being forced out. Particularly bad years, like 1782 and 1783, tended to check emigration because of the build up of rent arrears. Emigration involved a careful calculation of the relative advantages of staying or going rather than being the result of desperation. Highlanders moved in the hope of acquiring cheap land and bettering their circumstances. Letters from previous emigrants and information from soldiers who had returned from America created a positive image of a land of opportunity.

The American Revolution altered patterns of emigration from the Highlands. Numbers crossing the Atlantic dropped markedly. The emigration that still occurred was directed towards British North America. Before the Revolution they had moved mainly to North Carolina and New York state. Afterwards, they began to settle areas like Prince Edward Island, Nova Scotia. Highlanders who fought in the British army during the War of Independence and who chose to stay in America were given land along the St Lawrence or in Nova Scotia. Not all colonies were successful: Lord Selkirk's efforts to establish Highlanders at a site near modern Detroit failed because of high mortality from malaria. Such environments might be considered well suited to immigrants who were accustomed to the rigours of the Scottish Highlands, but the incomers were not used to clearing virgin forest. In addition, the shift from a partly commercialized economy back to pure subsistence production was seen by many as a step backwards.

Emigration from Ireland

Irish emigration to America began later, but on a more substantial scale than emigration from Scotland. There was an Irish presence in the West Indies as early as the 1630s. By 1666 the Irish formed 20 per cent of the population of Barbados, and in 1678 a third of the free inhabitants of the Leeward Islands. They emigrated to become planters, merchants and indentured servants at a rate of several hundred a year during the later seventeenth century. Ulster Protestants accounted for a third to a quarter of Ireland's population in the eighteenth century, but accounted for three-quarters of emigrants to America between 1700 and 1776. The first great wave of emigration from Ulster to New England in 1717–18 was organized by Presbyterian ministers. Hostility from the local population led emigrants from 1725 to go to Pennsylvania, penetrating up the Delaware and Cumberland valleys and across the Alleghenies. They were seen as ideal frontier colonists, a suitable shield against Indian attack.

Emigration from Ireland in the eighteenth and early nineteenth centuries has been overshadowed by the diaspora of the 1840s, but was nevertheless considerable, and drawn from a smaller population; the outflow in the eighteenth century was probably greater than in the seventeenth in terms of numbers, though not necessarily as a proportion of the population. It was, however, increasingly drawn from particular areas and social groups. The movement of Ulster Protestants of Scots descent formed a distinctive element in transatlantic migration. Having moved from Scotland in the previous century, they were already a mobile group and, when opportunities in Ulster began to dry up in the early eighteenth century, they started to emigrate to America. Protestant emigration from Ulster to the Delaware between 1729 and 1774 may have numbered 52 000, peak outflows being related to slumps in the linen industry. The 1760s marked an important watershed as emigration spread to new areas of southern and western Ireland. Emigration from Ireland, at this time, occurred against a background of economic expansion and relative prosperity. There was a rise in emigration in the early nineteenth century, much of it still from the north and south-east, from the better off rather than the poor, by individuals rather than families.

Large-scale emigration from Ulster to America began in 1717, when long leases granted in the 1690s began to run out and higher rents were charged (Dickson, 1966). Over 2000 a year left during the peaks of 1717–19, 1727–29, 1740–43 and the early 1750s. Overall, *c.*100 000 people may have left Ulster between 1717 and 1760, another 200 000 between 1770 and 1776. In the later seventeenth and early eighteenth centuries, despite having supported the government against the Jacobites, Ulster Presbyterians suffered nearly as much religious persecution as Catholics. The Test Act of 1704 barred them from holding civil and military offices, closed their churches and schools, and prohibited their clergy from conducting weddings and funerals. Several early parties of emigrants were led by Presbyterian ministers, but it may be dangerous to assume that, because the emigrants were Presbyterian, they were emigrating solely due to religious and political persecution. In the 1720s scarcity of food and rent rises also drove people out. During the more favourable 1730s, with better harvests and lower prices, emigration slowed. Later in the century, emigration was linked closely to the fortunes of the linen industry in Ulster, as many smallholders were part-time weavers. The emigration boom in the 1770s was connected with a disastrous collapse of the linen industry. In the 1730s and 1760s South Carolina imposed duties on Negro slaves, so encouraging European immigrants. In the 1760s Ulster emigrants to South Carolina could also obtain grants of 100 acres per family with an additional 50 acres for every family member, exempt from taxation for 10 years, with an additional grant to purchase tools. Emigrant agents, acting for captains, shipowners and sometimes land promoters, toured Ulster towns on market days, but they catered for existing demand rather than stimulated it. By the mid-eighteenth century, an increasing number of Protestant emigrants were less well off; smallholders, cottager/weavers, and even labourers, rather than farmers. The cost of passages to America fell from between £5 and £6 in the early eighteenth century to £3.5s by 1773, but a minimum of £10 was needed to keep an emigrant solvent until their first harvest, the equivalent of a year's wages for a labourer; as a result, many poorer people emigrated as indentured servants. Emigrants from Ulster often went straight to the frontier; in the 1790s half the settlers on the trans-Appalachian frontier were of Ulster descent. Though they were conservative, subsistence-oriented farmers, they usually did better than if they had remained in Ireland.

Catholics, mainly Irish speakers, were more isolated from information about emigrant opportunities and had a traditional, communal culture, which worked against individual initiative at a time when commercialization was only just starting to erode peasant insularity. Nevertheless, in the seventeenth and early eighteenth centuries there was some migration of Catholic Irish as indentured servants to the Caribbean. Irish Catholics who did emigrate to America in the seventeenth and early eighteenth centuries often led short, hard lives. Between 1783 and 1814 some 100 000–150 000 Irish emigrated to America – at least 5000 per year in the 1780s and 1790s, more than two-thirds of them from Ulster. Many of them were substantial tenants and artisans, as well as the indentured servants. Between 1815 and 1844, 800 000–1 million emigrated, twice the total for the previous 200 years. An increasing proportion of them, especially from the 1820s, were poor Catholics; subtenants, labourers and farmers' sons. In 1823–25 the British government gave Catholic emigration a boost by providing free passages and land grants in upper Canada. However, colonization of peat lands, seasonal migration to Britain and illicit distilling continued to provide alternatives to emigration.

The Social Origins of British Emigrants

What were the social backgrounds of British emigrants to America and how did they differ from the populations of their areas of origin? The first colonists were predominantly young and male, they were pioneers in a hostile environment who lived under what were, effectively, garrison conditions. The voyage of the Pilgrim Fathers in the Mayflower in 1620 was one of the first in which women and children were a significant component. A preponderance of men arriving as indentured servants perpetuated a male-dominated society in which men tended to marry late and women early, a society which was often volatile and unstable. In the first half of the seventeenth century, emigrants to New England were often recruited through personal contact by members of organizations such as the Virginia Company. The costs of emigration in the first half of the seventeenth century were substantial. The decision to emigrate might involve the liquidation of all the assets belonging to a person or family. During the seventeenth century a family might have to pay £30–£50 to transport themselves and their possessions across the Atlantic. This put emigration beyond the reach of the poorest (Table 4.2).

Table 4.2 Occupations of 242 Men Migrating to New England, 1635–38 (After Cressey, 1987)

Occupation	%
Clergy and professional	2
Yeomen	2
Husbandmen	20
Labourers	4
Servants	21
Textile trades	21
Woodworking trades	11
Leather trades	9
Food and drink	4
Transport and distribution	4
Metalwork and building	2

By the later seventeenth century a significant percentage of people moving to New England, and a far higher proportion of those emigrating to colonies further south, came as indentured servants, both male and female, who worked in farming, as craftsmen or sometimes as domestic servants. Indentured servants formed a majority of the emigrants from the British Isles to North America and the West Indies during the seventeenth century. The system of indenturing servants in the American colonies seems to have developed as a modification of apprenticeship and agricultural service (Middleton, 1996). Such people had their passages paid by an agent or potential employer, repaying the cost by being bound to work as a servant for a fixed number of years, often six or seven.

There has been considerable debate over whether indentured servants were drawn from the 'middling sort' of society or from its lower levels (Galenson, 1978). Indentured servants were sometimes portrayed as the dregs of society, recruited from unemployed labourers, vagrants and criminal element of society. The registers of indentured servants for Bristol between 1654 and 1679 list over 10 000 people with some details of their social backgrounds. Three-quarters were male, and most were probably in their late teens and early 20s (Souden, 1987). Where occupational details are available, 35 per cent came from yeoman backgrounds, only 10 per cent from labouring families, with a high proportion of apprentices and craftsmen. The typical indentured servant emigrant, then, was young, of middling to lower-middling status with at least some skills. In many respects they confirmed more to the image of betterment than subsistence migrants.

While not all the migrants necessarily came to Bristol with the specific intention of emigrating, indentured servants had a much wider pattern of geographical origins than contemporary apprentices; 39 per cent of indentured servants came from over 64km against only 15 per cent of apprentices. Many originated from wood-pasture districts like the Forest of Dean, areas which contributed relatively few migrant apprentices, but areas which were also noted for high levels of mobility, where the importance of rural industry rendered the population vulnerable to periodic slumps. Many also came from West Country cloth-making towns like Bath, Taunton and Wells, possibly for similar reasons. Although a majority of them were destined for work in agriculture, 57 per cent came from towns. Souden (1987) has suggested that the migratory patterns inside Britain of men and women who became indentured servants was probably a more accurate reflection of mobility among the lower ranks of society than contemporary patterns of movement by apprentices at one extreme, or vagrants at the other. Such servants were not the rogues, whores and vagabonds of popular image, but a distinctive element in the longer-distance mobility patterns of seventeenth- and eighteenth-century Britain.

Indentured servants provided the main labour force for American plantations before the widespread introduction of Negro slaves in the late seventeenth century. Conditions were often hard and in Maryland during the 1640s, 40 per cent did not survive their period of indenture. Their rights were safeguarded by colonial assemblies; they could not be severely punished without the permission of a Justice of the Peace. On expiry of their term they received some kind of payment: in seventeenth-century Virginia, 50 acres of land, clothing and a musket; in eighteenth-century North Carolina, merely £3 and a suit of clothes, grants of land tending to disappear in the eighteenth century unless in remote areas like Nova Scotia. Prospects for upward mobility after completing their service were variable. Some prospered and a few in Virginia became tobacco planters, but others remained tenants, cottagers and labourers. Most former servants in New England became wage-earners or small landholders. Further south on the Chesapeake, perhaps because of the high mortality levels, there was more scope for upward social mobility.

Following the 1718 Act, which led to the systematic adoption of transportation as a punishment for serious crimes, another category of emigrants which became increasingly important during the eighteenth century was transported convicts, although some transportation had occurred during the seventeenth century. After the Battle of Dunbar in 1650, up to 1000 Scottish prisoners were shipped to America by Cromwell's administration (Grainger, 1997). Such men, and Jacobites transported after the 1715 and 1745 Rebellions, could be considered as political prisoners, but the majority of people transported to America were petty criminals (Ekirch, 1985). The 1718 Act made it the main penalty for offences against property, the most frequent sort of crime. Between 1718 and 1775 two-thirds of felons convicted at the Old Bailey were transported to be sold as servants. The Scottish High Court of Justiciary, and its Irish equivalent, also used transportation as a punishment. Numbers of criminals transported from Scotland between 1718 and 1775 probably amounted to 700–800. From Ireland the figure was much higher; possibly around 16 000. From England came over 30 000, making a total of about 50 000 from the British Isles, about a quarter of British immigrants to America during the eighteenth century. Over 90 per cent were sent to Virginia, Maryland and Pennsylvania, the rest to the West Indies. They were sent to hard labour in the plantations, sometimes chained, with living conditions little better than those of Negro slaves. How different were they from ordinary British citizens and voluntary emigrants? A high proportion were drawn from the ranks of the unskilled and semi-skilled, the group most vulnerable to economic depression and poverty. They stole out of desperation rather than because they were hardened criminals. While most were convicted of petty theft, the crimes for which people were transported varied considerably: in Ireland people were often transported simply for vagrancy; in Scotland only for more serious offences

In the eighteenth century the social and geographical origins of emigrants to America were more diverse, but, overall, probably more skilled than in the seventeenth century. Slaves now did most of the hard field labour, and labour recruitment emphasized skills rather than muscle. The quality of indentured servants probably also rose. On the eve of the Revolution, 56 per cent of them claimed to be skilled workers. Bailyn's (1987) analysis of over 9000 people who emigrated between 1773 and 1776 has shown that there were two main migration streams with different social and economic characteristics. One comprised emigrants from southern England, especially London, and the other people leaving from northern England and Scotland (Table 4.3). The first group was characteristically young, single and skilled, predominantly male artisans and craftsmen of middling origins who had served all or at least part of an apprenticeship. They were leaving individually, or in small groups, to work as indentured servants in areas of established settlement in colonies such as Maryland, Pennsylvania and Virginia. Over 40 per cent of the emigrants who went through London gave residences as elsewhere in Britain, many having come long distances: 63 per cent of them had travelled over 80km; 26 per cent over 240km. Similar patterns occurred for other ports of departure such as Bristol, Greenock and Liverpool. Many long-distance migrants had probably not originally intended to emigrate.

Table 4.3 Origins of Emigrants to America, December 1773–March 1776 (After Bailyn, 1987)

England		**Scotland**	
Home Counties	592	Borders	470
London	2345	Western Lowlands	477
East Anglia	110	Eastern lowlands	291
SE. England	109	Perthshire	299
West Country	253	Highlands and	
Bristol	107	Hebrides	1099
Welsh Border	147	North East	80
East-Central	107	Far North	303
Midlands	229	Unknown	853
North	250		
Yorkshire	938		
Unknown	9		
Total	**5196**		**3872**

Emigrants from northern England, especially Yorkshire, and from Scotland were typically from agricultural backgrounds, more often moving as families with children, sometimes as part of large groups. In many cases they were leaving for less positive reasons than the first category of emigrants; to escape rising rents and deteriorating living standards, and were looking for new land on the American frontier. A fifth of the craftsmen who were emigrating claimed to be skilled, including people in specialist occupations such as backgammon-table makers, goldsmiths, gunstock makers and mathematical instrument makers. Over 80 per cent of the emigrants from southern

England were male. The figure for Yorkshire was only 67 per cent and for Scotland 50 per cent, indicating higher levels of family migration. For both groups, however, the impression was that emigration was not seen as a desperate escape, but as an opportunity to be seized (Table 4.4).

Table 4.4. Reasons for Emigrating, December 1773–March 1776 (After Bailyn, 1987)

	London	Yorkshire	Highlands
Positive reasons			
To settle	241	70	4
To better self	12	173	134
To follow occupation	100	49	3
Total	353	292	141
Negative reasons			
Unemployment	5	0	20
Poverty	0	0	114
High Rents	0	63	196
Bad economic conditions	0	22	0
Total	5	85	330
Combined total	**358**	**377**	**471**

Like their seventeenth- and early-eighteenth-century predecessors, such people were not necessarily poor. Some, at least, may have carefully considered the relative advantages of arriving in America as free emigrants having spent most of their capital on the passage, and emigrating as indentured servants thus saving their passage money, and using their term of service – usually four years at this period – to assess possible opportunities. Their motives for emigration combined positive and negative elements, with unemployment and poverty, rising rents and poor economic conditions being balanced by the desire to acquire land and to better themselves. Of English emigrants, 68 per cent were going as indentured servants against only 18 per cent of the Scots. Farmers were more likely than other occupations to travel in family groups but, for farmers and craftsmen, two-thirds of migrating families had no children, implying that they were carefully choosing the best time in their life cycle to emigrate. This suggests that emigration was a calculated strategy rather than a desperate move. Weavers came almost entirely from Lancashire and west Yorkshire rather than areas of declining preindustrial clothmaking, a high proportion of them from urban origins.

By the late eighteenth and early nineteenth century, and the start of mass migration, there were considerable short-term variations in the social background of the emigrant stream between years of peaks and troughs, reflecting economic cycles within Britain (Erickson, 1994). It has sometimes been assumed that English emigrants in the nineteenth century came predominantly from agricultural and rural-craft backgrounds, driven out by enclosure and, after 1815, agricultural depression, in contrast to the later nineteenth century when emigrants were overwhelmingly urban in origin. However, it has been suggested that labourers and weavers were too poor and were unable to afford to emigrate. At the end of our period, around 1830, farmers and labourers were outnumbered among emigrants by craftsmen in traditional trades whose skills had not changed much from preindustrial times. Half the men emigrating to America in 1831 from England and Wales were in craft or industrial occupations (Table 4.5). In 1827 39 per cent of all migrants came from larger towns, at a time when these accounted for only 28 per cent of the population (Erickson, 1994). Emigration from England in 1827–28 had involved a substantial proportion of workers from new industries due to a depression in the cotton industry (Erickson, 1994). In 1831 emigrants in the most rapidly changing and expanding industries, including textiles, metalworking and engineering, were over-represented. Emigration does not, then, seem to have acted as a major safety valve in reducing the English agricultural labour force. In 1827–31 only 21 per cent of English emigrants came from agricultural low-wage counties against 55 per cent from industrial high-wage ones.

Table 4.5 Occupations (per cent) of English and Welsh Male Emigrants to America, Aged 20 or Over, by Port of Arrival, 1831 (After Erickson, 1994)

	New York	Philadelphia	Boston	New Orleans
Agriculture	25.5	19.2	6.3	14.3
Labourers	10.0	4.6	15.0	–
Service	1.9	2.7	3.8	–
Crafts	35.4	40.4	18.7	14.3
Industry	14.7	19.9	52.4	2.8
Commerce and Professions	12.5	13.3	3.8	68.6

The Assimilation of Immigrants in America

The role of return migration across the Atlantic has often been ignored. While return migrants to Britain were fewer than those crossing to America, and are more poorly recorded, some people did return. Cressey (1987) suggests that around a sixth of migrants to New England in the seventeenth century came back to Britain. Sometimes this was only temporarily to take up legacies, collect rents and debts, or visit family and friends. Others saw a move to the New World as only a phase in their lives. Some returned permanently having failed to find success or happiness across the Atlantic.

The social background of seventeenth-century migrants to New England meant that levels of literacy for both men and women were higher than in England. People kept in touch with events in Britain through correspondence which, perhaps because of the distance over which it had to travel, was often carefully preserved. While news undoubtedly took longer to reach America than remoter parts of Britain, the mechanisms were similar and probably as reliable. As well as keeping people in touch with general and personal news, emigrant correspondence provided a means of transmitting back reports of success and favourable conditions, which encouraged other kin and friends to consider emigration.

The surge in emigration in the 1760s and 1770s was linked to a rapid spread of the American frontier (Bailyn, 1987). Emigrants often went straight to the frontier, Scots to northern New York state,

Irish Protestants to south-west Pennsylvania. By the early nineteenth century there were marked differences in emigrant destinations within America, depending on their occupational background (Table 4.5). Emigrants' ties with their homelands often remained strong and influenced the ease with which they became assimilated. Miller (1985) has claimed that a high proportion of Irish emigrants, especially Catholics, considered emigration to be involuntary exile (though most went voluntarily and few returned), and that this attitude, while perpetuating a sense of Irish identity in America, slowed the process of adaptation and assimilation to a new society.

Many emigrants crossed the Atlantic in response to inducements by land speculators to settle in particular areas. In the 1750s and 1760s, for instance, over 3.5 million acres in Nova Scotia were granted by the government to individuals and to syndicates who agreed to settle specific numbers of people. John Witherspoon, a Scot who had been appointed principal of Princeton College, formed a syndicate with a group of Glasgow merchants and acquired a large area of land at Pictou, Nova Scotia. They appointed recruiting agents at places like Fort William, Inveraray, Inverness and Portree, promising 150 acres for each family, and an additional 50 acres per family member, at a low rent and with the cost of their passage paid (Bailyn, 1985).

Movement did not end with emigration. The American colonies were peopled by the most mobile elements in British society and the patterns of migration which were a feature of Britain were often replicated in the New World (Horn, 1987). Rates of population turnover in British and American communities are not easy to compare. Social structures were different; in America there were considerable numbers of indentured servants, whose mobility would have been restricted during their period of service compared with British agricultural servants. Nevertheless, levels of population turnover in some Chesapeake communities in the later seventeenth century were similar to those in English communities like Clayworth and Cogenhoe (Chapter 2). Indentured servants who had served their time and were setting up on their own, or who had run away before the expiry of their term, were the most mobile element in colonial populations, paralleling society in England.

Mortality among migrants to Virginia and the West Indies was even worse than in the fen and marsh areas of England, where malaria was also a problem. About 40 per cent of emigrants to the Chesapeake area died within a few years, a great many from malaria, and the colony was only maintained by continuous immigration. New England, by comparison, provided a healthier environment and, by the later seventeenth century, life expectancy there may have been better than in England.

Emigration to Australia and South Africa

Although America was by far the most important destination for British emigrants during our period, movement to Australia and South Africa was starting to develop in the early nineteenth century. Australia was settled as a penal colony from 1788, when the vessels of the 'First Fleet' anchored in Botany Bay, which had not been visited by a British ship since Cook's initial exploration nearly 30 years previously. It was the longest voyage ever undertaken by such a large group, lasting eight months and bringing 736 convicts. Many of them came from London, but the rest were drawn from all over England. Forty convicts had died on the voyage – a remarkably low proportion considering its length and the conditions in which the convicts were kept. In 1790 and 1791 further fleets were sent. Of the convicts sent in 1791, 10 per cent died *en route* (Hughes, 1987). The Australian environment proved tougher than anticipated and the fledgling colony lived on the verge of starvation for several years. The length of the passage, the expense and the penal character of the colony put off free emigrants; only 20 had moved to Australia by 1800, though an increasing number of convicts who had served their time stayed and took up land grants (Richards, 1993).

In the early nineteenth century the colony grew slowly with about five vessels a year bringing up to 1000 convicts between them. In the years before Waterloo many convicts were pressed into the army or navy rather than being transported. After 1815 convict numbers increased to reach a peak in the early 1830s. From a population of *c*.7500 in 1800 the colony grew to 36 598 by the time of the first census in 1828. By the 1830s passage times from England had been cut to 110 days for some vessels, compared with 252 days for the First Fleet

Free migrants were not positively encouraged before the late 1820s. In 1828 there were only *c*.4500 free immigrants in Australia. The passage cost far more that the voyage to America; in 1828 £30 to Australia against £5 to Canada. From 1831 the colonies began using money from land sales to fund, in whole or in part, the passage of selected migrants (Richards, 1993). The criteria used for selection in the early years are not clear, but there seems to have been concern by the colonial administration to attract people with suitable skills rather than the poorest elements of society – such as unemployed agricultural labourers – who were precisely the people that the British authorities were anxious to see emigrating. There has been considerable debate as to whether early free immigrants to Australia were drawn from the poorest elements of British society or formed a broader cross-section. Assistance was generous, but rarely covered the total cost of passage and resettlement.

The shift towards assisted emigration to Australia prompts the more general question of whether emigration provided a mechanism for Britain to off-load the 'losers' of the Industrial Revolution. The 1820s and 1830s were certainly decades of rapid social change and mounting concern over the state of British society. Erickson, however, has challenged the view that emigrants at this time were necessarily the casualties of cyclical and structural changes in the British economy, suggesting that they were drawn disproportionately from high-wage industrial areas rather than from the poorest social groups. Positive motives were still clearly important despite the push factors.

South Africa was also a sideshow compared with the flood of emigration to North America. Captured from the Dutch in 1795, returned to them in 1803 and recaptured in 1806, it remained little more than a staging-post on the route to India until after 1815. The postwar depression and high levels of unemployment in Britain led to various schemes to aid the emigration of British settlers to South Africa. In 1820 Parliament voted £50 000 to transport settlers and, out of 80 000 applications, some 4000 people were chosen from all over Britain. This was the largest sponsored emigration scheme of its kind (Keegan, 1996). They arrived in 1820 with another 1000 or so emigrants who had paid for their own passages, receiving 100-acre holdings west of the Fish River on indifferent soils. A high proportion of the settlers were from urban backgrounds, many of them weavers and other artisans who had suffered in the depression. Within a few years more than half had given up their allotments, and returned to their crafts or started up as traders (Thompson, 1990). The limited success of the scheme did not encourage any follow up and the British settlers failed to assimilate with the Afrikaaner population, creating a rift which was to cause major problems later in the colony's history.

*   *   *   *   *

By the early nineteenth century, emigration from Britain was occurring against background conditions which were very different from those which existed when the first settlers founded Jamestown. British society had experienced the early phases of industrialization and was moving towards a mature industrial economy. While the industrial regions that had experienced the greatest transformations were scattered and still limited in extent, the socioeconomic changes they had generated affected every part of the British Isles, including the Scottish Highlands and the west of Ireland. In the next chapter we turn to the links between migration and industrialization, and the question of whether the onset of the Industrial Revolution involved fundamental changes in the nature and patterns of migration.

5

MIGRATION AND INDUSTRIALIZATION

Introduction

From the later eighteenth century, the pace of economic and social change throughout Britain accelerated in the early phases of the Industrial Revolution. There has been considerable debate over the timing of its onset. Deane and Cole's (1964) suggestion, that rapid economic growth occurred mainly after 1780, was widely accepted until recently. It is now considered that the growth of industrial production was fairly steady from the mid-eighteenth century to the 1830s, with no particular period of rapid acceleration. From the 1760s there was certainly a spectacular rise of output in some industries, such as textiles and iron, but initially these sectors were relatively small in relation to industry as a whole. Appreciation of this has revised downwards estimates of late-eighteenth–early-nineteenth-century economic growth. A pattern of steadier long-term economic growth makes it less likely that there was a sudden change in patterns of migration as a result of industrialization.

Many elements involved in the Industrial Revolution, such as the growth of population or the rise of output in various industries, can be isolated, but the complexity of the relationships between them is difficult to analyse. In terms of population growth the basic trends are clear. The population of England rose from 5.77 million in 1751 to 8.66m in 1801 and 13.3m in 1831. The population of Scotland rose more modestly, but still significantly from 1.27m in 1755 to 1.61m in 1801 and 2.36m in 1831. In Ireland growth was most spectacular of all, from *c*.2.2–2.6 million in 1750 to 6.8–7.2 million in 1821. By the early nineteenth century, British population was growing at an unprecedented rate yet the economy was able to absorb it with little change in living standards, though it is far from clear to what extent population growth responded to the demands of the economy or whether the economy was stimulated by demographic increase. Another notable trend was the rise in urbanization. In England and Wales the proportion of the population living in towns with over 2500 inhabitants rose from 24 per cent in *c*.1750 to 30 per cent in 1801 (de Vries, 1984). In Scotland there was an equally marked rise in the proportion of the population in towns with over 10 000 inhabitants; from 9 per cent in 1755 to 18 per cent in 1801. In Ireland, population growth was largely a rural phenomenon and urbanization at this period was much more modest.

While mortality in major cities, including London, undoubtedly fell from high late-seventeenth–early-eighteenth-century levels, much of this urban growth was due to immigration. However, the Industrial Revolution did not only affect the towns. Many early factories were located in rural areas, often in quite remote locations, because of the need for water power. In addition, agriculture experienced major changes. In England agricultural change had been continuous and cumulative from the sixteenth century. However, the later eighteenth century saw major transformations in many lowland areas with the Parliamentary Enclosure of open fields, while in the early nineteenth century this process was extended to upland districts with the enclosure of waste. In Lowland Scotland the pace of agricultural change was even faster. Changes in the seventeenth and early eighteenth centuries had been much slower than in England (Whyte, 1979). From the 1760s into the early nineteenth century, the countryside and rural society were changed by a major shift to commercialization which included: enclosure and the removal of open fields; the development of more sophisticated crop rotations, improved livestock breeding and grazing management; the amalgamation of holdings; the removal of cottars and subtenants; and considerable reclamation of waste. Similar processes of commercialization occurred in the more fertile areas of eastern, southern and central Ireland. The Scottish Highlands and western Ireland were peripheral to industrialization, but were nevertheless affected by them. In these regions substantial population growth occurred in more traditional, conservative societies, which were slower to adapt to change, and in poorer environments with more limited resource bases. Here the shift to commercialization came later and often more traumatically.

These economic, social and demographic changes were closely associated with migration, but the nature of these links are not easy to identify. Migration was both an independent and a dependent variable in relation to economic and social change. Early writers considered that the volume of population movement in Britain increased with the Industrial Revolution, and that growing labour mobility was an underlying factor which allowed industrialization to occur. They believed that this involved a major change in kind rather than in degree, and that the nature of migration in the period of industrialization was distinctly different from preindustrial times. The popular image of British industrialization involved an agrarian society which was uprooted, then displaced by an urban-centred industrial economy, with agriculture providing abundant labour for the growing industrial sector (Nicholas and Shergold, 1987). This idea was implicit in Zelinsky's (1971) mobility transition model, in which the volume and extent of movement increased dramatically with modernization, in addition to showing significant changes in the origins, destinations, pathways and character of migrants (Chapter 1).

How did labour markets cope with regional imbalances in the supply and demand for labour? Little is known about the age, gender and occupational biases of migrant streams or the origins, destinations and distances travelled. Early suggestions that the growth of industry in the north of England encouraged a long-distance migratory flow of workers from the overpopulated, increasingly impoverished rural south, have been shown to be wrong (Redford, 1926). The traditional view was that levels of isolation were relatively high in preindustrial times, producing distinct regional differences between rural areas. From the late eighteenth century levels of isolation fell, with regions becoming more uniform in their characteristics and more fully integrated into Britain's economy and society. However, the nature and extent of this transition has been debated. Langton (1984) has suggested that industrialization highlighted the differences between regions. With the growth of distinctive regional economies, national integration remained limited. Industrializing Britain was a mosaic of regional economies, within which migration operated predominantly over short distances.

Many studies have emphasized continuity in patterns of migration from the preindustrial period into the nineteenth century. Clark and Souden (1987) have suggested that while the total volume of migration may have increased towards the end of the eighteenth century, movement remained predominantly short-distance. Redford (1926) and Tranter (1985) has also suggested that internal migration during the Industrial Revolution was predominantly over short distances. Despite Deane and Cole's (1964) assertion that levels of inter-county migration roughly doubled between the early eighteenth and early nineteenth centuries, there seems to have been no obvious widening of the geographical range of movement until the late nineteenth century (Perry, 1969; Lawton, 1978). Tranter (1985) believed that the growth and spread of rural industry, lack of urban and regional mortality crises, and, in England, stricter application of settlement laws and tougher legislation against vagrancy discouraged long-distance movement throughout the eighteenth century. The early phases of the Industrial Revolution had little impact on this pattern. Not until the second half of the nineteenth century did this diffuse, local pattern of mobility give way to movement which was increasingly concentrated on a few specific regions. Early industrialization was a gradual, evolutionary process. Large-scale methods of production emerged only slowly. Large manufacturing complexes were the exception rather than the rule during the first half of the nineteenth century, and most factories were located in areas where there was plenty of existing craft industry and labour.

Sources

In some respects sources for migration in the sixteenth and seventeenth centuries provide better overviews of migration than those for the late eighteenth and early nineteenth centuries (Southall, 1991). This is partly due to the wider-ranging nature of earlier sources, such as church court depositions, and partly to a lack of research on migration during the early phases of industrialization. For the beginnings of the Industrial Revolution, there is something of a hiatus; sources such as church court depositions and apprenticeship registers either fade out or become less useful. Settlement records exist, but are not representative of a wide range of society. The published census does not provide details of place of birth until 1841 and census enumerators' books do not become available until the mid-nineteenth century. As a result, ideas about migration in the late eighteenth and early nineteenth centuries have sometimes been based on untested hypotheses derived from earlier or later periods, notably from Ravenstein's work (Chapter 1). In any case mid-nineteenth century census data are misleading for they tend to show migration as a disruptive influence, with individuals making permanent transitions from traditional to modern societies, from rural to urban.

On the other hand, new sources become available which shed light on some characteristic features of migration and mobility at this time, for example early trade union records (Southall, 1991) or company records which contain details of the origins of employees. Settlement records provide a good deal of information on movement among the poorest sectors of society (Chapter 2). As literacy increased, working-class autobiographies begin to appear. Though few in number and not necessarily representative, they shed light on aspects of migration which are poorly covered by other sources, such as decision-making processes and the frequency of very short-distance moves within particular settlements (Crosby, 1991).

Inter-county migration in the early nineteenth century has been studied by Nicholas and Shergold (1987), using the records of 10 151 men and women who were transported to New South Wales between 1818 and 1839. The offenders were mainly petty criminals; nearly 90 per cent had committed offences against property and 67 per cent were first offenders. Their occupational profile was thought to have been similar to the working population as a whole. The source provided data on county of birth and county of residence when arrested, with no indications of intermediate moves. Of the sample as a whole, 32 per cent had moved, mostly as young, unmarried people. Inter-county migration was measured as the distance between the largest towns in each county and occurred over medium rather than short distances; half of it between 48km and 177km with a median of 95km. As intra-county moves were not recorded, however, this technique overemphasizes the importance of moves over medium-scale distances. More of the migrants were rural- rather than urban-born; 51 per cent had moved to non-contiguous counties, again suggesting that medium rather than short-distance migration was normal, representing a break with the pattern of preindustrial migration. Migrants were more literate than non-movers. Migrants who were literate tended to move greater distances than those who were not. Movers were significantly more skilled in terms of their occupations than non-movers. The implication was that migration was not a flood of unskilled rural workers forced out of a changing agricultural economy, but a high-quality labour flow. At a national scale, patterns of movement were dominated by the pull of London and high levels of mobility between adjoining industrial counties like Lancashire and Cheshire, Lancashire and Yorkshire, or Staffordshire and Warwickshire. There was no evidence of a marked flow of labour from southern rural to northern industrial England.

Pooley and Turnbull (1998) have pioneered a new approach to the study of migration in Britain, involving the assembly of a large sample of lifetime migration biographies derived from the researches of individual genealogists and family historians. Details of 16 091 individuals born between 1750 and 1930 were obtained. While there is nothing new about the sources used, or the techniques of analysis, the creation of such a substantial database has allowed patterns of migration to be studied at local, regional and national scales. As the authors admit, data from the later eighteenth and early nineteenth centuries are not as complete and accurate as those for later periods. In particular, the number of short-distance moves made within particular settlements or localities is undoubtedly underestimated. Nevertheless, the richness of the data set has allowed them to test a range of hypotheses relating to migration and industrialization.

Their data have allowed a range of research questions relating to the links between migration, urbanization and industrialization to be tackled, including the testing of Ravenstein's hypotheses with more detailed data than was available to him. It was also possible to relate changes in migration through time to Zelinsky's mobility transition model and to infer motives for migration. In the sample males were over-represented, as were people who lived to old age, while those who died in childhood were under-represented. The geographical distribution of the sample was quite close to that of the population overall, though people living in very large towns in the earlier part of the period were under-represented. Inevitably, there was a bias towards those in higher socioeconomic groups. Information on people born in the eighteenth and early nineteenth centuries was more scanty than for those born later.

Most moves in all periods were short-distance (Figs 5.1 and 5.2), a conclusion which clashes with some findings (Nicholas and Shergold, 1987). Most migration into towns was from their immediate surrounding

Figure 5.1 Migratory moves, 1750–99, from Pooley and Turnbull's sample (*Source*: Pooley and Turnbull, 1998)

Figure 5.2 Migratory moves, 1800–19, from Pooley and Turnbull's sample (*Source*: Pooley and Turnbull, 1998)

areas. Only London had a truly national migration field. Mean migration distances remained little changed until the 1880s. There was little support for Zelinsky's transition from low to high levels of mobility in the nineteenth century. While turnpikes, faster stagecoaches and then railways cut travel times substantially before the late nineteenth century, they only did so for the small proportion of the population who could afford to use them. Non-pedestrian travel for ordinary people was not a feature of the early phases of industrialization. Pooley and Turnbull also emphasize the danger of imposing modern concepts of 'short distance' and 'long distance' on to earlier societies. A move of 50km might seem a short distance today, but in the eighteenth century it would have represented more than a long day's walk, or several hours travel by horse and cart. Moves exceeding this distance only amounted to a fifth of those recorded in the sample.

Long-distance moves were relatively unimportant in all periods studied. Most regions experienced similar trends, save for the Scottish Highlands which were characterized by more long-distance movement than other areas. Rural–urban movements were less important than expected. Most moves occurred within a settlement, or to one of a similar size. Moves to large settlements were balanced by migration from larger places to smaller ones. Movement up the urban hierarchy was more likely to occur earlier in life, with some tendency for people to move to smaller places later on. Migration was more commonly undertaken as part of a family group than singly, again differing from accepted ideas, though young, single migrants were more likely to move long distances and up the urban hierarchy. Occupation, education and income were more significant in determining differences in migration than gender. Employment and marriage were the commonest reasons for movement though short-distance moves undertaken to change housing were probably under-represented in the data set. Women were more likely than men to move for marriage and family reasons rather than for employment.

The most important finding was that neither the level nor the nature of mobility changed dramatically after 1750, while patterns of movement were also very stable. There was no significant increase in the mean distance moved, or in the amount of long-distance migration, from the late eighteenth to the late nineteenth centuries. Farmers and agricultural labourers were less mobile than professional men or skilled workers, but the range of variation in length of residence between occupations was not great. There was more variation in the average distances moved by different social groups between 1750 and 1839 – 16.7km for agricultural labourers and 19.4km for farmers against 85.9km for professionals and 97.8km for skilled non-manual workers.

A high proportion of all moves in the later eighteenth and nineteenth centuries occurred within regions. Intra-regional movement was predominantly short-distance; over half of all moves within regions were under 50km. Within regions, migration from the countryside to the towns, and upwards within the urban hierarchy, was less important than expected. There was little evidence that industrialization increased the distinctiveness of regions in terms of their migration patterns. Britain was characterized by a number of well-integrated regional migration systems within which people moved easily and frequently, mainly over short distances. Levels of interchange between regions were relatively low. Moves within settlements accounted for nearly a third of all recorded ones, even in the late eighteenth/early nineteenth centuries when such moves were under-recorded. Of moves between settlements, most were between ones with populations of less than 5000. Migration from places with under 5000 inhabitants to ones with more than 5000 accounted for under 12 per cent of moves in each region. The local scale of most movements suggests that migration was not socially disruptive. Migration was most common for young adults, but, in terms of total numbers, more people moved as part of a nuclear family; single people tended to move further than families. A problem of this approach, however, is that each move – whether merely from one side of a village street to the other or between a rural area and a major city – is given equal weighting, but is unlikely to have been of equal significance to the people involved.

Migration and Industry: Regional and Local Examples

Despite the preponderance of short-distance migration, industrial communities might attract more long-distance movers than agricultural ones. Long and Maltby (1980) showed that there was more long-distance migration to industrial parishes in the Yorkshire Dales than to agricultural ones in lowland Yorkshire. Long-distance migrants to industrial communities in the Dales came predominantly from established textile areas elsewhere in Yorkshire. Skipton attracted most long-distance migrants among the Dales parishes studied, especially from places along the main east-west turnpike, such as Kendal, Kirkby Lonsdale, Lancaster, Sedbergh and Settle.

In Calverley, between Leeds and Bradford, there was a considerable turnover of population, but most of the movement was within a 16km radius of place of birth (King, 1997). Of males listed in the baptism and marriage register 60–70 per cent had textile-related occupations. Enclosure of waste from the mid-eighteenth to the early nineteenth century created new holdings and stimulated local-scale migration. There was a correlation between surges of out-migration from Calverley and the enclosure of commons and wastes in surrounding parishes. The enclosure of land in Calverley caused in-migration from Leeds, while the normal operation of the land market caused a constant trickle of families of freeholders and tenants into and out of communities. Townships had a fairly stable core of families and by the late eighteenth century, most people, once they moved into Calverley, were living out a significant proportion of their lives there. Rural industries allowed more people to stay in the community for longer, generating closer kin links. But there was also a steady stream of individuals and families moving into and through the parish. Increasingly, they only stopped temporarily. In the late eighteenth century only a quarter of immigrant families left subsequently. There is little evidence that much of the movement was influenced by the Settlement Laws, though vagrancy was a problem. The textile mills had a high turnover of labour, but much cloth production was still done by households of independent weavers who were much less mobile.

In examining migration during the early phases of industrialization, it must be emphasized that the most dynamic, rapidly expanding sectors of the economy; cotton, coal mining and iron smelting for instance, employed only a small percentage of the workforce. Many of the locations of early industrial sites were rural rather than urban, sometimes relatively remote, but often in areas where there was already a pool of labour engaged in domestic industry. Industrialization in such areas was a gradual rather than a sudden process. Migration to early factories involved, overwhelmingly, movement within the countryside, predominantly over short distances. Much early industrialization was merely the intensification of pre-existing forms of work. The evolution from domestic production to factory industry did not involve marked changes in patterns of population mobility. Most early cotton mills were small; ones employing 50 workers or less were much more common than those with 500 or more, though the size of the larger mills increased rapidly (Berg, 1985).

Nevertheless, some factory owners experienced problems in attracting a suitable workforce to remote water-power sites, especially people with appropriate skills. There was often a prejudice against factory employment. Early factories had to rely on casual labour, frequently with a high rate of turnover. At New Lanark, David Dale employed children from poorhouses in Edinburgh and Glasgow; *c*.500 worked there in 1799. Samuel Oldknow at Mellor and Samuel Greg at Styall used child apprentices from London institutions, as did various West Riding woollen mills. Such apprentices formed a quarter or even a third of the workforce in some early mills (Redford, 1926).

Many aspects of migration in the early phases of industrialization are highlighted by Pooley and D'Cruz's (1994) study of Benjamin Shaw, a mill worker born in 1772, who wrote an autobiography in 1826 providing information on 167 moves made by 39 members of his family. Benjamin's father, Joseph, was born in Garsdale, West Yorkshire, in 1748. He lived and worked in and around the nearby village of Dent for much of his early life. He made a brief move to the town of Kendal, but his wife, Isabella, does not seem to have liked the place and they returned to Dent. They made several short-distance moves in the Dent area to obtain better accommodation for their growing family. In 1791 Joseph went south to the factory village of Dolphinholme, near Lancaster. The decision to move was partly due to lack of work in Dent, especially for Joseph's growing children. The choice of Dolphinholme was based on information from a carrier who came from Dent, but had gone to work in Dolphinholme, as well as from the mill owner himself who visited Dent on a recruiting drive. The move was not a success, for within three weeks Joseph quarrelled with the mill owner over wages and was dismissed with the rest of his family. Joseph returned to Dent but the children, including Benjamin who had been taken on as an apprentice, stayed. Joseph subsequently returned and was taken on again, though at a lower wage. In less than two years the mill began laying off workers. Three of the children died in 1792–93 and most of the family returned to Dent, leaving Benjamin at Dolphinholme for a brief period before moving to Preston with his wife in 1795. His parents followed, though his mother died soon after.

The Shaws's story highlights a number of features which were probably typical of migration at this time. First, the number of moves made over very short distances, in and around Dent for instance, which would not have been identified from any other kind of source. A third of all moves made by the family were within rather than between settlements. Second, it emphasizes the importance of migration by families and, in this context, the importance of wives as well as husbands in the decision-making processes which led to migration. Some moves, such as from Dent to Dolphinholme, were based on a careful evaluation of possible advantages. Others were precipitated by traumatic events such as a death in the family. Nor was migration a simple stepwise progression from countryside to town. As many of the moves made by members of the Shaw family were made within the countryside as to urban locations; the pattern was more one of circulation within a region which was reasonably familiar. Distances moved were short; 70 per cent were under 30km, mostly undertaken on foot. This case study also emphasizes the importance of rural industrial villages in the transition of people from a proto-industrial rural setting to an industrial urban one.

As we have seen, rural–urban migration was an important component of population movement in preindustrial Britain. There has been considerable debate about how the volume, pattern and character of migration to urban centres changed during the early phases of industrialization, as well as about the contribution of migration to urban growth. Key questions include; did cities grow more by migration or natural increase at this period? Did urban in-migration increase with the acceleration of industrialization? How responsive was the rural population to employment demands generated by urban growth? What was the relative importance of push and pull factors in rural–urban migration?

It is clear that there was a steady shift of population from rural to urban throughout the period. Only briefly during the Napoleonic Wars, when the demand for agricultural labour was especially high, was this net movement checked. While mortality in larger towns and cities may have been less severe than in the late seventeenth and early eighteenth centuries, in-migration continued to account for a substantial proportion of urban growth, as high as 90 per cent in some quinquennia, though more usually around 60 per cent (Floud and McCloskey, 1994). During the 1810s and 1820s mortality rates improved sufficiently for more and more urban growth to be accounted for by natural increase rather than migration. As late as 1851, however,

55 per cent of the population of Manchester, 56 per cent of Glasgow's and 58 per cent of the inhabitants of Liverpool had been born in a different county. However, Pooley and Turnbull (1998) have shown that rural–urban migration was less important in the migration system than has sometimes been supposed, and that there was also significant movement down the urban hierarchy and back to the countryside. The predominantly local character of rural–urban migration meant that most people were not irrevocably severing their links with the countryside and were moving to places where they probably already had contacts, thus easing the process of assimilation.

It has been too easily assumed that migration between the countryside and the towns operated in only one direction and involved the permanent separation of rural dwellers from their agrarian roots. The significance of reverse movements from town to country is brought out by Tidswell's (1993) study of mobility in early nineteenth-century Scotland, from details of suspects and witnesses in the precognitions of the Lord Advocate's Department. That two-way movement between town and countryside was associated with considerable occupational mobility is also shown by working-class autobiographies. The case of Alexander Somerville, born in 1811 in the village of Oldhamstocks in East Lothian, is instructive. Starting as a farm labourer, he moved around East Lothian as a woodsman, a worker at a lime kiln, as a harvester, sheepshearer and drain-digger. He then moved to Edinburgh as a sawyer, but a trade depression forced him back to the countryside as a hay-mower, fence-maker and general labourer. He returned to Edinburgh as a market gardener, but went back to the countryside as a sheepshearer and harvester, before enlisting as a soldier and, eventually, emigrating to Canada. Somerville's movements suggest that the distinction between 'temporary' and 'permanent' migration, however sharply drawn in theory, may be difficult to distinguish in practice.

Some economic historians have extrapolated back to the early nineteenth century, using gravity models applied to post-1850 data. These have shown that for inter-county migration in the later nineteenth century, movement was related to levels of wages in the source county and to those in the destination county, the distance between them and the supply of non-agricultural jobs in the destination. This suggests that migrants responded to economic factors and were sensitive to wage differentials, but also to the costs imposed by distance. However, there appears to have been relatively little mobility between different industrial areas within Britain during the early phases of the Industrial Revolution, and even large, rapidly growing towns, like Manchester and Glasgow, drew most of their migrants from their own immediate hinterland. Declining textile areas, like East Anglia and the West Country, provided very few migrants to the expanding textile areas of Lancashire and Yorkshire.

Some longer-distance movements to the growing industrial towns did occur. In many cases they involved skilled workers and were heavily dependent on personal contacts setting up patterns of chain migration. An example was the migration of Scottish engineers to the industrial centres England, of whom the best known were John Rennie and James Watt. An instance of this is the links between Galloway and the Manchester cotton industry. William Cannan from Kirkcudbrightshire moved to Chowbent, near Leigh in Lancashire, in the 1770s and set up a machine-making business. James McConnel, his nephew, was apprenticed to him in 1781. In 1784 McConnel was joined by John Kennedy, the son of a neighbour of Cannan's family in Galloway. In 1791 McConnel and Kennedy set up their own textile machine-making business in Manchester and soon moved into cotton spinning. Their main rival was a firm run by Adam Murray and his brother John, both from Galloway, who had also served their apprenticeships under William Cannan. James Kennedy, John's brother, and John McConnel, the half brother of James, were also involved in the firm of McConnel and Kennedy, which recruited at least some of its workforce from Galloway and used its Scottish connections to good effect in developing their marketing strategies.

Another kind of movement of skilled workers, less directed but still structured, was that of tramping artisans. The practice of skilled artisans tramping in search of work went back to the early eighteenth century for some groups (Hobsbawm, 1950–51). The system, widespread by the nineteenth century, was designed for single men. No provision was made for men travelling with wives and children. With large-scale unemployment in the 1830s and 1840s the system came under pressure and became a kind of poor relief. It is not entirely clear whether tramping was done by all young men in certain trades after completing their apprenticeship in order to widen their experience or whether, and to what extent, it was a provision against unemployment in an economy where economic integration between regions was still incomplete, so that a man might escape the effects of recession by migration. Southall (1991) has examined the Steam Engine Makers'

Society, founded in 1824. Upon showing their membership certificate to the secretary of each branch the artisan would get supper, lodging, breakfast and a penny for every mile he had travelled since he had last been relieved, but he was not allowed to refuse any work that was offered to him. Tramping was more frequent in summer than in winter when unemployment tended to be greater, suggesting that a voluntary element was involved. But tramping was also concentrated in periods of economic depression (Table 5.1).

Table 5.1 Tramping Artisans in the Steam Engine Makers' Society, 1835–40 (After Southall, 1991)

Year	Number of Reliefs	Members Travelling >322km	Mean Distance km per Tramp	% Members on Tramp
1835/6	11	0	26.4	1.5
1836/7	44	0	84.0	3.4
1837/8	223	3	107.5	8.8
1838/39	295	4	98.8	11.1
1839/40	846	43	253.0	16.8

Although the volume of long-distance rural–urban migration was a relatively small component of total population movement, it nevertheless had some effects. By 1851 the percentage of people aged 45 and over was significantly higher in areas of net out-migration, such as the Scottish Highlands, north and central Wales, and parts of the south west of England, while the percentage aged 15–45 was highest in the industrial areas (Langton and Morris, 1986). The proportion of the population born outside the county of enumeration in 1851 was high in industrial areas, such as south Lancashire and west Yorkshire, but low in rural ones like the East Riding, East Anglia, Lincolnshire, Kent and Sussex.

Migration and Agricultural Change: Southern England and Lowland Scotland

The later eighteenth and early nineteenth centuries saw important changes in the agricultural labour force in England which affected the nature and patterns of mobility. The decline of living-in agricultural servants , especially in southern England and after 1815, must have reduced the local circulation of adolescents and young adults. By 1831 farm servants formed 40 per cent or more of the agricultural labour force only in the North and West Ridings of Yorkshire, Cumberland, Westmorland, Lancashire, Cheshire and Derbyshire (Armstrong, 1988). There was more demand for labourers employed by the week, day or at piecework rates. There was no significant expansion of the agricultural workforce in England and Wales between 1700 and 1800, and only a modest expansion between 1800 and 1851. Taken with the overall growth of population, this implies a substantial shift of employment from agriculture to industry and the service sector, and from rural to urban areas (Floud and McCloskey, 1994). Between 1760 and 1840 the percentage of the male workforce occupied in agriculture in England and Wales fell from around 53 per cent to around 29 per cent, while that in industry rose from 24 per cent to 47 per cent (Floud and McCloskey, 1994). At regional and local levels, however, the impact of agricultural change upon population mobility is less clear.

There has been considerable debate over the impact of Parliamentary Enclosure of open fields on the demand for labour in the countryside, and thus on patterns of mobility. It is important to appreciate that Parliamentary Enclosure of arable land was heavily concentrated in a belt of country stretching from southern England, through the Midlands into lowland Yorkshire (Turner, 1980). Even within this zone, many parishes had already been enclosed by the mid-eighteenth century. Early ideas about Parliamentary Enclosure saw it as driving out smallholders, cottagers and squatters (Hammond, 1911; Armstrong, 1989). The orthodox modern view is that Parliamentary Enclosure created more demand for labour, even in the Midlands where arable was replaced by pasture (Chambers, 1972). The new agricultural systems provided more regular, seasonally secure employment and did not cause out-migration by ejecting those who had depended on the commons. On the other hand, Snell (1985) believes that settlement data show increased male seasonal unemployment in much of southern and eastern England in the late eighteenth and early nineteenth centuries. Much of the work of ditching and hedging was done by mobile pieceworkers who followed the enclosure awards. Crafts (1977) suggested, however, that while there was not a large-scale expulsion of labour from the countryside as a result of Parliamentary Enclosure, there was still significant out-migration at a local scale, especially in the Midlands where there was widespread conversion of arable to pasture. This supports Hoskins's (1957) suggestion that enclosure and the conversion of arable to pasture in Leicestershire cut the labour force to a third or quarter of that needed in the open fields, leading to migration into industrial villages like Wigston Magna. Enclosure has certainly been associated with population decline between 1801 and 1811 in some parishes in Cambridgeshire and Leicestershire (Armstrong, 1988). In addition, settlement records suggest that more people were examined after enclosure than before. It is likely, however, that there was little long-distance migration due to displacement resulting from enclosure. The enclosure of upland waste, especially in northern England and Wales, during the early nineteenth century may well have led to local-scale influxes of people as areas of waste were converted into improved pasture and arable, requiring a greater labour force (King, 1997).

While the expansion of parks by landowners, sometimes with the removal of villages, the existence of open and close villages (Chapter 2), and land reclamation may all have contributed to local population movement, the overall impression is that the decline of farm service and the effects of the settlement and poor laws reduced levels of mobility in southern England in the late eighteenth/early nineteenth centuries. Escott's (1988) study of Binfield in Berkshire between 1779 and 1801 identified agricultural labourers as the least mobile sector of society. This is emphasized by the marked gradients in wages which existed within southern England between rural areas and the towns and, at a broader scale, between southern England and the industrializing north. In the later 1830s, following changes to the poor law, attempts were made by some parish authorities to transfer poor families to cotton mills in northern England, but such instances were exceptional.

One feature of population mobility which developed rapidly in many lowland areas of England was the use of temporary migrant labour at harvest time. In France seasonal migration had been widespread in the sixteenth and seventeenth centuries, a vital complement to a sedentary population (Hufton, 1974), but in England it was relatively unimportant before c.1640. It was specifically allowed under the 1662 Settlement Act and in the later seventeenth century, it became increasingly common with harvest workers moving from upland areas of England to East Anglia and the south Midlands. By the late eighteenth century, seasonal migration had become a major element in English rural society (Collins, 1976), associated with rising agricultural efficiency and specialization, and with the increasing cultivation of crops, like woad and flax, requiring a lot of temporary labour (Kitch, 1992; Thirsk, 1997)

Seasonal migration was facilitated by patterns of contrasting farming regions; labour was able to exploit variations in the timing of harvests between hill and vale, light and heavy soils. Mobility out of clay-soil arable areas of southern England was especially high. In these areas root or fodder crops were not grown extensively so that full employment in summer occurred only during the cereal harvest. Light soil areas provided more continuous work, with little outflow of labour. Grass-to-corn migration occurred after the hay harvest. Workers moved from the cheese-making areas of north Wiltshire to the southern chalklands, from the Vale of Somerset to Mendip, Derbyshire to north Nottinghamshire, the Yorkshire Dales to the East Riding, and from Wales to Hereford and Shropshire. Migratory task gangs developed in southern England after the new Poor Law with men and women working under overseers, moving from farm to farm for the grain harvest and hop picking, then returning to their parishes of settlement at the end of the season (Armstrong, 1989; Snell, 1985). Temporary labour was also drawn from industrial areas. In the 1760s and 1770s harvest wages were higher than in textile manufacturing or lead mining. But by the 1820s the stream of industrial workers was drying up in some areas; urban populations were becoming more isolated from the countryside, losing agricultural skills while urban wages were higher. Rural cottage industry was also in decline (Collins, 1976).

This shortfall was met by harvesters from Scotland and, especially, Ireland. Scottish harvest migration to northern England, and to a lesser extent East Anglia, was well established by the late eighteenth century. The flow was checked during the Napoleonic Wars, leading to increased use of Irish labour. Irish harvesters came to Britain from the late seventeenth century, but not until the early nineteenth century were they seen as indispensable (Collins, 1976; Johnson, 1967). In the 1790s there were under 10 000 of them, but soon after 1815 there were *c.*20 000 and by 1846–47, there were *c.*75 000, encouraged by population pressure in Ireland, high wages in England and fast, increasingly cheap steamship services from 1816. In Lincolnshire, where local labour was scarce in the reclaimed Fens, farmers relied entirely on them. In central-southern England and the West Midlands they were also important. In Sussex there were only a few Irish harvesters in 1820, but by 1834 they were replacing urban workers. They travelled under gang masters, who negotiated contracts with the farmers. They might spend three months or more in England, working at successive harvests in different areas: arriving at Liverpool and starting with the hay harvest in Lancashire and Cheshire; moving to Derbyshire and north Nottinghamshire for the hay and corn harvest; then to Cambridgeshire, Lincolnshire and Yorkshire for the corn harvest; and back to Lancashire and Cheshire for lifting potatoes. Their acceptance of lower rates of pay sometimes caused friction with local labour, but farmers saw them as hardworking and cheap (Collins, 1976).

If rural society in southern England was becoming less mobile in some ways and more inward looking, the reverse was true in the Scottish Lowlands. During the late eighteenth and early nineteenth centuries, society in Lowland Scotland changed rapidly with agricultural improvement and the development of industry. The pace of change was unprecedented by Scottish standards and dramatic compared with much of England. It was associated with, and facilitated by, high levels of population mobility at a range of scales from local movements within estates to a large-scale redistribution of population from the Highlands and Southern Uplands towards the Central Lowlands.

Some agricultural change, precipitating population movement, occurred in the early eighteenth century. Dodgshon (1981) has identified a substantial reduction of cottars and tenants on pastoral farms in the eastern Borders at this time, associated with a decline in subsistence arable production on upland farms and a shift to full commercial livestock farming. The population movements which resulted from this attracted no contemporary comment, probably because dispossessed families were absorbed by the expanding local woollen industry. In Galloway the removal of tenants to create large cattle parks under direct landlord management precipitated the Levellers Revolt of 1724–25 (Dodgshon, 1981). Agricultural change in many parts of the Lowlands accelerated from the 1760s, causing major changes in rural society. Devine (1994) has shown that in sample areas there was a steady, though rarely drastic, reduction in tenant numbers and a much larger scale removal of subtenants and cottars.

There seems, however, to have been more tenant displacement in upland areas where the subsistence arable element was abandoned in favour of commercial livestock production (Devine, 1994; Dodgshon, 1983). On the Douglas estates in south Lanarkshire tenant numbers fell by 54 per cent between 1737 and 1774. Over much of the Lowlands the new farming systems demanded a more efficient and rational use of labour. By the 1790s the use of subtenants and cottars was under widespread attack. The scale of cottar dispossession was substantial, but its impact has yet to receive much detailed research (Devine, 1994). However, a study of the factors influencing migration between 1755 and the 1790s in selected Lowland counties shows that the effects of cottar displacement were far from simple; cottar clearance was not strongly identified as a key variable in the process of out-migration, suggesting that many cottars were redeployed locally. In many areas there was a shift of population within parishes from the countryside to villages and small towns (Devine, 1994). In the parish of Stonehouse in Lanarkshire, for instance, the rural population in 1696 was *c*.600, that of the village of Stonehouse *c*.272. A century later 467 people lived in the rural part of the parish against 593 in the village.

Long-hire labour had been an element in pre-improvement rural society (Chapter 2), but was now developed more extensively and systematically, with systems of six-month or one-year contracts, and a tradition of high levels of mobility between employers (1984). Under such systems, numbers of permanent farm workers were closely tied to the size of the farm. Additional seasonal labour needs were met by temporary labour obtained locally from estate villages and industrial centres or, increasingly, from the Highlands and, by the early nineteenth century, Ireland. The new improved farming systems, with their emphasis on root crops as well as cereals, probably required more rather than less labour compared with the pre-improvement open-field systems. The overall impact of these changes was to generate a high level of mobility among the rural population, a good deal of the movement operating within the countryside rather than between rural areas and the towns. Occasionally turnover can be quantified. Houston and Withers (1990) cite the village of Kippen in Stirlingshire, where two-thirds of the families resident in 1789 had disappeared by

1793. Movement of farm servants at the end of six-month contracts was frequent, though mostly over short distances, often within the hinterlands of particular hiring fairs. In the north-east, workers lived on the farm in communal bothies and were normally single. On marriage they might obtain the tenancy of a small croft on the margins of the improved land. In the Lothians and Berwickshire it was normal to find married farm workers living in cottages beside the farm (Devine, 1994).

Former cottars either had to adjust to the new labour systems or move to other employment, but this did not necessarily involve removal from the estate. Landlords were keen to retain surplus population. This was often achieved by the establishment of planned estate villages. Although one or two examples are known from the late seventeenth and early eighteenth centuries, the main period of foundation, in the later eighteenth and early nineteenth centuries, coincided with the most rapid phase of agricultural improvement. Over 300 new centres were established throughout Scotland (Lockhart, 1981). In many cases the aim was to provide centres of artisan employment servicing the agricultural population, but also catering for more distant markets. Many were centres of textile manufacture, particularly linen. Lockhart (1987) has shown that recruitment to a sample of such villages in north-east Scotland was overwhelmingly local, with 90–95 per cent of household heads – mostly tradesmen, labourers and fishermen – being drawn from within a 40km radius. Much of this movement probably operated within estates, though skilled workers, and especially entrepreneurs, were often drawn from further afield, attracted by handbills and newspaper advertisements.

Agricultural improvement in Lowland Scotland also involved extensive reclamation of waste land. Lowland bogs were drained, sometimes using outside labour, as in the case of Kincardine Moss west of Stirling. In 1768 Lord Kames brought in 170 families from Highland Perthshire to clear the peat, paying no rent for several years (Flinn, 1976). Other rough pasture areas held jointly between several proprietors were divided, enclosed and improved. In the north-east new agricultural frontiers were established in many areas by allowing people to occupy and improve areas of waste at the margins of cultivation, rent free for a number of years, creating a fringe of crofts which provided a reservoir of seasonal labour for the larger farms (Devine, 1984). Developments of this kind must have generated a lot of small-scale local mobility and, less often, some long-distance movement.

Population change in Scotland during the later eighteenth century can be studied by comparing parish totals in Webster's census of 1755 with the first official census in 1801. Most rural parishes in the Lowlands grew more slowly during this period than would have been expected from the national rate of increase, suggesting some out-migration, while many, in areas like upland Aberdeenshire and Angus, and the upland parts of Ayrshire and Lanarkshire, experienced a fall in population to a degree implying substantial out-migration. On the other hand, many purely agricultural parishes in arable-oriented areas gained population by 20 per cent or more, suggesting that a good deal of movement was intra-regional and rural–rural, though longer-distance flows into the Central Belt were also significant (Devine, 1994).

Some features of geographical mobility within the new rural society of Lowland Scotland have been established by Houston (1983) from a series of population listings for the Berwickshire parish of Greenlaw in the late 1830s. The listings identified all those who moved into and out of the community at the two main hiring times of Whitsunday and Martinmas. During this period there were 385 incomers and 295 outgoers among a total population of *c*.1350. Movement was frequent but overwhelmingly local in character; 60 per cent of those leaving moved within a 16km radius. Most moves were between Greenlaw and the arable Merse to the south and east. Longer-distance movements reflected contacts with Edinburgh and the important agricultural market of Dalkeith, but there was little other evidence of contacts with the towns. Of single men who had moved, 37 per cent had stayed in their previous parish for only six months and 70 per cent for under a year. Mobility was concentrated in the 15–24 age group for women, but for men was more spread out between 15 and 34. There was no significant difference between the average distances moved by men and women, though families migrated over shorter distances, on average, than single adults. As Berwickshire depended to a considerable extent upon married farm workers, who may well have been less inclined to move as often as single workers, levels of turnover may have been lower than in some parts of the Lowlands.

Migration and the Periphery: The Highlands

During the eighteenth century the economy and society of the Highlands were brought into closer contact with the rest of Britain. Before the eighteenth century there was little permanent movement of population from the Highlands to the Lowlands, and even less in the reverse direction. Although increasing commercial influences are evident in the early eighteenth century, the pace of change only accelerated after the defeat of the 1745 Jacobite Rebellion. The progressive integration of Highland chiefs-turned-landlords into British society, and their adoption of more expensive lifestyles, generated growing demands for cash, which led to the widespread commercialization and restructuring of their estates. At the same time, population growth caused growing pressure on traditional farming systems (Dodgshon, 1998).

From the 1760s, roughly parallel with changes in the Lowlands, estates in the Highlands began removing tacksmen, the former clan gentry and middlemen, amalgamating holdings, raising rents and shifting towards large-scale cattle ranching, followed later by commercial sheep farming. All these affected traditional society and caused people to be displaced. The scale of population removal in these early 'clearances' was considerable, but the effects were piecemeal and often protracted, providing time for adjustment. As with the Borders earlier in the century, many people were probably re-absorbed locally, while there was also significant migration to Lowland industrial villages and towns (Gray, 1990). Between 1755 and 1801 this gradual seepage of labour, poorly recorded but significant in scale, caused a substantial drop in the populations of many parishes in a zone from Argyll through Dumbartonshire and Stirlingshire to Perth, Angus and the interior of the north-east (Withers, 1988).

In the mid–later eighteenth century changes in the north and west Highlands were still limited. There was little permanent migration to the Lowlands. Emigration – generated by rising rents and periodic threat of famine – to North America by large parties under the leadership of local tacksmen was more characteristic (Chapter 4). Despite steady population growth in a marginal environment, the inhabitants were sustained by the cattle trade, fishing and by-employments such as kelp burning.

The rapid spread of commercial sheep farming into the north and west Highlands in the late eighteenth and early nineteenth centuries brought more drastic changes. While Parliamentary Enclosure had displaced people at a local scale in England and agricultural improvement in Lowland Scotland had led to significant population mobility, there was no precedent for the thoroughness and intensity of population removal which occurred on some Highland estates in the process which has become known as the Clearances. While the eviction of people on particular estates occurred over an extended period between the 1760s and the mid-nineteenth century, at a local scale depopulation was often sudden and dramatic. Commercial sheep rearing, introduced by farmers from southern Scotland and northern England, began to spread through the southern Highlands in the 1760s and 1770s. By the 1780s it had reached Ross-shire and by the turn of the nineteenth century, Sutherland. The collapse of cattle and kelp prices after 1815 made the new farming systems even more attractive to estate owners in the northern Highlands. It had been possible to combine the rearing of cattle for Lowland and English markets with traditional peasant agriculture, but commercial sheep farming had to be undertaken on a large scale to be viable. The better-quality valley lands – which were cultivated by peasant smallholders – were required by sheep farmers for their winter grazing, so that the old and new farming systems were incompatible. The only solution for estate owners was to clear the existing population out of areas suitable for sheep. The aim of most landowners before 1815 was not to drive out the population, but to resettle it. People were still seen as a resource rather than a burden and lingering paternalism still helped shape proprietors' attitudes. On many west-coast estates this involved moving the inhabitants out of the interior glens and relocating them in crofting townships (planned sets of smallholdings) on the coast, often on previously unimproved land of dubious quality. The hope was that they would be able to make a living by combining agriculture with crafts or fishing.

While agricultural changes in the southern and eastern Highlands during the later eighteenth century involved a thinning of the population, the continuing focus on arable farming and cattle rearing had prevented wholesale depopulation. Although instances of substantial numbers of people being removed from their holdings are known from the 1770s – 80 tenants were moved to make way for sheep at Aberarder near Loch Laggan in 1770 (Richards, 1982) – large-scale clearances really began in the 1780s, with the worst being after 1810. The removal of the local population was accompanied by a smaller influx of prosperous farmers from pastoral areas of southern Scotland, such as Annandale, Nithsdale and Tweeddale, as well as from northern England.

As Richards (1982) has discussed, definitions of 'clearance' are not precise. The removal of tenants was sometimes gradual and not all moved unwillingly. It is the large-scale clearances that were carried out on short time-scales which have attracted most attention from historians. The most notorious occurred on the Sutherland estates, covering nearly a million acres in northern Scotland, in the early nineteenth century. Plans for redeveloping the estates were conceived during the boom years before 1815, but were largely executed during the postwar slump. The aim of the Sutherland family's estate managers was to clear glens, like the Strath of Kildonan and Strathnaver, to introduce sheep farming and to relocate the population on the coast in new planned settlements, where it was hoped that the expansion of the fishing industry and a range of manufactures would provide them with a living, and the estate with a further source of income.

The plan was well-intentioned but ill-executed, with tenants driven unwillingly from their homes which, in some cases, were burnt to prevent re-occupation. Many thousands of people were involved. The later clearances of 1819–20 alone affected *c*.5700 people, about a quarter of the population of the county of Sutherland (Richards, 1982). Many settled on the lands which had been assigned to them, in villages like Brora, Dornoch, Helmsdale and Port Gower. However, estate officials had unreasonable expectations that men who had previously only worked the land would take readily to the sea, especially when they lacked the capital for boats and equipment, as well as the necessary skills to use them. The postwar economic slump meant that fishing and manufacturing failed to develop on the scale that had been hoped for so that most settlers remained smallholding crofters. Some were, perhaps, no worse off than they had been before, but, for others, clearance brought even harsher conditions than they had been used to. Of the tenants and subtenants cleared in 1819–29, 69 per cent settled elsewhere on the Sutherland estates, but 8 per cent moved to neighbouring estates and 20 per cent moved out of the county, while 3 per cent emigrated. Neighbouring landowners accommodated some evicted tenants, but often on poor-quality land at inflated rents. Others, who drifted south into Ross-shire, may eventually have filtered into the Lowlands (Richards, 1982).

After about 1820, with economic recession and continuing growth of population, people uprooted by clearances for sheep farming could no longer be seen as potential assets. Clearance schemes were often combined with assisted emigration, as in the removal of the population of the island of Rhum (*c*.500) in 1826 (Richards, 1982). Once expelled from places and lands to which they had strong ties, the displaced tenants were often unable or unwilling to settle on the lands that they were reallocated. So initial clearance often precipitated further migration within the Highlands, to the Lowlands or abroad.

In the late eighteenth and early nineteenth centuries, high population levels were maintained in many parts of the north and west Highlands by temporary seasonal migration, partly to the Lowland harvest, but also to industrial work such as the bleachfields of the Vale of Leven near Dumbarton. While much migration to the Lowlands from the southern and eastern Highlands was permanent, there was far less permanent migration from the far north and west during the early nineteenth century, as earnings from seasonal migration were used to shore up the traditional smallholding economy (Withers, 1988).

Seasonal migration to the Lowlands began in the later seventeenth century, but greatly increased in the later eighteenth century, with market centres, such as Doune and Drymen, along the Highland edge developing as hiring fairs, and Edinburgh becoming the gathering point for workers making for the Lothian harvest. By the end of the eighteenth century a contemporary suggested that half the young women in the southern Highlands went to the Lothian harvest. Few families in this region could have paid their rents without the earnings of seasonal labour in the Lowlands. By the early nineteenth century other forms of seasonal work were developing, including gutting herring in north-east fishing ports and on the Clyde. Seasonal migration first developed in the more accessible southern and eastern Highlands. In the early nineteenth century seasonal labour was drawn increasingly from the more remote areas of the north and west Highlands. The collapse of the kelp industry after 1815, a decline in the west-coast fishing industry, a fall in cattle prices, continuing population growth, and the demobilization of soldiers after the Napoleonic Wars made the economic position of much of the population in this area difficult. Temporary migration from the Highlands was encouraged by the reduction of cottars in the Lowlands between *c*.1780 and *c*.1820, which removed reserves of seasonal labour. The contraction of hand-loom weaving after *c*.1830, and the concentration of weaving in the towns, meant that the families of weavers were less readily available for harvest.

Highlanders also migrated to Lowland towns in increasing numbers in the later eighteenth century. Withers (1985) has shown that each of the main Lowland towns, from Greenock and Glasgow through Stirling and Perth to Dundee, recruited Highlanders from distinct, though overlapping, hinterlands within the southern Highlands and that, as time went on, migration spread further north and west to more remote districts. Lobban (1969) has shown that the proportion of Highlanders in Greenock, small in the early eighteenth century, had reached 30 per cent of the population by 1791–1805. Most eighteenth-century migrants were drawn from areas of the south-west Highlands relatively close to the town. It was only in the nineteenth century that a significant proportion of Highland migrants was drawn from the more remote north and west.

Another way in which the growing problem of overpopulation and underemployment in the Highlands, especially the north and west, was ameliorated in the late eighteenth and early nineteenth centuries was through military recruitment. This had started in the late seventeenth century from estates whose owners were loyal to the government. It increased in the mid-eighteenth century during the Seven Years' War, especially from the estates of former Jacobite families, whose owners were keen to rehabilitate themselves with the government. Military recruitment, for foreign service or the militia, reached a peak during the Napoleonic wars. Estimates of the total numbers of men who enlisted, from a total population of only *c*.300 000, exceed 75 000. At a local scale the impact was even greater. Skye, with a population of *c*.16 000, provided *c*.3680 men for the British army between 1793 and 1805 (Richards, 1982). There was often an element of compulsion about enlistment, with the threat that families who did not produce recruits might not have their tenancies renewed. The Northern Isles, with a strong seafaring tradition, sent many men to the Royal Navy and the merchant service during the same period. The demographic effect of the removal of so many men has not been studied in detail, but must have included substantial effects on fertility.

The Irish in Britain

While the movement of Highlanders to the Lowlands represented a major redistribution of the population within Scotland, the largest flow from the economic periphery to the industrial core of Britain in the late eighteenth and early nineteenth centuries was undoubtedly the migration of the Irish. Although massive emigration from Ireland to Britain is often associated with the Great Famine of the mid-1840s, large-scale movement to Britain began half a century earlier. Migration increased in the last decade of the eighteenth century and again after Waterloo, rising from the 1820s into the 1830s. In terms of the growth of the Irish population in Britain, the fastest rate was probably between the late 1780s and 1821, with a more rapid rate of increase even than after the Great Famine (Davis, 1991). Numbers of baptisms in Glasgow's Catholic chapel, providing an approximate measure of Irish immigration into the city, rose most rapidly between 1800 and 1810 (Handley, 1943). Between 1815 and 1845 perhaps half a million Irish settled in Britain against around a million migrating to America. The 1841 census listed over 289 000 Irish-born people in England, of whom 75 000 lived in London and nearly 106 000 in urban Lancashire, with 126 000 in Scotland.

It is not clear to what extent migration streams to Britain and America differed. Pre-Famine emigrants to both destinations tended to be drawn from the ranks of farmers and tradesmen rather than the poorest social groups. Nevertheless, despite the steady fall in the cost of transatlantic passages, it was still much cheaper to move to Britain, making it, potentially, a more attractive destination for families, the very poor and those with least skills. But the issue is clouded by the fact that many emigrants to America had to travel to Britain in order to embark, and some may have decided to stay, while there were also large numbers of seasonal migrants from Ireland in early nineteenth-century Britain.

Most studies have focused on the push factors behind Irish emigration at this period, the Malthusian pressures of overpopulation, poverty, land hunger and starvation. Ireland, by European standards, was certainly poor in terms of average income per head, which was about half that of Britain. Population grew from *c*.4 million in the 1780s to *c*.5 million in 1800, and 8.2 million by 1841 (O'Grada, 1994). Industrial decline also encouraged emigration. In most Irish counties the proportion of the workforce in industry fell between 1821 and 1841. The cotton and woollen industries declined in the early nineteenth century (O'Grada, 1993), and the linen industry also experienced problems. Periodic political and economic crises in Ulster sent waves of hand-loom weavers to Scotland, especially after the 1798 rising and during the 1820s and 1830s (Davis, 1991). Pre-Famine emigrants were drawn predominantly from the wealthier provinces of Ulster and Leinster rather than the poorer ones of Connacht and Munster. Protestant migrants from Ulster were more literate than their Catholic counterparts from the south and also spoke English.

Yet to focus purely on push factors is an oversimplification. A revisionist school of Irish economic and social history has questioned many of the assumptions outlined above. Mokyr (1983) suggests that the Irish had different, rather than worse, patterns of consumption compared with the British. They were poorly housed and clothed, something which struck English visitors forcibly, but enjoyed cheap fuel and a diet which was better than in most parts of Europe, probably superior to that of many English agricultural labourers. He also concluded that the scale of food shortages and famines between *c.*1740 and 1845 has been exaggerated, and that dependence on potatoes was an advantage in that they were less subject to price fluctuations than wheat, the dietary basis for the English labourer, though there may have been some deterioration in the diet of the Irish rural population during the first half of the nineteenth century. As regards population pressure, the ratio of population to cultivable acres in Ireland was not significantly worse than in England and Wales or Scotland.

Some of the problems in Ireland were relieved by seasonal migration to Britain. By 1841 there were nearly 58 000 Irish seasonal agricultural workers in Britain, mostly men. They gradually ousted Welsh and Scottish seasonal labour in England. By the 1820s they were displacing Highlanders from harvest work in west-central Scotland and by the 1830s, in the Lothians (Davis, 1991). As with seasonal migration from the Highlands, this flow was conservative in outlook, representing a continuation of traditional movements within Ireland from the west to the lowlands of the east and south. It acted as a substitute for permanent emigration in areas like Connacht, western Ulster and western Munster, helping maintain the traditional peasant economy (O'Grada, 1994).

The impact of large-scale emigration on Irish society has been given far less consideration that its effects on destination areas (Mokyr, 1983). Arguably the outflow should have improved conditions in the labour market for those who remained in Ireland, but because so much of the emigration came from relatively prosperous areas like Ulster and Leinster, it did not relieve population pressure where it was most severe, in the west. Mokyr (1983) has claimed that the Irish population was already a residual one by the time of the Famine. He has tried to establish whether the emigrants were better educated, more skilled, more willing to adopt new work regimes and take risks than those who stayed, but his results were inconclusive, due principally to the difficulty in applying quantitative measures to such intangible variables. The unskilled, illiterate character of most Irish emigrants suggests that they were not very different from the population they had left, but the preponderance of young, economically active people among the migrants may have increased the dependency ratio in the remaining Irish population.

Irish emigration to Britain occurred in a series of definite streams, linking particular source areas and destinations: from the South West, especially Cork and Limerick, to Bristol, South Wales and London; from Dublin to Liverpool; and from Ulster to Glasgow. Movement was facilitated by the development of regular steamship services across the Irish Sea. Competition brought fares down drastically during the 1820s and 1830s. In 1818 the fare for steerage on the first Belfast-Glasgow service was 14s. By the late 1820s it had fallen to as low as 3s. and by 1833 to 6d. (Handley, 1943). So much emphasis has been placed on the push factors that drove people out of Ireland that it is easy to overlook the influences which attracted them to Britain: the high wages in industrial areas; the availability of work, such as hand-loom weaving or labouring, which was similar to what they were used to in Ireland; the increasing knowledge of England generated by growing contacts through army service or seasonal migration; and the existence of growing Irish communities in all the main British towns.

The Irish chose, overwhelmingly, to settle in urban environments. South-western Scotland was one of the few areas in which substantial numbers of Irish migrants settled as permanent agricultural workers (Devine, 1991; Handley, 1943). By 1841 nearly half the Irish-born in Britain were concentrated in London (17.6 per cent), Liverpool (11.9 per cent), Glasgow (10.7 per cent) and Manchester (8.3 per cent). Regionally, the main foci outside London were Lancashire and west-central Scotland. A problem in studying Irish communities in Britain during the early nineteenth century is the lack of quantitative information about them, especially on occupation, residence and family structure. There has been a tendency to use details from the 1841 and 1851 census and enumerators' books, and project them backwards. Irish communities were rapidly augmented by children born in England who do not, of course, figure as Irish in any census, but it is difficult to be sure to what extent second and third generations acknowledged themselves as Irish.

Irish immigration to industrial areas like Lancashire was not very significant before the eighteenth century. By the turn of the nineteenth century they were settling in larger numbers. In 1797 Manchester was said to have over 5000 and there was already a strong Irish community in Liverpool. The failure of the Irish potato crop in 1821, followed by famine in 1822, caused a further large influx. Much research on Irish immigration to Britain has focused on a few large cities, notably London, Manchester, Liverpool and Glasgow. The Irish have been portrayed as the outcasts of urban society in social, economic, political and religious terms (Pooley, 1989). Many studies have set out to demonstrate that they were a segregated group, explicitly or implicitly using a 'ghetto' model. However, definitions of segregation are highly subjective. More recently, it has been stressed that this is only a partial picture and the diversity of experience of the Irish in Britain has been emphasized (Davis, 1991). By 1851 there were 31 British towns with Irish-born populations exceeding 1000. These centres had varying economic and social structures, different political patterns and diverse job opportunities. Within them, the Irish took up a range of occupations. All large towns had plenty of low-skilled employment, while some, in addition, had specific labour market characteristics which attracted the Irish, whether in heavy industry, textiles or construction. Additionally, there was a small, under-researched influx of skilled and professional Irish, much more widely scattered residentially, more easily assimilated into British society, and as segregated from working-class Irish as their British middle-class counterparts. Some towns, notably Bristol, Dundee, Edinburgh, Hull and Newcastle, were more liberal in their response to the Irish than main reception centres like Glasgow, Liverpool and Cardiff. In the west of Scotland the Irish obtained jobs in mines and mills from which they were largely excluded in northern England (Davis, 1991). In Glasgow the Irish posed little threat to local Scots because of the high proportion of skilled jobs in the city, but in Liverpool, lacking in manufacturing industry, Irish immigration led to social and political tensions from early in the nineteenth century.

In London there was no dominant industry, unlike Lancashire and the west of Scotland. A high proportion of Irish went into the service sector, though the complexity and marked subdivision of the labour market made it difficult for newcomers to find places unless assisted by kin and friends. By the mid-nineteenth century there was a concentration of Irish in transport, construction, labouring, food and drink, and clothing. Unfortunately, the skilled trades which attracted the Irish – such as shoemaking and tailoring – were depressed industries, in which working conditions and wages were deteriorating. Women found work as servants and in clothing manufacture, where the pay was very poor. Many men and women without skills worked as street sellers. There seems to have been less of a shift of Irish into skilled occupations in London than in Welsh or Scottish towns (Lees, 1979). In towns generally, the lowest grades of building workers were rapidly monopolized by the Irish. In Liverpool in 1833 there were over 700 Irish hod-carriers, while in Stockport in 1835, 80 per cent of bricklayers' labourers were Irish. The Irish also dominated the workforce in canal construction. Many migrated as hand-loom weavers; others became miners.

There has been considerable debate over the nature of Irish communities in British towns and cities. The economics of the housing market forced them into low-rent areas, where they displaced other slum dwellers. The popular contemporary image of the Irish living in ghettos has been challenged in recent years. Social class and employment opportunities were more significant than ethnicity in determining patterns of Irish settlement (Davis, 1991). Modern studies have shown that while Irish families might dominate individual back streets, courts and alleys, occasionally with up to 75 per cent of households originating from Ireland, they did not dominate whole neighbourhoods, but coexisted with low-income families from a range of origins (Lees, 1979). But while the Irish were not separated physically and lived in mixed neighbourhoods, they did interact heavily amongst themselves, patronizing Irish pubs, shops and businesses, using networks of friends and kin. Although there was a high rate of turnover of individual Irish families, their mobility, like that of the working classes in general, was usually over very short distances, within rather than between districts. In London areas like Holborn, Southwark and Whitechapel, which were sought out by the Irish in the early nineteenth century because of the availability of cheap housing and local employment, continued to hold large Irish populations late into the century. On the other hand, some people of Irish birth were scattered through virtually every residential area in the capital (Lees, 1979). This pattern of concentration and dispersal was a feature of other large cities like Liverpool and of smaller towns like Lancaster (Pooley, 1989)

The increase in immigration from Ireland after 1815 produced a panic reaction from some sectors of the press, which expressed fears of the impact of an influx of strangers whose acceptance of low wages, alien speech and religion, and doubtful loyalty to Britain threatened to corrupt the British working classes. The Irish were blamed for the existence of slum conditions in British cities and for spreading disease such as cholera and typhoid. They provided convenient scapegoats for many urban problems which were more general in nature (Davis, 1991). On the other hand, English and Scottish employers often valued them as workers. Despite their reputation for drunkenness and rowdiness, Scottish mill owners preferred them to Highlanders as being less proud and more flexible. Popular stereotypes of the Irish, including the comic 'Paddy' and the drunk, fighting navvy, were reinforced by the British press. The Irish were seen as feckless with their earnings and were associated with crime and disorder, as well as faction fighting, but some of the 'Irish crime rate' may have been due to discriminatory, heavy-handed policing (Swift, 1989). While English emigrants to the colonies were seen in a positive light as 'empire builders', Irish migrants to Britain were considered as less-civilized failures and a subversive influence on society (Davis, 1991).

The role of the Catholic church in providing Irish communities in British cities with a sense of identity has received a good deal of attention, but it is clear that the growth of the church was slow during the first 30 years of the nineteenth century and that the proportion of Irish immigrants who were regular churchgoers was low at this time (Davis, 1991). In Glasgow in the 1830s there was only one priest for 11 000 Catholics, under 30 per cent of whom attended mass regularly (Devine, 1991). The Catholic church was to become a major agent of social and cultural change, helping to convert the traditional rural culture of Irish immigrants to an urban and industrial setting, but this occurred mainly in the second half of the century. The Irish did, nevertheless, while adopting an urban life style, retain a distinct identity which separated them from much English and Scottish working-class culture. It must not be forgotten, though, that the Irish were not socially and culturally homogeneous; there were marked differences between Catholic and Protestant, between people from different regions of Ireland, and in the socioeconomic background of the immigrants. In Glasgow, where the Irish immigrants were split roughly evenly between Catholic and Protestant, Orange Lodges were proliferating by the 1820s and 1830s, leading to sectarian tensions (Devine, 1991).

Were the Irish in Britain any better off than they would have been if they had stayed at home ? This is difficult to answer; with the earnings of children taken into consideration, an Irish family might earn three times as much in Britain as in Ireland, but against this was offset the loss of benefits like cheap fuel, possibly higher housing and living costs, and much worse overcrowding. For families to survive, women and children had to work, while many male jobs were casual, producing a fluctuating income. There was much poverty and scope for upward social mobility appears to have been less than among Irish immigrants to America. Nevertheless, Lees (1979) has pointed out that quite modest improvements in material circumstances, not registered by any change in occupational status in census designations, might make a considerable difference to the comfort of an Irish family.

The impact of the Irish on British society has been seen as profound, both by contemporaries and recent historians. The Irish were widely considered to have increased inequality in British society, driven down wages, increased social problems in cities and reduced rural–urban migration (Redford, 1926). More positively, they are thought to have provided cheap labour for British industry, generating significant economic expansion. On the other hand, the Irish influx contributed only moderately to the overall growth of population and to the expansion of particular towns (Davis, 1991). The impact of Irish immigration on the British labour market during the Industrial Revolution has been analysed by Williamson (1989), who points out that it had little effect on the market for skilled labour.Nevertheless, because immigration was predominantly of adults with low dependency rates and high labour participation, their impact on the unskilled workforce was even greater than their numbers might superficially suggest. His conclusion, however, on the basis of quantitative modelling, was that, overall, Irish immigration made little difference to British development, directly causing little of the growing inequality or even the industrial growth in mid-nineteenth-century British society. He considered that the presence of the Irish did stifle migration from poorer agricultural areas to industrial centres, but whether higher wages in northern towns without the Irish would really have drawn people out of the rural south of England is open to debate (Davis, 1991).

6

Conclusion

We have reviewed migration in Britain from Tudor times to the main phase of the Industrial Revolution. During this period British society changed markedly: from an overwhelmingly rural population employed mainly in agriculture to a substantially urban, industrial one; from a strongly localized society to one where transport improvements, rising literacy and more rapid dissemination of news brought people into contact faster and more comprehensively with national and international events. Yet, in terms of the patterns of mobility which characterized society, there were fundamental continuities. Most movement remained local, within communities or between neighbouring ones. Whether we are considering a sixteenth century farm servant or a working-class family in mid-nineteenth-century London, their moves, while perhaps frequent, were mostly undertaken over distances which were short enough to allow them to remain in touch with family and friends. Long-distance moves; out of a community, and especially out of a region, were relatively infrequent. Yet, throughout our period, some people were prepared to travel long distances in search of suitable opportunities, despite the time this might take, or the difficulties, hardships and sometimes dangers involved. If conditions on an emigrant ship with only 1.7m of space between decks or in an early-nineteenth-century Manchester slum seem bad, it is easy to forget how meagre living conditions were for an English agricultural labourer or an Irish cottager in their areas of origin.

As so much movement was local in scale, within settlements, between adjacent parishes, from the countryside to a nearby town or back again, much of it cancelled out in that most communities were neither substantial net gainers nor losers. Yet communities which gained or lost population on a significant scale as a result of migration did exist. The expansion of Britain's urban system would have been impossible, given prevailing levels of mortality, without a steady inward flow of migrants. The landscape remains of former communities, depopulated by out-migration, sometimes voluntary, sometimes forced, can be found in every part of Britain from Connemara and the Hebrides to lowland England. The period at which depopulation occurred may vary from the fifteenth century to the nineteenth, but the underlying influences prompting the outflow of population in different areas at different times were often strikingly similar.

The effect of all this local-scale mobility was seen in the high levels of turnover which have been demonstrated for both rural and urban communities, though it should be remembered that it has been possible to calculate turnover rates for only a handful of communities. The impact of high turnover, even if the exchange of population was overwhelmingly with neighbouring parishes, is difficult to gauge, but must have been considerable in terms of the choice of potential marriage partners, the spread of information, skills and experience, and the scattering of kin and friends through a range of neighbouring communities which were, nevertheless, still easily accessible. Macfarlane (1978) has emphasized the 'individuality' of English society in the preindustrial period: high levels of population movement were a significant part of this which, by the seventeenth century, can be extended to other parts of the British Isles, including Wales and Lowland Scotland.

The patterns which have been identified were similar in many respects to those in societies elsewhere in Western Europe, but there were some notable differences. The levels of turnover found in Early-Modern rural communities in England and Lowland Scotland were higher than in many continental peasant societies, where owner occupation reduced the movement of farming families and reliance on family labour greatly reduced the number of farm servants employed. On the other hand, the corollary of the dominance of peasant proprietorship in poorer upland areas like the Massif Central or the Alps, was the need to earn money by seasonal migration to lowland rural areas and towns, a pattern which was common in the sixteenth and seventeenth centuries on the continent, but which developed later in Britain (Hufton, 1974; Viazzo 1989).

Despite the changes in transport technology, some features of preindustrial mobility are a feature of life today. Marriage partners are still mainly drawn from a very limited geographical radius, reflecting contacts generated through neighbourhood, workplace and social circles. Pooley and Turnbull (1998) have shown that the basic frameworks of population mobility did not change between the later eighteenth and the twentieth century. Had data been available, the probability is that there would have been an equal degree of continuity between the late sixteenth and late eighteenth centuries. The transport developments of the late eighteenth and early nineteenth centuries had little effect on increasing the average distance moved by ordinary people. When Benjamin Shaw left Dolphinholme in 1795 to look for work in Preston, he walked – and suffered from frostbitten feet as a result (Crosby, 1991).

Today much migration is still over short distances, within rather than between settlements. Long-distance movement is easier than in the past in some respects: transport improvements, the advertising of many job vacancies nationally, the willingness of firms to meet relocation costs, all facilitate mobility. Yet the expense and complications involved in buying and selling private houses, the limited stock of housing for rent, and the difficulty of swapping local authority housing between different areas undoubtedly reduces mobility, while public transport systems and the motorway network often allow people to change their workplace without moving their residence.

This book has highlighted research on migration in preindustrial Britain at a range of scales from the individual to inter-regional, national and international flows. An impressive amount of work in this field has been undertaken in recent years by scholars from a variety of disciplines, bringing with them different techniques and approaches. However, this book has also highlighted some of the major gaps in our knowledge. Some can never be completely filled due to the limitations of surviving historical sources. However, there is still plenty of scope for new research. The availability of increasingly powerful and sophisticated computer database packages offers prospects for local-scale studies of migration which relate population movement to the life cycles and family backgrounds of individuals, as well as to the broader social and economic character of communities. King's (1997) work on the Yorkshire township of Calverley provides a good example of what can be achieved by research at this scale. Despite the range and variety of sources which have been considered in this book, there are still new sources to identify and explore, as well as increasingly sophisticated ways of analysing established ones. Much research on Early-Modern migration has been empirical rather than theoretical. Many of the theoretical frameworks used in historical studies of migration are based on ideas generated in the 1960s, including those of Zelinsky, while the earlier work of Ravenstein still casts a long shadow. However, more recent ideas, such as those of Giddens, which emphasize the social and cultural meaning of migration within the context of the development of modernity, are beginning to have an impact on research (Pooley and Turnbull, 1998).

The impact and importance of migration on British society during our period is also evident in literature, song and folk memory. On the negative side, the sense of alienation which pervades the modern folk history of the Scottish Highlands and Ireland centres on powerful images of forced emigration and exile, expressed in communities of Irish and Highland origin all over the world. By contrast the optimistic pantomime image of Dick Whittington symbolizes the positive side of migration with the aspirations of betterment migrants to the towns. It is worth remembering how far back such aspirations go: the real Dick Whittington was a contemporary of Chaucer. The gypsy rover, the travelling journeyman, the wandering beggar, the soldiers and sailors leaving their sweethearts or returning from the wars are familiar stereotypes in ballad and folk song. The practical, workaday side of migration was expressed in the bothy ballads of north-east Scotland, where farm servants moved regularly from one employer to another, sometimes thankfully, as in the farm worker who penned his farewell to a hard master:

> So fare thee weel Drumdelgie, for I maun gang awa
> Fare thee weel Drumdelgie, with your weety weather and a'
> Fare thee weel Drumdelgie, I bid ye all adieu
> I leave ye as I got ye, a most unceevil crew !

His relief at leaving, and his implicit hope for better conditions in his next position, illustrate the combination of push and pull factors which permeate, and complicate, all research on migration in the past.

Bibliography

Adams, I. H., and Somerville, M., *Cargoes of Hope and Despair*, Edinburgh: John Donald 1993.

Alldridge, N., 'The population profile of an early modern town: Chester 1547–1728', *Annales de Demographie Historique*, 1986, pp. 115–31.

Appleby, A. B., *Famine in Tudor and Stuart England*, Liverpool University Press 1978.

Armstrong, D., 'Birth, marriage and death in Elizabethan Cumbria', *Local Population Studies*, 53, 1994, pp. 29–41.

Armstrong, W. A., 'Labour I: rural population growth, systems of employment and incomes', in G. E. Mingay (ed.), *The Agrarian History of England and Wales*, VI 1750–1850, Cambridge University Press 1989, pp. 641–728.

Armstrong, A., *Farmworkers in England and Wales: A Social and Economic History, 1770–1980*, Iowa State Press 1988.

Bailyn, B., *The Peopling of British North America: An Introduction*, London: Tauris 1986.

Bailyn, B., *Voyagers to the West: Emigration from Britain to America on the Eve of the Revolution*, London: Tauris 1987.

Bailyn, B., and Morgan, M. *Strangers Within the Realm. Cultural Margins of the First British Empire*, London: University of N. Carolina Press 1991.

Baines, D., 'European emigration 1815–1930: looking at the emigration decision again', *Economic History Review*, 47, 1994, pp. 525–44.

Banks, S., 'Nineteenth-century scandal or twentieth-century model? A new look at "open" and "close" parishes', *Economic History Review*, 41, 1988, pp. 51–73.

Barry, J., 'Introduction', in J. Barry (ed.), *The Tudor and Stuart Town, 1530–1688: A Reader*, London: Longham 1990.

Beier, A. L., 'The social problems of an Elizabethan country town: Warwick, 1580–90', in P. Clark (ed.), *Country Towns in Pre-Industrial*

England, Leicester University Press 1981, pp. 46–85.

Masterless Men: The Vagrancy Problem in England, 1560–1640, London: Methuen 1985.

Ben Amos, I. K., 'Failure to become freemen: urban apprentices in early modern England', *Social History*, 16, 1991, pp. 155–72.

Beresford, M., *The Lost Villages of England*, London: Lutterworth 1954.

Berg, M., *The Age of Manufactures, 1700–1820*, London: Collins 1985.

Bogue, D. J., *The Principles of Demography*, London: Wiley 1969.

Boulton, J., *Neighbourhood and Society: A London Suburb in the Seventeenth Century*, Cambridge University Press 1987.

'Wage labour in seventeenth-century London', *Economic History Review*, 49, 1996, pp. 268–90.

Brodsky-Elliot, V., 'Single women in the London marriage market: age, status and mobility', in R. W. Outhwaite (ed.), *Marriage and Society: Studies in the Social History of Marriage*, London: Europa 1981, pp. 81–100.

Buckatzsch, E. J., 'Places of origin of a group of immigrants into Sheffield, 1624–1799', *Economic History Review*, 2, 1949–50, pp. 303–6.

Bumstead, J. M., *The People's Clearances, 1770–1815*, Edinburgh University Press 1982.

Canny, N., 'Migration and opportunity: Britain, Ireland and the New World', *Irish Economic and Social History*, 12, 1985, pp. 7–32.

Chambers, J. D., *Population, Economy and Society in Pre-Industrial England*, London: Oxford University Press 1972.

Clark, P., 'The migrant in Kentish towns, 1580–1640', in P. Clark and P. Slack (eds), *Crisis and Order in English Towns, 1500–1700*, London: Routledge 1972, pp. 117–63.

Clark, P. (ed.), *The Transformation of English Provincial Towns, 1600–1800*, London: Hutchinson 1984.

Clark, P., 'A crisis contained? The condition of English towns in the 1590s', in P. Clark (ed.), *The European Crisis of the 1590s*, London: Allen and Unwin 1985, pp. 44–66

'Migration in England during the late seventeenth and early eighteenth centuries', in P. Clark and D. Souden (eds), 1987, pp. 213–52.

'Migrants in the city: the process of social adaptation in English towns, 1500–1800', in Clark and Souden (eds), 1987, pp. 267–91.

Clark, P., and Souden, D. (eds). *Migration and Society in Early Modern England*, London: Hutchinson 1987.

Coleman, D. A., and Haskey, J. C., 'Marital distance and its geographical orientation in England and Wales, 1979', *Transactions of the Institute of British Geographers*, 11, 1986, pp. 337–55.

Collins, E. J. T., 'Migrant labour in British agriculture in the nineteenth century', *Economic History Review*, 29, 1976, pp. 38–59.

Constant, A., 'The geographical background of inter-village population movements in Northamptonshire and Huntingdonshire, 1754–1943', *Geography*, 33, 1948, pp. 78–88.

Corfield, P. J., *The Impact of English Towns, 1700–1800*, Oxford University Press 1982.

Cornwall J., 'Evidence of population mobility in the seventeenth century', *Bulletin of the Institute of Historical Research*, 40, 1967, pp. 143–52.

Crafts, N. F. R., 'Determinants of the rate of Parliamentary Enclosure', *Explorations in Economic History*, 14, 1977, pp. 177–99.

Cressey, D., 'Kinship and kin interaction in early-modern England', *Past and Present*, 113, 1986, pp. 38–69.

Coming Over: Migration and Communication Between England and New England in the Seventeenth Century, Cambridge University Press 1987.

Crosby, A., 'The Family Records of Benjamin Shaw, mechanic of Dent, Dolphinholme and Preston, 1772–1841', *Record Society of Lancashire and Cheshire*, 130, 1991.

Cullen, L. M., *The Emergence of Modern Ireland, 1600–1900*, London: Batsford 1981.

Davis, G., *The Irish in Britain, 1815–1914*, London: Macmillan 1991.

Deane, P., and Cole, W. A., *British Economic Growth, 1688–1950: Trends and Structures*, Cambridge University Press 1964.

Desbrisay, G., 'Authority and Discipline in Aberdeen, 1650–1700', Unpubl. Ph.D. Thesis, University of Aberdeen 1989.

Devine, T. M., *The Tobacco Lords*, Edinburgh: John Donald 1975.

'Temporary migration and the Scottish Highlands in the nineteenth century', *Economic History Review*, 32, 1979, pp. 344–59.

Devine, T. M. (ed.), *Farm Servants and Labour in Lowland Scotland, 1770–1914*, Edinburgh: John Donald 1984.

Irish Immigrants and Scottish Society in the Nineteenth Century. Edinburgh, John Donald 1991.

Devine, T. M., *The Transformation of Rural Scotland. Social Change and the Agrarian Economy, 1660–1815*, Edinburgh University Press 1994.

De Vries, J., *European Urbanisation, 1500–1800*, London: Methuen 1984.

Dickson, R. J., *Ulster Emigration to Colonial America, 1718–1775*, Belfast: Routledge 1966.

Dodgshon, R. A., *Land and Society in Early Scotland*, Oxford University Press 1981.

'Agricultural change and its social consequences in the Southern Uplands of Scotland, 1600–1780', in T. M. Devine and D. Dickson (eds), *Ireland and Scotland, 1600–1850*, Edinburgh: John Donald 1983, pp. 46–59.

From Chiefs to Landlords, Edinburgh University Press 1998.

Donaldson, G., *The Scots Overseas*, London: Hale 1966.

Earle, P., 'The female labour market in London in the late seventeenth century and early eighteenth century', *Economic History Review*, 42, 1989, pp. 328–53.

Ekirch, A. R., *Bound for America: The Transportation of British Convicts to the Colonies, 1718–1775*, Oxford: Clarendon 1987.

Erickson, C. (ed.), *Leaving England*, London: Cornell University Press 1994.

Escott, M. M., 'Residential mobility in a late eighteenth century parish: Binfield, Berkshire, 1779–1801', *Local Population Studies*, 40, 1988, pp. 20–35.

Field, R. K., 'Migration in the later Middle Ages: the case of the Hampton Lovett villeins', *Midland History*, 8, 1983, pp. 29–48.

Finlay, R., *Population and Metropolis: The Demography of London, 1580–1650*, Cambridge University Press 1981.

Flinn, M. (ed.), *Scottish Population History*, Cambridge University Press 1976.

Floud, R., and McCloskey, R., *The Economic History of Britain Since 1700*, 2nd edn, Cambridge University Press 1994.

Fogelman, A., 'Migration to the thirteen British North American colonies, 1700–1775: new estimates', *Journal of Interdisciplinary History*, 22, 1992, pp. 691–709.

Fox, H. S. A., 'Servants, cottagers and tied cottages during the later Middle Ages: towards a regional dimension', *Rural History*, 6, 1995, pp. 125–54.

Galenson, D. W., '"Middling people" or "common sort"? The social origins of some early Americans re-examined', *William and Mary Quarterly*, 35, 1978, pp. 499–524.

Galley, C., 'A model of early-modern urban demography', *Economic History Review*, 48, 1995, pp. 448–69.

Gemery, H. A., 'European emigration to North America, 1700–1820: Numbers and quasi-numbers', *Perspectives in American History*, 1, 1984, pp. 283–342.

Gillespie, R., 'Migration and opportunity: a comment', *Irish Economic and Social History*, 13, 1986, pp. 90–5.

Goose, N. R., 'In search of the urban variable: towns and the English economy, 1500–1650', *Economic History Review*, 39, 1986, pp. 165–85.

Goose, N., 'Urban demography in pre-industrial England: what is to be done?', *Urban History*, 21, 1994, pp. 273–84.

Grainger, J. D., *Cromwell Against the Scots: The Last Anglo-Scottish War, 1650–1651*, Edinburgh: Tuckwell 1997.

Gray, M., *Scots on the Move: Scots Migrants, 1750–1914*, Edinburgh: Economic and Social History Society of Scotland 1990.

Grigg, D. B., and Ravenstein, E. G., 'The laws of migration', *Journal of Historical Geography*, 3, 1977, pp. 41–54.

Gwynn, R., 'The number of Huguenot immigrants in England in the late seventeenth century', *Journal of Historical Geography*, 9, 1983, pp. 384–95.

Hammond, J. L., and Hammond, B., *The Village Labourer*, London: Longman 1911.

Hampson, E. M., 'Settlement and removal in Cambridgeshire, 1662–1834', *Cambridge Historical Journal*, 2, 1926–28, pp. 273–89.

Handley, J. E., *The Irish in Scotland*, Glasgow: John S. Burns and Son 1943.

Hey, D., *An English Rural Community: Myddle Under the Tudors and Stuarts*, Leicester University Press: 1974.

Hey, D. (ed.), *Richard Gough: The History of Myddle*, London: Penguin 1981.

Hobsbawm, E. J., 'The tramping artisan', *Economic History Review*, 3, 1950–51, pp. 299–320.

Holderness, B. A., 'Personal mobility in some rural parishes of Yorkshire, 1777–1822', *Yorkshire Archaeological Journal*, 42, 1967–70, pp. 444–54.

'"Open" and "Close" parishes in England in the eighteenth century', *Agricultural History Review*, 20, 1972, pp. 126–39.

Pre-Industrial England, London: Dent 1976.

Horn, J. P. P., 'Moving on in the New World: migration and out-migration in the seventeenth-century Chesapeake', in Clark and Souden, 1987, pp. 172–211.

Hornsb,y S. J., 'Patterns of Scottish emigration to Canada, 1750–1870', *Journal of Historical Geography*, 18, 1992, pp. 397–406.

Hoskins, W. G., *The Midland Peasant*, London: Macmillan 1957.

Houston, R. A., '"Frequent flitting": geographical mobility and social structure in mid nineteenth-century Greenlaw', *Scottish Studies*, 27, 1983, pp. 31–47.

'Geographical mobility in Scotland, 1652–1811: the evidence of testimonials', *Journal of Historical Geography*, 11, 1985, pp. 379–94.

The Population History of Britain and Ireland, 1500–1750, London:

Macmillan 1992.

Houston, R. A., and Whyte, I. D., *Scottish Society, 1500–1800*, Cambridge University Press 1989.

Houston, R. A., and Withers, C. W. J., 'Population mobility in Scotland and Europe, 1600–1900: A comparative perspective', *Annales de Demographie Historique*, 1990, pp. 285–308.

Hufton, O., *The Poor of Eighteenth-Century France, 1750–1789*, Oxford: Clarendon 1974.

Hughes, R., *The Fatal Shore*, London: Collins Harvil 1987.

Huzel, J. P., 'The demographic impact of the Old Poor Law: more reflections on Malthus', *Economic History Review*, 33, 1980, pp. 367–81.

Johnson, J. H. J., 'Harvest migration from nineteenth-century Ireland', *Transactions of the Institute of British Geographers*, 41, 1967, pp. 97–112.

Jones, E., 'The Welsh in London in the seventeenth and eighteenth centuries', *Welsh History Review*, 10, 1980–81, pp. 461–79.

Jones, H., 'The evolution of Scottish migration patterns: a social-relations-of-production approach', *Scottish Geographical Magazine*, 102, 1986, pp. 151–64.

Population Geography, London: Chapman 1990.

Kent, D. A., '"Gone for a soldier": family breakdown and the demography of desertion in a London parish, 1750–91', *Local Population Studies*, 45, 1990, pp. 27–42.

Keegan, T., *Colonial South Africa and the Origins of the Racial Order*, London: Leicester University Press 1996.

Kent, J. R., 'Population mobility and alms: poor migrants in the Midlands during the early seventeenth century', *Local Population Studies*, 27, 1981, pp. 35–51.

King, S., 'Migrants on the margin? Mobility, integration and occupation in the West Riding, 1650–1820', *Journal of Historical Geography*, 23, 1997, pp. 284–303.

'Reconstructing lives: the poor, the Poor Law and welfare in Calverley, 1650–1820', *Social History*, 22, 1997, pp. 318–38.

Kitch, M., 'Capital and kingdom: migration to later Stuart London', in A. L. Beier and R. Finlay (eds), *The Making of the Metropolis: London, 1500–1700*, London: Longman 1986, pp. 224–51.

'Population movement and migration in pre-industrial rural England', in B. Short (ed.), *The English Rural Community*, Cambridge University Press 1992, pp. 62–84.

Kussmaul, A., *Servants in Husbandry in Early-Modern England*, Cambridge

University Press 1981.

General View of the Rural Economy of England, 1538–1840, Cambridge University Press 1990.

Kyd, J. G. (ed.), "Scottish Population Statistics', *Scottish History Society*, 3rd ser., vol. 44, Edinburgh: 1952.

Landau, N., 'The laws of settlement and the surveillance of immigration in eighteenth-century Kent', *Continuity and Change*, 3, 1988, pp. 391–420.

'The regulation of immigration, economic structures and definitions of the poor in eighteenth-century England', *Historical Journal*, 33, 1990, pp. 541–72.

'Who was subjected to the Laws of Settlement? Procedure under the Settlement Laws in eighteenth-century England', *Agricultural History Review*, 49, 1995, pp. 139–59.

Landers, J., *Death and the Metropolis: Studies in the Demographic History of London, 1670–1830*, Cambridge University Press 1993.

Langton, J., 'The Industrial Revolution and the regional geography of England', *Transactions of the Institute of British Geographers*, 9, 1984, pp. 145–67.

Langton, J., and Morris, R., *An Atlas of Industrializing Britain, 1780–1914*, London: Methuen 1986.

Laslett, P., 'Clayworth and Cogenhoe', in P. Laslett (ed.), *Family Life and Illicit Love in Earlier Generations*, Cambridge University Press 1977, pp. 50–102.

Lee, E. S., 'A theory of migration', in J. A. Jackson (ed.), *Migration*, Cambridge University Press 1969, pp. 282–97.

Lees, L. H., *Exiles of Erin: Irish Migrants in Victorian London*, Manchester University Press 1979.

Levine, D., and Wrightson, K., *The Making of an Industrial Society: Whickham, 1560–1765*, Oxford: Clarendon 1991.

Lobban, R. D., 'The Migration of Highlanders into Lowland Scotland, 1750–1890', unpubl. Ph.D. Thesis, University of Edinburgh 1969.

Lockhart, D. G., 'The planned villages', in M. L. Parry and T. R. Slater (eds), *The Making of the Scottish Countryside*, London: Croom Helm 1981, pp. 249–70.

'Migration to planned villages in Scotland between 1725 and 1850', *Scottish Geographical Magazine*, 102, 1986, pp. 165–80.

Long, M., and Maltby, B., 'Personal mobility in three West Riding parishes, 1777–1812', *Local Population Studies*, 24, 1980, pp. 13–25.

Lovett, A. A., Whyte, I. D., and Whyte, K. A., 'Poisson regression analysis and migration fields: the example of the apprenticeship registers of

Edinburgh in the seventeenth and eighteenth centuries', *Transactions of the Institute of British Geographers*, 10, 1985, pp. 317–32.

Lucassen, J., *Migrant Labour in Europe, 1600–1900*, London: Croom Helm 1987.

Lynch, M., 'Urbanisation and urban networks in seventeenth century Scotland', *Scottish Economic and Social History*, 12, 1992, pp. 24–41.

Mabogunje A. L., 'Systems approach to a theory of rural-urban migration', *Geographical Analysis*, 2, 1970, pp. 1–18.

MacCarthy-Morrogh, M., *The Munster Plantation: English Migration to Southern Ireland, 1583–1641*, Oxford: 1986.

McClure, P., 'Patterns of migration in the late Middle Ages: the evidence of English place-name surnames', *Economic History Review*, 32, 1979, pp. 167–82.

Macfarlane, A., *The Family Life of Ralph Josselin*, Cambridge University Press 1970.

The Origins of English Individualism, Oxford: Blackwell 1978.

Macinnes, A. I., *Clans, Commerce and the House of Stuart, 1603–1788*, East Linton: Tuckwell Press 1996.

McIntosh, M. K., 'Servants and the household unit in an Elizabethan English community', *Journal of Family History*, 9, 1984, pp. 3–23.

A Community Transformed: The Manor and Liberty of Havering, 1500–1620, Cambridge University Press 1991.

MacPherson, A. G., 'Migration fields in a traditional Highland community, 1350–1850', *Journal of Historical Geography*, 10, 1984, pp. 1–14.

Martin, J. M., 'The rich, the poor and the migrant in eighteenth-century Stratford on Avon', *Local Population Studies*, 20, 1978, pp. 38–48.

Marshall, R. K., *The Days of Duchess Anne: Life in the Household of the Duchess of Hamilton, 1656–1716*, Edinburgh: 1973.

'Wet nursing in Scotland, 1500–1800', *Review of Scottish Culture*, 1, 1984, pp. 43–51.

Middleton, R., *Colonial America*, Oxford: Blackwell 1996.

Millard, J., 'A new approach to the study of marriage horizons', *Local Population Studies*, 28, 1982, pp. 10–31.

Miller, K. A., *Emigrants and Exiles: Ireland and the Irish Exodus to North America*, Oxford University Press 1985.

Mills, D. R., 'The poor laws and the distribution of population *c*.1600–1860 with special reference to Lincolnshire', *Transactions of the Institute of British Geographers*, 26, 1959, pp. 185–95.

Lord and Peasant in Nineteenth-Century Britain, London: Croom Helm

1980.

Mitchison, R. M., 'The making of the old Scottish poor law', *Past and Present*, 63, 1974, pp. 58–93.

Mitchison, R. M., 'North and south: the development of the gulf in Poor Law practice', in Houston and Whyte (eds), 1989, pp. 199–225.

Mokyr, J., *Why Ireland Starved: A Quantitative and Analytical History of the Irish Economy, 1800–1850*, London: Allen and Unwin 1983.

Nicholas, S., and Shergold, P. R., 'Internal migration in England, 1818–1839', *Journal of Historical Geography*, 13, 1987, pp. 155–68.

O'Grada, C., *Ireland Before and After the Famine*, Manchester University Press 1993.

A New Economic History, 1780–1939, Oxford: Clarendon 1994.

Ommer, R. E., 'Primitive accumulation and the Scottish *clann* in the Old World and the New', *Journal of Historical Geography*, 12, 1986, pp. 121–41.

Overton, M., *The Agricultural Revolution in England*, Cambridge University Press 1996.

Pain, A. J., and Smith, M. T., 'Do marriage horizons accurately measure migration? A test case from Stanhope parish, County Durham', *Local Population Studies*, 33, 1984, pp. 44–8.

Palliser, D. M. 'A regional capital as a magnet: immigrants to York, 1477–1566', *Yorkshire Archaeological Journal*, 57, 1985, pp. 111–23.

Parton, A., 'Poor law settlement certificates and migration to and from Birmingham, 1726–57', *Local Population Studies*, 38, 1987, pp. 23–9.

Patten, J., 'Rural-urban migration in pre-industrial England', *Oxford University School of Geography Research Papers*, 6, 1973.

'Patterns of migration and movement of labour to three pre-industrial East Anglian towns', *Journal of Historical Geography*, 2, 1976, pp. 111–29.

Percival-Maxwell, M., *The Scottish Migration to Ulster in the Reign of James I*, London: Routledge 1973.

Perry, P. J., 'Working class isolation and mobility in rural Dorset, 1837–1936: a study of marriage distances', *Transactions of the Institute of British Geographers*, 46, 1969, pp. 121–41.

Phillips, C. B., 'Town and country: economic change on Kendal, *c.*1550–1700', in P. Clark (ed.), 1984, pp. 99–132.

Pickles, M. F., 'Labour migration: Yorkshire *c.*1670 to 1743', *Local Population Studies*, 57, 1996, pp. 30–49.

Pooley, C. G., 'Residential mobility in the Victorian city', *Transactions of the Institute of British Geographers*, 4, 1979, pp. 258–77.

'Segregation or integration? The residential experience of the Irish in mid-Victorian Britain', in Swift and Gilley (eds), 1989, pp. 60–83.

Pooley, C. G., and D'Cruz, S., 'Migration and urbanisation in North West England, *c.*1760–1830', *Social History*, 19, 1994, pp. 339–58.

Pooley, C. G., and Turnbull, J., *Migration and Mobility in Britain Since the Eighteenth Century*, University College of London Press 1998.

Poos, P. L., *A Rural Society After the Black Death: Essex, 1350–1525*, Cambridge University Press 1991.

Porter, J., 'A forest in transition: Bowland, 1500–1650', *Transactions of the Historical Society of Lancashire and Cheshire*, 125, 1974, pp. 40–60.

'Waste land reclamation in the sixteenth and seventeenth centuries: the case study of south-eastern Bowland, 1550–1630', *Transactions of the Historical Society of Lancashire and Cheshire*, 127, 1978, pp. 1–23.

Pound, J., *Poverty and Vagrancy in Tudor England*, London: Macmillan 1986.

Raftis, J. A., *Tenure and Mobility. Studies in the Social History of the Medieval English Village*, Toronto: Pontifical Institute of Medieval Studies 1964.

Ramsay, G. D., 'The recruitment and fortunes of some London freemen in the mid sixteenth century', *Economic History Review*, 31, 1978, pp. 526–40.

Rappoport, S., 'Social structure and mobility in sixteenth-century London', *London Journal*, 9, 1983, pp. 107–35.

Worlds Within Worlds: Structures of Life in Sixteenth-Century London, Cambridge University Press 1989.

Razi, Z., *Life, Marriage and Death in a Medieval Parish: Economy, Society and Demography in Halesowen, 1720–1400*, Cambridge University Press 1980.

Redford, A., *Labour Migration in England, 1800–1850*, Manchester University Press 1926.

Reed, M., 'Economic structure and change in seventeenth-century Ipswich', in P. Clark (ed.), *Country Towns in Pre-Industrial England*, Leicester University Press 1981, pp. 88–141.

Rich, E. E., 'The population of Elizabethan England', *Economic History Review*, 2, 1950, pp. 242–65.

Richards, E., *A History of the Highland Clearances*, vol. I., London: Croom Helm 1982.

'How did poor people emigrate from the British Isles to Australia in the nineteenth century?', *Journal of British Studies*, 32, 1993, pp. 250–70.

Robinson, P., *The Plantation of Ulster: British Settlement in an Irish Landscape, 1600–1620*, Dublin: Gill and Macmillan 1984.

Rosen, A., 'Winchester in transition, 1580–1700', in P. Clark (ed.), *Country Towns in Pre-Industrial England*, Leicester University Press 1981, pp. 144–95.

Schofield, R., 'Age-specific mobility in an eighteenth century English parish', in Clark and Souden (eds), 1987, pp. 253–66.

Schofield, P., 'Frankpledge lists as indices of migration and mortality: some evidence from the Essex lists', *Local Population Studies*, 52, 1994, pp. 23–9.

Sharlin, A. J., 'Natural decrease in early-modern cities: a reconsideration', *Past and Present*, 79, 1978, pp. 126–38.

Shaw, F. J., *The Northern and Western Islands of Scotland: Their Economy and Society in the Seventeenth Century*, Edinburgh: John Donald 1979.

Short, B., 'The evolution of contrasting communities within rural England', in B. Short (ed.), *The English Rural Community*, Cambridge University Press 1992, pp. 19–43.

Sinclair, Sir John, *Statistical Account of Scotland*, 21 vols., Edinburgh: 1791–99.

Sirault, M., 'Physical mobility in Elizabethan Cambridge', *Local Population Studies*, 27, 1981, pp. 65–70.

Skipp, V., *Crisis and Development: An Ecological Case Study of the Forest of Arden, 1570–1674*, Cambridge University Press 1978.

Slack, P., 'Vagrants and vagrancy in England, 1598–1664', in Clark and Souden (eds), 1987, pp. 49–76.

Smout, T. C., 'Lead mining in Scotland, 1650–1850', in P. L. Payne (ed.), *Studies in Scottish Business History*, Edinburgh: Cassel 1967.

Landsman, N. C., and Devine, T. M., 'Scottish emigration in the seventeenth and eighteenth centuries', in N. Canny (ed.), *Europeans on the Move: Studies on European migration*, Oxford: Clarendon 1994.

Snell, K., 'Parish registration and the study of labour mobility', *Local Population Studies*, 33, 1984, pp. 29–44.

Snell, K. D. M., *Annals of the Labouring Poor: Social Change and Agrarian England, 1660–1900*, Cambridge University Press 1985.

'Pauper settlement and the right to poor relief in England and Wales', *Continuity and Change*, 6, 1991, pp. 375–415.

'Settlement, Poor Law and the rural historian: new approaches and opportunities', *Rural History*, 3, 1992, pp. 145–72.

Solar, P. M., 'Poor relief and English economic development before the Industrial Revolution', *Economic History Review*, 48, 1995, pp. 1–22.

Somerville, A., *The Autobiography of a Working Man*, London: 1848.

Southall, H., 'The tramping artisan revisits: labour mobility and economic distress in early Victorian England, *Economic History Review*, 44, 1991, pp. 272–96.

Souden, D., 'Movers and stayers in family reconstitution populations', *Local Population Studies*, 33, 1984, pp. 11–28.

'Migrants and the population structure of later seventeenth-century provincial cities and market towns', in P. Clark (ed.), 1984, pp. 133–68.

'"East, west – home's best"? Regional patterns in migration in England', in Clark and Souden (eds), 1987, pp. 292–332.

'"Rogues, whores and vagabonds"? Indentured servant emigration to North America and the case of mid-seventeenth-century Bristol', in Clark and Souden (eds), 1987, pp. 150–71.

Spufford, M., *Contrasting Communities*, Cambridge University Press 1974.

Stapleton, B., 'Migration in pre-industrial southern England: the example of Odiham', *Southern History*, 10, 1988, pp. 47–93.

Stouffer, S. A., 'Intervening opportunities and competing migrants', *Journal of Regional Science*, 2, 1960, pp. 1–26.

Styles, P., 'The evolution of the law of settlement', in P. Styles, *Studies in Seventeenth-Century West Midlands History*, Kineton: Roundwood Press 1978, pp. 175–204.

Swain, J. T., *Industry Before the Industrial Revolution: North East Lancashire, c.1500–1640*, Manchester: Chetham Society, 1986.

Swift, R., and Gilley S. (eds), *The Irish in Britain, 1815–1939*, London: Pinter 1989.

Taylor, J. S., 'The impact of pauper settlement, 1691–1834', *Past and Present*, 73, 1976, pp. 42–74.

Poverty, Migration and Settlement in the Industrial Revolution, Palo Alto, CA: Society for the Promotion of Science and Scholarship 1989.

Thirsk, J., 'Industries in the countryside', in J. Thirsk, *The Rural Economy of England*, London: Hambledon 1984.

England's Agricultural Regions and Agrarian History, 1500–1750, London: Macmillan 1987.

Alternative Agriculture, Oxford University Press 1997.

Thompson, L., *A History of South Africa*, London: Yale University Press 1990.

Tidswell, D., 'Mobility from place of birth in early nineteenth-century Scotland', in A. H. Dawson (ed.), *Scottish Geographical Studies*, Dundee and St Andrews: University of Dundee, Dept of Geography 1993, pp. 176–85.

Tinley, R., and Mills, D. R., 'Population turnover in an eighteenth century Lincolnshire parish in comparative context', *Local Population Studies*, 52, 1994, pp. 30–8.

Tranter, N., *Population and Society, 1750–1960*, London: Longman 1985.

Tupling, G., *The Economic History of Rossendale*, Manchester: Chetham Society, 1927.

Turner, M., *English Parliamentary Enclosure: Its Historical Geography and Economic History*, Folkestone: Dawson 1980.

'Distribution and persistence of surnames in a Yorkshire dale, 1500–1750', *Local Population Studies*, 54, 1995, pp. 28–39.

Viazzo, P., *Upland Communities: Environment, Population and Social Change in the Alps Since the Sixteenth Century*, Cambridge University Press 1989.

Walton, J., 'Proto-industrialization and the first industrial revolution: the case of Lancashire', in P. Hudson (ed.), *Regions and Industries*, Cambridge University Press 1989, pp. 41–68.

Wareing, J., 'Changes in the geographical distribution of the recruitment of apprentices to the London companies, 1486–1750', *Journal of Historical Geography*, 6, 1980, pp. 241–9.

'Migration to London and transatlantic emigration of indentured servants, 1683–1775', *Journal of Historical Geography*, 7, 1981, pp. 356–78.

White, P. E., and Woods, R. J. (eds), *The Geographical Impact of Migration*, London: Longman 1980.

Whyte. I. D., *Agriculture and Society in Scotland in the Seventeenth Century*, Edinburgh: John Donald 1979.

'Marriage and mobility in East Lothian during the seventeenth and eighteenth centuries', *Transactions of the East Lothian Antiquarian Society*, 19, 1987, pp. 17–30.

Population mobility in early modern Scotland', in Houston and Whyte (eds), 1989, pp. 37–58.

'Urbanization in early-modern Scotland: a preliminary analysis', *Scottish Journal of Economic and Social History*, 9, 1989, pp. 21–37.

Whyte, I. D., and Whyte, K. A., 'Continuity and change in a seventeenth-century Scottish farming community', *Agricultural History Review*, 32, 1985, pp. 159–69.

'The geographical mobility of women in early modern Scotland', in L. Leneman (ed.), *Perspectives in Scottish Social History*, Aberdeen University Press 1988, pp. 83–106.

Williams, G., *Recovery, Reorientation and Reformation: Wales, c.1415–1642*, Oxford University Press 1987.

Williamson, J. G., 'The impact of the Irish on British labour markets during the Industrial Revolution', in Swift and Gilley (eds), 1989, pp. 134–62.

Williamson, J., 'Coping with city growth', in Floud and McCloskey (eds), 1994, pp. 332–56.

Withers, C. W. J., 'Kirk, club and cultural change: Gaelic chapels, Highland societies and the urban Gaelic subculture in eighteenth-century Scotland', *Social History*, 10, 1985, pp. 171–92.

'Highland migration to Dundee, Perth and Stirling, 1753–1891', *Journal of Historical Geography*, 11, 1985, pp. 395–418.

Gaelic Scotland: The Transformation of a Cultural Region, London: Routledge 1988.

Wolpert, J., 'Behavioural aspects of the decision to migrate', *Papers and Proceedings, Regional Science Association*, 15, 1965, pp. 159–69.

Woodward, D., 'The determination of wage rates in the early modern north of England', *Economic History Review*, 47, 1994, pp. 22–43.

Wrigley, E. A., 'A simple model of London's importance in changing English society and economy, 1650–1750', *Past and Present*, 37, 1967, pp. 44–70.

'A note on the lifetime mobility of married women in a parish population in the later eighteenth century', *Local Population Studies*, 18, 1977, pp. 22–9.

'The effect of migration on the estimation of marriage age in family reconstitution studies', *Population Studies*, 48, 1994, pp. 81–97.

Wrigley, E. A., and Schofield, R. S., *The Population History of England, 1541–1871: A Reconstruction*, Cambridge University Press 1989.

Wright, S. J., 'Sojourners and lodgers in a provincial town: the evidence from eighteenth-century Ludlow', *Urban History Yearbook*, 17, 1990, pp. 14–35.

Wrightson, K., *English Society, 1580–1680*, London: Hutchinson 1981.

Wrightson, K., and Levine, D., *Poverty and Piety in an English Village: Terling, 1525–1700*, London: Academic Press 1979.

Zelinsky, W., 'The hypothesis of the mobility transition', *Geographical Review*, 61, 1971, pp. 219–49.

INDEX